FAT

*The Story of My
Life with My Body*

Nonfiction
 by
Jean Braithwaite

Published by
Snake~Nation~Press

Acknowledgments

Chapter 1, "Time Slices," was published in the winter 2010 issue (295.1) of the *North American Review*. Chapter 2, "Sweet Things," was originally published as "Sweet" in *Bayou 42* (2004). Chapter 18, "Activism," was published as "Fat Pride" in *The Sun 379* (July 2007). "The Man with No Nose" (from Chapter 19) was published under the headline "Our Bodies, Our Imaginations" in the *New York Times* Sunday Fashion and Style section, December 12, 2004. "Penis Envy, and Other Theories" (excerpted mostly from Chapter 10) was published in *All Rights Reserved* in fall 2010. An essay with the same title as the book was published in *Black Rock and Sage* 2005 and reprinted in *Notes on Teaching English* (volume 30, May 2006), but only a paragraph or two from that essay remains in this book.

Notes

The names of some of the individuals who appear in this book have been changed, either for privacy, or because I couldn't remember the actual name. Otherwise, all events are portrayed just as they actually occured, within the limits of fallible human memory.

Published by Snake Nation Press
Valdosta, Georgia 31601

Printed and bound in the United States of America.

Copyright © Jean Braithwaite 2011

All Rights Reserved
A number of the stories in this debut collection have appeared elsewhere, in a slightly different form.

This is a work of fiction. Names, characters, place and incidents either are the product of the author's imagination or are used fictitiously. Any resemblance to actual persons, living or dead, business establishments, events or locales, is entirely coincidental.

No part of this book may be reproduced in any form, except for the quotation of brief passages, or for non-profit educational use, without prior written permission from the copyright holder.

ISBN: 978-0-9825430-4-7

Design by Force Street Media

FAT

The Story of My Life with My Body

Nonfiction
 by
Jean Braithwaite

Published by
Snake~Nation~Press

Dedication

Thanks to the Norman Mailer Writers Colony for the fellowship that enabled me to finally finish the manuscript to my satisfaction. Thanks to Pat Okker, Trudy Lewis, and my other important professors at the University of Missouri. Thanks to Averill, who gave me the idea. Thanks to Laura and Helen, the centers of my emotional life at the dissertation stage. Thanks to all my other friends, family, teachers, and lovers of all time, whether or not you appear in this book and whether or not you are still speaking to me (and… sorry!). Special thanks to my father, who promoted my intellectual ambitions early and proudly. This book is dedicated to the two transcendent women in my life—my mother and my mate—who don't necessarily endorse all its contents, and also to fat and fat-fearing women everywhere who may stumble on this message in a bottle and incorporate it into their thoughts and feelings about life with their bodies. You're why I made the effort.

Chapter 1

Time Slices:
My Body Fat and Thin

The beginning of fall, University of Missouri, trying to finish the PhD program

In the week before school started, without actually saying anything untrue, I deliberately gave one of my English Department colleagues the impression that I have cancer, or HIV, or some other deadly illness, though in fact I'm fairly sure I don't. No history of cancer anywhere in my family, no risky sex, intravenous drugs, blood transfusions, etc etc, and I don't feel sick. But, of course, I have gone from a size 28 pants to a size 10 in the last year. Or to be more precise, it's a little longer: two semesters plus two summers. One summer plus one semester ago, around about size 22-20, is when people in the department first started noticing I wasn't quite as fat, and the excruciating compliments began. Most people quit bothering me after one strained exchange. But fresh people keep turning up, like Denise for instance, who was away during spring semester, and of course the change is even more dramatic for them.

Out of the corner of my eye I saw Denise do a double take. "Hello," I called out, and waved my arm so as to cover the side of my face while, without breaking stride, I continued briskly through the rows of desks toward the xerox machine. She followed me, beaming. "Good to see you again," I said, and it sort of was—I always enjoyed Denise's company—though my body wanted to cringe away from her gaze. I've wished I could wave a wand and beglamor the senses of everyone who knew me as a fat woman, prevent them from seeing any change. I can't make myself pretend to have the standard feelings, and I don't know how to explain why I don't.

"Nice to see *you*," Denise said, with a warm extra significance. She gave me that look, long familiar to me, the confident congratulating smile, the appreciative sweep of the eyes that says you'll be happy to be looked at *now*, the subject of your body is not taboo *now*, we can rejoice together at the way you surely have improved your life. Now that you're thin.

I braced myself for whatever direction Denise would take me next. For years women smaller than me have gabbed on about the repulsiveness of their own excess weight while tactfully refraining from seeming to notice my body. For years I have kept my mouth shut whenever people discuss the proper ways to eat and exercise, reluctant to look as ridiculous as a fat woman pontificating on these subjects must look. I knew myself as an abstemious and vigorous person, even an ascetic, but of course other people didn't see me that way. The zones of silence have gradually frozen over: I've had no practice steering the course of a conversation about my body shape, and I helplessly respond in the most minimal, literal-minded way to whatever people happen to say first. As a sort of compromise with my own secret agenda, though, I allow myself to answer with uncooperative sincerity, to signal distress nonverbally.

The answer to "You look great" is always "Thanks, so do you," and a withdrawal of my eyes that says Drop it. When I'm lucky, that's the end of it. The answer to "How much weight have you lost?" is always "I don't ever keep track of my weight." The answer to "You're so thin!"—since it doesn't have to be interpreted as a compliment or a question—is simply a pained smile.

"How did you do it?" Denise said.

This exact combination of words was a new one, and I felt a bitter trickle of pleasure at the new avenue of evasion it opened up. "Well…" I said. I let my face drop, long and grave. "Actually it's not something I set out to do at all." That's true, I thought, and even my face isn't dishonest, because my foremost emotions about "it" aren't light-hearted. Is it my fault if people's prejudices blind them to the possibility that my attitudes about fat and thin are different from theirs?

Denise's face plummeted too, and I felt a little guilty, but it would be all right in a second, because her next line would be Are you sick and my truthful answer would be No, not as far as I know.

"So it wasn't intentional?"

"No, it wasn't."

"Well," she said. We looked at each other steadily for a moment. My mind felt a sense of acceleration, speeding forward on a track it did and didn't want to be on, fueled by righteous self-justification, pushing further and further into a territory of shame and anxiety. The two sets of feelings sat layered on each other without mixing, oil and water. I found no difficulty meeting the compassion in Denise's face with my own frank look. "Anyway," she said at last. "You look great."

"Thanks," I said. I smiled bravely, and the smile was not a lie either, because there is danger, I *am* going into danger and I don't know what will happen to me next. "Looking good is something."

"I'm sorry," she said. "I hope you'll be all right."

"Me too," I said. Not a lie. All year I've worried: Have I accidentally slipped into anorexia again, or Won't I inevitably bounce back fatter than ever, like 90-some-humongous-percent of all weight-loss cases, or What will become of my bone density decades from now?

Bone density is a serious business: my grandmother and her sisters all lived into their nineties but only my grandmother stayed thin. Oh she was proud of herself! The fat sisters' knees and hips wore out eventually, but their spines stayed intact. One day as my grandmother twisted to open a door she had the first of many spontaneous vertebral fractures, and she spent her last years of life in pain and incapacity. Fat women don't get osteoporosis. But no one ever talks about the health risks of not being heavy enough.

So all right, set aside the question of my bones, I'm 40 and can put off thoughts of post-menopause for a year or two anyway. In light of the Denise episode, my mental health seems a more pressing concern. I mean, what the hell is wrong with me? Denise isn't the only person to be affected by my peculiar reactions since this whole business began. I've seriously offended at least two faculty members and a secretary, not to mention my mother. Somehow I've got to get hold of myself.

My best friend Laura takes me shopping for school clothes and my body in the dressing room mirror looks elongated to the point of distortion, like an El Greco figure. These days I juggle two images of myself. Me of two summers ago, with the fat body I'd had for my whole adult life, pretty much, and me now, this fall, verging on gaunt, looking like a weirdly middle-aged version of my pubescent body at 13, or my anorexic body at 20. Those periods were so short, compared to the rest of my life, that I don't feel confident identifying the person in the mirror as the real me. Most people would figure this thin person to be the central core of me, newly escaped from the prison of my surrounding fat. I can't, and don't want to, share in this attitude.

On the other hand, the self-image I formed at puberty and self-destructively pursued for most of a decade never did completely leave me. Over the years, in dreams I've often been thin, inhabited a body much like this one without registering it as something strange, and even in waking life I've caught myself a couple of times recently thinking that at least it's nice to see my face again, the distinct features reemerging like a rockscape after snowmelt, no longer blurred and softened. I'm ashamed how I want to keep looking at myself in the dressing-room mirror, ashamed of finding the El Greco figure elegant.

I'm quiet for a long time after we leave the store, and I can feel Laura wondering about my thoughts. "Do you miss being fat?" she says.

"Sort of," I say. "No, not exactly."

Being fat is a great big pain in the ass. Getting appropriate clothes was a real undertaking for me. The ordinary styles of women's underpants chafed away to nothing between my thighs. And besides… they kept my crotch as warm as a sauna, and I worried about smelling bad. Thin people have a higher proportion of skin per pound—a higher "surface-to-volume ratio"—so heat escapes from them more easily than from a fat person. For years I wore men's boxer shorts instead of underpants, to give my body a little better ventilation. It worked, but no place in Columbia, Missouri sold boxers in a size 5X except for the fantastically expensive men's store. I dealt with big-and-tall companies on the web, by phone. Last time, two summers ago, I bought six pairs of underwear, which took 10 days to arrive and cost around 50 dollars total with shipping and handling. Now I can buy underpants at Walmart any day for a fraction of that. This is one of a number of ways that a fat person's life requires extra planning.

On airplanes I tried to get in early, to arrange myself so I wouldn't get in people's way more than I had to. Sometimes I lifted the armrest and let my thigh bulge over into the next seat. It wasn't completely impossible to wedge myself in between the dividers, but then the plastic creaked in an alarming way, and some of me spilled over the top anyway. Of course people didn't like sitting by me. Often they asked the stewardess to move them; once a man slammed the armrest back down onto my thigh. I had to worry whether the seatbelt would go around me, and if it didn't, decide whether to ask for the extender or just to fake it, keeping my hand over the end of the unfastened belt. And I had to make damn sure I wouldn't need to use the airplane toilet. I could just squeeze into the compartment, but I couldn't spread my legs inside it.

When I shopped around for an apartment, I checked carefully that the toilet wasn't tucked into some kind of niche or too close to the wall, and even on a well-placed toilet, there was barely enough room to maneuver my hand between the toilet seat and the front of my body. I often wondered how people even fatter than me managed in the bathroom. Most bathtubs were a tight squeeze, too, and I barely fit under the steering wheel in my car, with the seat put back to the furthest notch. I drive a Geo Prizm, so people fatter than me at my biggest are forced to own larger cars, presumably. My pants size was 28, which is the largest pants size available at Lane Bryant. It made me feel a little precarious to be right on the edge like that, especially since, as a matter of fact, the 28s were a little on the tight side. I knew that if I got even a smidgen fatter, life would be even more difficult.

Will be more difficult, if I refatten from this thinness.

"It's physically easier to move through the world now," I say. "But to me that doesn't seem like the main point."

"What's the main point?" Laura says, and such is her generosity and grace that she genuinely sounds more interested than dutiful.

Even though of course I was prompting Laura to prompt me for more information about my feelings, I'm not ready with my answer. The first thing that pops into my head—that I still *am* a fat person—sounds too crazy. I don't want to scare Laura. I consider other ways of formulating my emotional state. I'm disoriented in my present and afraid about my future. I feel defensive about my recent past, and humiliated by other people's haste to dissociate the me of this moment from the fat woman I have been. "I hate it that everyone acts like I'm a better person than I was before, when I know I'm not." And there's something else: how can I possibly make my book work now? "If anything, I liked myself better last year than I do this year," I tell Laura.

"You were more relaxed then," Laura says. "More sure where you were going next."

"It isn't fair! Thin-me is suddenly getting all this credit for all the things fat-me did all along, for the last 20 years. I *never* overate. I *always* exercised. I was *always* careful about nutrition."

Laura embraces me. "I know it, you've always eaten healthier than anybody else I know. That person—fat-you—was my best friend. And I'm glad I knew you then. You changed the way I look at people."

Philosophers use the concept of the *time slice* to do justice to the complexity of personal identity and change. At my age, a year is only one-fortieth of my total experience of life—not enough to make me see myself as a completely different person. But I'm clearly not exactly the same, either, because, well, look at me. I'm the same size now that I was at 13 or 20, but I don't want to identify myself with either of those desperately immature girls. I look radically different from last year, but I don't want to think I've changed fundamentally. The thing is, you can think of people as four-dimensional entities. Me-of-two-summers-ago and me-of-this-fall are both cross-sections of my life taken through the dimension of time, in the same way that you can imagine taking cross sections of any object—a lamp, for instance. It's wide at its base, then as you move upward it narrows to some kind of waist or stem, then it flares out fat again at the lampshade end. You wouldn't say it wasn't all the same lamp, but on the other hand you wouldn't say the base and shade are identical things. For different philosophical purposes, you might take thicker or thinner time slices of the same individual. Here's a reprise of February-me, a time-slice cut paper-thin:

February, this year
A professor on my dissertation committee is the first to hail me: "You look wonderful—what are you doing different?" The calculations take me less than half a second. "Wonderful" plus "different" equals didn't look wonderful before. "Look" plus "what are you doing" equals that your body's shape, whether attractive or unattractive, is something you caused. All of which adds up to congratulating me for abandoning the bad behavior that made me look bad. Excuse me for not feeling complimented.

"I'm not doing anything different," I say, clenching my jaw and averting my face. I'm *not*, I tell myself. Not the way she means it, anyway.

The floodgates open. More compliments every day. You look great, you look so much better, so healthy! You look thin, oh, you look so thin, you've really lost a lot of weight, haven't you? I bet you feel a lot better. The smiling brightness in their voices and faces that says Of course you're pleased to hear this. What can I say? I am not at all pleased that *thin* is a synonym for admirable.

It isn't even true that I look thin. I'm still a fat woman, just not *as* fat as before. And I'm very afraid this may be a step in the wrong direction. It isn't *true* that I look wonderful. My skin hangs on me like oversized clothes, and my fat doesn't stay firmly in place like it used to, but flows around, liquid. When I bend my neck forward, deep creases form, and soft layered curves squish out under my chin. Like a meat pudding. I look like something badly wrapped, barely contained, oozing. I think of jellyfish, of fleshy fungus slowly creeping, of magma sloshing over the edge of lava pools. It's like puberty again but with the video running in reverse. I look at my shrinking breasts. They're a pair of balloons saved from a party, a few weeks later, that most of the air has seeped out of. The limp skin looks simultaneously stretched-out and deflated. I have the skin of a sixty-year-old woman. It pleats on my neck, arms, thighs, buttocks. If I swing an arm or a leg up in the air, flesh rolls in a wave along the limb.

Oh, you look so *good*! Everybody in the department has to say it at least once. I know the intention isn't to harass me but I bristle anyway. If my mother could see me she would let me have it, for not considering other people's feelings. What do I owe to other people's feelings and what do they owe to mine? My shame and fear. My anger.

March

Before spring break I write to my mother. Wouldn't it be irresponsible not to? What if she keels over from shock at the airport? *…think I should warn you in advance that I've gotten significantly less fat…* I can't bear to call myself thin, partly because I'm not—size 20 is still fat, a little fat, anyway—and partly for other reasons. *Surely you must know that I love you and have a high opinion of your judgment…* But. *We are unlikely to agree on this subject. Can we please not talk about it, for now?* I worked on the letter for weeks, scrubbing it clean of the suppressed anger in the first draft, and the second. 40 years old, all that should be behind me. Laura and my best male friend, Andy, preview the final version. Nobody could read this as punitive in its intentions, right? No, no, they say, it sounds honest and kind.

"What did I ever do," my mother says on the phone, "to deserve an uptight, defensive, *pissy* letter like this?"

August

At size 10 I'm pretty haggard, with loose skin hanging off me in folds like a drenched parachute. This time I tell my mother nothing in advance. I figure, so she didn't like my letter, she can be a little surprised this time.

"Oh, my god," she says, dropping her suitcase. "You look awful."

"Thank you," I say, "I am not under the misapprehension that I look good, despite a parade of witnesses testifying to the contrary."

"Go to the hospital," she says. "I'll pay."

With my mother on the banks of the Mississippi, May 2001.

Me in Fall 2002. Mom: "You look awful." Everyone else: "You look great."

She calms in a day or two, seeing me eat volumes of oatmeal, rice, tortillas, and beans, just like always.

September, now, 2002, still at the mall

"But I'm getting used to thin-you, too," Laura says. "I didn't think I would make the adjustment so quickly, but you look like you to me now."

"To me I don't."

"I think you just need more time to grow into thin-you a little."

"I don't even know that I'm going to *stay* thin-me." What if this is just the narrow part of the lamp? What if there's still another lampshade flare in my future? Like the other time.

November 1981

I'm on the cusp of adulthood, not quite 20, when I finally manage to give up the shameful vice of eating. I've tried this before, hundreds of times in my teenage years, but always unsuccessfully, growing fatter and fatter in fits and spurts until now I am something less than human, my body utterly obscene.

Winter 1982

And now I'm gloriously thin again, with a new boyfriend, all new clothes, a habit of running miles every day, and my whole redeemed life stretching out in front of me.

Spring 1983

So how come I'm not happy? Why does sex seem so uninteresting, why do my running injuries never seem to heal, why do I crave food constantly, how come eating less food on average than I did at age 14 now makes me gain weight, even though I exercise at least as much?

December 1983

My great epiphany: endlessly resisting appetite is not how life is supposed to be. I will be guided only by the promptings of my own body, eating enough not to be constantly hungry, stopping when I feel full. I won't weigh myself. My body will find its own equilibrium. Whatever that is, no matter how fat, I swear, the orchestral music rising around me—I'll never diet again!

Now

How well am I keeping those promises?

The English Department has a picnic at the beginning of every fall semester. Laura and I are talking to the linguistics professor when I notice somebody noticing me. Beverley is in charge of some intramural program and has her office in a different building, so it's been a year since I've run into her. I try to get around behind Laura, hide myself, but too late. Next thing I know, Beverley has my arm and starts to gush.

"I had to look twice, and I still wasn't sure it was you! You're hardly recognizable. You've been doing just marvelous things to your body!" Beverley has just become the new record-holder for Most Disagreeably Worded Compliment. I go rigid.

"*I* don't think so," I say. The response doesn't strike me as intelligible, so I tack on the line that had such an effect on Denise. "Actually, I never set out to do this."

"Oh, I'm so sorry!" Beverley is visibly stricken. She drops my arm and backpedals fast, groping for some other conversational direction. "And here I'm always setting out to do it but not succeeding."

"Yes, that's the more usual procedure." I'm aiming for a dry humor, a tone that will shift us upward and away from my individual life to lofty social commentary, but my voice comes out wrong: even to me it sounds tight and cold, adversarial. The mouths of Laura and the professor make startled Os. They show their palms, spreading their arms slightly to either side as if they wanted to link hands with Beverley and me, as if they were getting ready to form a human bridge across a dangerous chasm. Rescue and Recover! their body language says. I want to help out too, smooth things over, but it's like I'm not even there now. High up over the arctic, the pilot has gone into convulsions and the plane will continue forward on auto-pilot until it crashes. I have time to notice Beverley's looks: well-groomed in a way that strikes a judicious balance between professional crispness and the plushness of the body she has to clothe. She is soft at the edges, bottom-heavy and a slight belly as well—a matronly body. How she must hate it.

I've always thought of Beverley as average-sized, but then I always classified other women as average unless they were big enough to be in my league, or nearly so. Whereas when I was anorexic, everybody looked tubby to me. I wonder if Beverley has gained weight this last year or if it's only my frame of reference that has shifted.

In the car on the way home I seek Laura's reassurance. "How awful was I?" I say. "Tell me the truth."

"You were pretty hard on her," Laura says. "She felt it very much." There's a Jane Austen-y echo to her words—Mr. Knightley scolding Emma for humiliating Miss Bates—and I wonder if Laura is making a deliberate allusion.

"I didn't mean it to hit her so hard," I say. I marshal my arguments: I meant no harm; I was only trying to protect my own sense of myself. People shouldn't make those assumptions about other people's lives. To praise the thin is, by direct implication, the same thing as to scold the fat. And the fat *don't deserve it.*

"Isn't she exactly the kind of person you meant to help with your book?" Laura says gently.

"Oh, god," I say. "I'm utter scum."

On Monday morning I walk into Beverley's office and give my name to the secretary. I've worked out in my mind that if Beverley doesn't see me now then leaving a note will be sufficient. I have the wording worked out already too. But she comes out to meet me and looks glad. She's been tossing and turning over this too, I think.

"I wanted to say I'm so sorry for embarrassing you." I talk fast, to get the gist of it out before she can say anything that might deflect me from my planned course. "I didn't mean to, and of course I *know* you didn't mean to hurt my feelings either."

"I was just going to email you, to apologize."

"It wasn't your fault. I should have done better, but the whole subject is just so painful for me."

"I understand completely," she says. "You're so kind." Of course, she's still under the impression that I have cancer. Mortal illness will buy you a lot of faux-pas forgiveness points. It's like I have a get-out-of-jail-free card in my hand, but I've already decided it would be cheating to keep it.

Beverley and I look at each other; it's clear we're not done yet. I try to gather my thoughts and she speaks first. "I do want to offer you my… my very best wishes. If you—I mean… it's none of my business, of course.…"

"I'm not sick," I say. "As far as I know."

"Oh, I'm so glad!" she says. She means it, I can see. She's genuinely relieved and happy for me. At the moment. Later on, in a few hours, when the feelings of guilt and pity she's accumulated over the weekend have had a chance to dissipate, then she may start to wonder just why the hell I put her through all that. Already her face registers a little puzzlement, behind the willed opacity characteristic of a person who is determined not to ask any questions that might not be polite.

"I think I should try to explain myself," I say. But the task is gigantic, superhuman, undoable. I want to tell Beverley she is guilty of nothing, not just toward me, but in her life with her own body. But there is no way to say this without being insulting in exactly the same way I have felt insulted this last half-year: Yes, though I barely know you and you have never broached the subject, I fully understand how this part of your life works, better than you do yourself, perhaps…. This is definitely the wrong tack. I think instead about how to describe my life.

Myself at 14, call her Time Slice #1a, fired up with the will to excel, putting herself on the road to self-loathing and failure. Myself at 20, Time Slice #1b, triumphantly thin, but no different, really, certainly no more skilled at living life, pursuing exactly the same half-baked goals by even more immoderate strategies, headed for physical catastrophe sooner or later. I hope I have nothing in common with 1a or 1b but maybe I do.

I think of myself in my moderate 30s, Time Slice #2, stable and content in my own daily life, but socially shrouded, keeping my thoughts on the subject of fat and thin unexpressed to almost everyone. I miss 2. Even if I don't get fat again, the fact that she existed means that I will always be connected to her fat, always have protective feelings toward her body. I don't want to be separated from 2, but her privacy is beyond recovering for me now. If I do get fat again—some future Time Slice 4?—few people will say anything about it directly, but their silence won't fully conceal their pity, contempt, exasperation: *After all that, how could she just let herself go again?*

The hypothetical #4 is no use to me just now. I force myself to turn my attention away from her frustrations and focus on just this moment. "Okay," I say to Beverley. "First, do you know what a time slice is?"

Chapter 2

Sweet Things

1967, Austin, Texas

In the cookie aisle of the grocery store I was trying to persuade my mother to buy a fancy kind with a jam filling and she was arguing that I would like a cheaper kind just as well. This was the willful perversity of the powerful—how could my mother sincerely believe that she was more of an expert about my desires than me? No doubt she had some ulterior motive, moralizing, or trying to trick me, keep me in my place.

"This package only has half as many cookies," she said.

"Well, so? All you have to do is *buy two packs*." My teenage sister Anita had stayed out of the campaign, gazing away from me with an air of bored superiority. But she had to be impressed by the airtight case I was making. I sneaked a look at her. Her dark hair had been made wavy by wearing curlers to bed, which meant she would be going out on a date later. She had a round, pretty face and the hair curved softly around the sides. I was deeply ambivalent about my older sister. On the one hand, she was obviously someone worth looking up to; she had all the skills of a parent, could drive my little brother and me to the movies, use the good scissors to cut a firm straight line, or pop popcorn when she wanted. On the other hand, she was silly, giggling on the phone or spending an hour in front of the dresser mirror in our bedroom, perfecting her makeup. I already knew I wanted to be a different kind of girl, daring and tough rather than feminine and sweet.

"Anita, look at these," I said. I tugged on her arm and held up the package of jam cookies, making them undulate in the air. I smiled enticingly.

She turned suddenly and snapped at me. "You little snot, you don't even know how lucky you are—you can eat whatever you want!"

I was dumbfounded. What was she talking about? I couldn't eat anything except what somebody else fixed for me or bought me. *She* was the one who had the freedom to do as she pleased, I was always subject to someone else's arbitrary rules. When Anita took Dan and me to Dairy Queen, she was the one who insisted one sundae or ice cream cone was the limit, though I knew she had more money in her purse and could easily have bought a second round for us even if she didn't want one herself. At home I was pressed to eat more of what I wanted only a few bites of (meat, eggs, casserole) or some of what I had never wanted any of in the first place: green beans with their brassy sourness like hitting two adjacent piano keys simultaneously, slimy stringy spinach, cooked carrots or squash which had a morbid fleshy texture not decent in any vegetable. Meanwhile, foods I wanted the most were measured out with a miserly hand, a few shoestring potatoes shaken from their can or the rare homemade dessert with dinner: No, *one* piece is *enough*. It was grossly unfair.

On television I had seen advertisements for a toy called the Easy Bake Oven and the thought of it played in my mind occasionally. Should I ask for an Easy Bake Oven for Christmas? It looked like a big toy, and if I got it, then I couldn't expect much else. Besides, the girls in the ads were obviously the kind who liked to dress up and play with dolls. But they got cake all the time, because they made it themselves. Would an Easy Bake Oven give *me* the license to eat cake every day?

"How about this?" My mother's voice sounded more conciliatory. "If you want to get these cookies, but take just one in your lunch bag instead of two we'll do that."

"No," I said, choking up from the combined injustices of my mother and my sister.

"One of these or two of those," my mother said, in an ostensibly patient voice under which the steel rang clearly. Silently I put the jam cookies back on the shelf, swallowing my tears. I wouldn't deign to participate in this travesty of compromise. What was my sister *talking* about? It was no use asking for an Easy Bake Oven, I decided. Even if I got it, it wouldn't be the same for me as for the girls on TV. Really I had known that all along.

For Christmas I got my first two-wheeler, and I loved it.

1971, Tucson, Arizona

My best friend in fourth grade was Mona Smith who was slightly older than me and more settled in her preferences. She was passionate about horses: I became a horse-worshipper too. She made fun of me for liking the fourth-grade teacher. Once I had very much admired Mrs. Miller's red hair and the coordinated pantsuits she wore—they were stylish without being a handicap as dresses were. But under the influence of Mona's teasing I pretended first indifference, then dislike for Mrs. Miller. Mona's definite attitudes were magnetic. I felt toward her a mix of admiration, bafflement, and superiority that was not completely unlike what I felt toward my older sister before she grew up and lived on her own, before my parents moved to Arizona with Dan and me.

"Mrs. Miller, how much do you weigh?" Mona asked out of the blue one day. The question made no sense to me. Kids often asked each other how tall they were, but they didn't ask adults. And fourth-graders didn't compare their weights in the 1970s. Of course, everyone understood it was bad to be fat. Fat Roger was one of the neighborhood boys with whom I played a plastic-bat-and-tennis-ball version of baseball in the streets of our new subdivision on the edge of town. For serious competitors, the thing to do, when you were in the outfield, was shout "Hey batter, batter, batter, *swing*" to throw off the timing of the kid at the plate. But when Roger came to bat, it was wittier to yell, "Hey, hey, Roger, get your *weight* into it," and then howl with laughter. Roger always smiled as though he enjoyed the joke too, and it never occurred to me to think he suffered. Roger was fat, therefore he deserved our scorn. Fat kids were greedy, everybody knew that. I wasn't fat, so I wasn't anything like Roger.

Mrs. Miller hesitated a long time before answering Mona. "Um…" Her eyes shifted away from Mona's gaze as though she were a shy or guilty child and *Mona* were the teacher. "A hundred and three pounds." Her voice was so meek that I suspected her of making some kind of joke, though the point was obscure to me. The school nurse weighed us kids and measured our height every year, and I reported the rising figures at home with pride. Was Mrs. Miller ashamed that her number was too low? I was vaguely aware that grown-up women paid attention to their weight, but I had no grasp of the details. Perhaps Mrs. Miller was actually boasting while pretending the opposite, like when I acted disappointed with a math assignment that got a higher grade than Mona's.

My mother owned a bathroom scale (which I had gotten on for projects such as weighing my guinea pig), and she drank diet Fresca, which I had sipped. As the fluid first touched your tongue, the flavor seemed exotically interesting if not completely enjoyable—much of the pleasure consisted in being sophisticated, as when asking for a taste of a parent's beer—but in a second or two, as the stinging bubbles burst, the flavor veered off in a crazily metallic direction. It tasted like something meant to be drunk by robots, not human beings. But still, once the aftertaste faded, it could seem worth taking a second sip. Fresca was best poured over ice cream, where its bubbles were neutralized in the melt and refreeze. The ice cream would turn into a mass of jagged edges, adventurous as the lunar landscapes from TV, and the Fresca's peculiar flavor was diluted down to a tolerable metallic garnish that reminded me of another ambivalent pleasure: the crunching silver balls that were one of the decoration options for our annual Christmas cookies. Just the same, I preferred fruit-flavored drinks to any soda. Even the regular sugared kind of sodas had that searing, difficult texture. Why were they called "soft"?

The palate has to be trained to embrace certain challenges. Carbonation, just like coffee or jalapeno peppers, has to be encountered many times, practiced, before it becomes genuinely attractive. In the fourth grade I did not yet really like chocolate, which seemed to harbor flavors beneath the sweetness that were adult, alien, and perverse.

Similarly, the mind has to be trained before complex cultural values and beliefs come to seem satisfyingly self-evident. But some tastes come to us more readily than others. The appetite for sweetness is a childhood universal around the world. Evidence suggests that it's biological, built into us from birth. Likewise the delicious pleasure of looking down on other people. Feeling superior does not require fully articulated reasons. I was smarter and stronger than Mona; my family's habits were more correct than Mona's; and Roger was just contemptible, beyond the pale by anybody's standards.

It seemed to me that other children generally had access to more sweets than I did. When Mona spent the night at my house, there would be some special treat that was planned, oatmeal molasses cookies that my mother made, or else a trip to a hamburger place where we could order any three things, as long as one was a hamburger. My second thing was always french fries and then I agonized over the choice between milkshake and apple pie. But at Mona's house, along with the special treat—say, ice cream and fudge sauce for after dinner—there would also be many other things that didn't seem to be extra or unusual but just part of daily life. Poptarts at breakfast, cookies in the afternoon, candy in the cupboard which was easy to grab any time. Also we could help ourselves to soda from Mona's fridge, but because I didn't like soda I classified it differently in my mind, not as a sweet treat, but an ordinary beverage which my family just happened not to bother with, apart from my mother's Frescas. Candy, on the other hand, I understood as something that was being deliberately restricted. At home it was only for Halloween or Easter.

I took it as given that the laxer standards of Mona's mother were wrong and my mother's ways were right, though I gladly exploited the difference when I was at Mona's. I believed I knew all about nutrition, since I had learned the four food groups in school: milk-and-milk-products, meat-and-fish, bread-and-cereal, fruit-and-vegetables. But I was under the impression that my own mother's strictures were primarily economic, that the taint of unwholesomeness that infused the idea of candy in my mind was because of the money spent to get it, money that, except on rare holidays, should be thriftily saved instead of squandered on unnecessary luxury. I had an allowance now myself—25 cents a week—which I could have used to buy snacks, but I almost never did. It was foolish to invest in things that would simply be consumed, instead of long-lasting value like marbles or comic books.

"Mom, Mrs. Miller weighs 103 pounds."

"That's very nice, Mona, but I don't think—"

"Don't you wish *you* weighed 103 pounds, Mom?" I understood Mona's needling by the tone but not its content. Mrs. Smith was a perfectly ordinary-looking mother. Her outfits were less glamorous than Mrs. Miller's, certainly—patterned dresses for the most part—but after all, Mrs. Miller was a *teacher*.

"Mona! It's very rude to talk about people's weight!"

It *was*? Why?

Mrs. Smith had just been to the grocery store and she brought out a bag of chocolate-chip cookies. We could have three apiece, she said.

We didn't stop at three, of course. Left alone at the kitchen table, why would we? But we felt awkward out there, the potential for exposure inhibited us, and Mona had the idea of smuggling the bag into her bedroom instead. There, sitting cross-legged on Mona's star-patterned quilt, all in private among Mona's dozens of horse figurines and *Black Stallion* novels, laying out the cards for one of our endless games of double solitaire, we were completely released from the pressure of adult scrutiny.

My scientific curiosity was inflamed. For normal cooked foods, the non-sweet, non-cellophane-wrapped kinds, my parents never set portion limits. Obviously that was unnecessary because of the natural boundary of fullness one reached—even for baked potato or corn on the cob—after which the idea of eating more was repugnant. Was there a natural limit to the number of cookies one wanted to eat? I had never reached it, but then I had never been in a situation where I was allowed to make the experiment.

We laid out cookies in front of us, out to the side of our cards, three in a row. For some reason neat rows were more satisfying than eating them directly from the bag. And for some reason three was the perfect number to fill a row. I was used to feeling a certain anxiety as I approached the halfway point of any treat, the moment when the resources remaining would be equal to, and then less than, those that had already been eaten through. The sense of poverty would increase as the fractions shrunk, one third left, one fourth left—I would try to conserve, but the end was inevitable—one eighth left, one bite left, nothing. But now, as Mona and I ate, we replenished our cookies instantly from the bag so that there were *always* three in front of us. It reminded me of the magic wallet in the fairy tale (the story said "wallet" but the picture showed a *bag*) that could never get empty no matter how many coins were spent. The freedom was a relaxation as complete as what I felt on Friday afternoon when school was over and I didn't have to think about it again for days and days, and even though bedtime was coming I had a flashlight ready under my pillow and a new stack of library books and no need to ration my pleasure.

Too late, I realized that I should have been counting the cookies, to know how many would make me full. The continuous replenishing made it harder to keep track. I had moved along my row in order, replacing the one I had just eaten and then picking up the one to the right of it to eat next. But had I gone through the whole cycle twice or three times? I wished Mona's mother had bought something other than chocolate chip. Jam cookies would have made a very appealing subject for experiment. I had already known I wasn't *that* fond of chocolate, so it proved little if I began to get tired of it. But still, still… an opportunity like this didn't come every day.

After four times three cookies, or else five times three, I began to find the sight of them in front of me less attractive. Had I hit the wall, my fullness limit? The sensation was not as clearcut as for ordinary food. Perhaps I would begin to think about stopping. I ate now without replenishing, and the sight of the cookies dwindling before my eyes was almost a relief, like a chore that is half done, then two-thirds done, then three-quarters done, then finally finished. The cookies were dry in my mouth and tiresome to chew. Their flavor had shifted in a complicated way. The oppressive, heavy chocolate of the chips seemed to have spread itself thinly over the inside of my mouth, so it was everywhere, yet less distinct. The chocolate was the key to my discomfort, yet it was the only thing that relieved the dullness of the body of the cookies. I finished the row; I would certainly stop here.

The sight of Mona continuing to set out her cookies made me restless. At home when Dan and I had some treat, I always took care to consume mine more slowly than he did so that a time would come when I still had something but he had nothing. No matter how slowly he tried to eat, I could eat slower; my will was stronger and he always cracked first. Now I looked at Mona and took stock of myself. Had I really hit the wall or did I want one more? Well, there was a way to be sure. I took another cookie straight from the bag and bit it. When I had it in my mouth, crumbs lying along my tongue like thick dust, I didn't want it anymore. So I was full; it *was* possible to get full of sweets just like ordinary food. I finished the cookie feeling certain it would be a long time before I wanted another. A minute later, though, something pulled me toward the bag again. Something—what? A desire to change the acrid flavor inside my mouth, maybe, or the feeling that it wasn't fair for Mona to get more than I did. It felt magnetic, the draw of the memory of sweetness: do that again. Get more of *that*. It felt as though my teeth themselves were clamoring to chew again. Was this what "sweet tooth" meant? The phrase had always puzzled me. Every kid I knew had a sweet tooth. Did adults not have them? Did Mrs. Smith have one and my mother not?

I bit another cookie which became a burden the second it touched the inside of my mouth. Yes, I thought, exactly as not-good as the last one—how come I forgot? But when it was gone some itch, some pull, still persisted and eventually I decided to take just one more. I can't say how many times I took just one more and how many times, chagrined and astonished, I confronted again the strange glitch that my memory had suddenly developed, before I shook myself free. After all, the bag wasn't infinite, really. I began to worry about how we would get it back to the kitchen and how suspiciously light it would weigh then to Mrs. Smith's hand.

"We better leave some, Mona."

"I know. Don't be so bossy. You ate more than I did, anyway."

"I did *not*."

"Yes, you did. This is you: *rowf rowf*." Mona put her head down and pretended to gobble like an animal at the opening of the cookie bag.

Now

Several times I've tried to explain what the cookie afternoon meant to me, without complete success. "A binge," a friend of mine called it, but it wasn't that, not for me at least. I didn't know enough yet to binge. I was completely innocent of the dieting merry-go-round so many other women and girls were on, the cycle of deprivations and temptations and shame that Mona, perhaps, already knew even prior to puberty. For me there were five years yet to go before the snap wouldn't snap on my favorite pair of pants, six or seven years before I fully comprehended my sister's anger in the cookie aisle, and guessed at the possible humiliations of Mrs. Smith. Losing three, gaining four; losing five, gaining ten; losing twenty, gaining thirty.

Mona and I had sneaked cookies, yes, but that was only a matter of disobeying someone else's rules. True bingeing requires a sense of sin, that feeling of weakness and tearing like damp paper giving way, a succumbing to desires that you yourself recognize as forbidden, obscene, in the full knowledge that self-loathing must inevitably follow.

The afternoon of the cookies was neither the beginning nor the end of my relationship with sweets, nor was it even an important emotional landmark, except in retrospect. At the time I felt no guilt, no overwhelming desire, though later these emotions were familiar to me as breathing. Then my love-hate affair with sugar went on and on, more sordid and secret when I was fat than when I wasn't, more stormily intense when I was starving myself than when I wasn't. By then there were landmark incidents, events in our relationship history, eruptions and reconciliations and renunciations. Over the years, I broke up with sugar many times, and many times drifted back to it. Even after I gave up dieting forever, vowing always to eat the food I needed not to be hungry—nutritious foods, the ordinary ones where I could be sure there was no mismatch between appetite and hunger, nothing sweeter than fruit—even then I sometimes wavered. Why shouldn't I do what everyone else did? I hated making myself conspicuous in front of other women, refusing food they had cooked. Oh, are you on a diet? No. The same old rage, same old shame. And a flicker of the old attraction too. Yes, even after I had stayed away for years at a time, even after I had convinced myself by countless experiments that it was simpler and pleasanter to turn down the first slice than to take it and find myself wishing helplessly for a second slice which I would never be able to ask for, never, not while the complacent thinner women around me chatted, amiably deploring their fat thighs and bottoms…. Even then, sometimes, sugar could still lure me back for one last fling.

Chapter 3

Physical Education

On the edge of puberty in the Age of Aquarius…
At the end of sixth grade the school nurse measured me at 98 pounds and 60 inches tall—five feet exactly. It could be no coincidence, I felt, that both figures stood right at major boundaries at exactly the time I was to leave elementary school behind. Something significant must be about to happen to me, something lay just ahead, parts of me which had been latent until now, mere potential, like seeds, were about to quicken and emerge. In the early 1970s, it was still possible for a girl my age to feel proud of her increasing size. On the playground equipment I felt myself strong and fast, in class I felt my intelligence. I loved the Beatles and Cat Stevens; I was against Nixon, the Vietnam War, and pollution. The Age of Aquarius was dawning and I would surely grow up to change the world.

That summer when we visited my grandparents' farm in rural Utah my mother asked my grandmother if she owned a bathroom scale.

"Yes, but it doesn't work very well. If I just do even a few deep-knee bends, and get on it again, it'll say I weigh five pounds less."

My father assumed one of his stock joking faces, the character of the good-hearted moron, "Well, Mary, by all means: do a few deep-knee bends!"

"So what do you weigh?" my mother asked her mother.

"With or without the knee-bends?" said my father, but both the women ignored him. They were intensely engaged with each other and he and I were superfluous.

"Oh," my grandmother said, smiling coyly. There was a pause before she answered. "A hundred and twenty-nine. What do you weigh?"

"Oh," my mother said. "A hundred and twenty… eight." She looked archly at my grandmother as she stretched out the last word. My mother's face and voice didn't match what I understood to be the content of this conversation. Information had been requested and provided, but the exchange didn't seem to be completed after my mother's answer. The air between the two women felt anticipatory, charged, like the instants between "get set" and "go" when I ran against other girls in PE class. But what was at stake between them?

"And a half," my mother said, dispelling the tension. They laughed and changed the subject.

Mom, my grandma, and me. I know my body will always be perfect.

My parents watched a good deal of the 1972 Olympics on television. I was excited by the Olympic fanfare and flag, and the running in of the flame. I had read the Greek myths in *My Book House* and I thought those different gods and their attributes were so appealing. It would be beautiful to really believe in a whole pantheon of gods, the way the Greeks did. Was it possible to make yourself believe things you didn't, just by wanting to and practicing, entering into that frame of mind? But a modern person would have to keep quiet about it, or people would think they were crazy. The best thing would be if you could turn beliefs off and on at will.

During a commercial break, my father held a banana aloft like a torch and ran with it around the living room, lifting his knees high. He stopped by the side of the television and jogged in place with an exaggerated expression of solemnity. I recognized this face as one from the repertoire of my father's yokel shtick. "Teams of relay runners have passed this banana from hand to hand, running through the day and through the night without pause. See how the banana skin shines"—now he was doing his Howard Cosell voice—"like the very dream of Olympic gold itself! Not since it started its long journey, from the top of Mt. Olympus in Greece, has the Olympic banana been at rest for even an instant." My mother laughed, but I didn't look at my father. He was interfering with my sacred mood. "Never ceasing, never peeled, never dropped—whoops! ah, good catch!"— he juggled it from one hand to the other—"Neither snow, nor rain, nor sleet shall stay this faithful banana from the swift completion of its appointed rounds." I longed for Zeus to hurl one of his thunderbolts at my father. Just a small one. Enough to knock him out for a couple of minutes.

Some of the gymnastic equipment in the Olympics was similar to playground equipment I used, but other things were exotic, like the rings. "The iron cross," said the announcer, "is the most physically taxing and painful position of all the ring exercises." It looked like it. The man doing the iron cross had his arms spread almost as wide as they would go. His trunk was perfectly upright and his legs perfectly horizontal with the toes pointed. Under each arm I could see a little triangle of muscle connecting the arm to his back, like the web in a duck's foot. When I held my own arms out I couldn't feel

31

any web and I was alarmed for the man on TV. It looked as though his strength was barely preventing the rings from pulling him apart. His face was grim and after a few seconds his shoulders were visibly trembling.

"It may take a lot of strength to do that," my mother said. "But it's not very attractive." I agreed: it was hard to keep looking at that stretched web. But still, there was something exalted about the most difficult trick of all. To pour yourself out unstintingly, will yourself to hold fast, for the glory, for the approval of passionate gods.

1976 Olympics

The Japanese and Soviets were neck and neck in the team gymnastics event when a man on the Japanese team made a strange little half-hop and bobble as he dismounted from the rings, letting out a little dismayed yip as he did so, though his performance received a 9.7, a very high score. Announcers later explained that the man had broken his kneecap during the floor exercises but concealed the injury from everyone in order to compete as scheduled on the pommel horse and rings. The TV showed replays of the dismount repeatedly. In hindsight the man's agony was apparent. He dropped from a height of eight feet, turning three somersaults on the way down, landed—the right leg buckled but the left foot stuck firm—yipped, then recovered himself to stand tall with arms raised. Over and over the clip repeated until my mother cried out at the television, making a sudden, sharp sound with her mouth full open like a dog barking.

"That's terrible! Stop it! Kim—" She appealed to my father. "They shouldn't keep glorifying that. It's just plain stupidity! To do that with a broken bone!" He murmured something in assent. I thought my mother coarse-minded not to appreciate the sacrifice and pride that motivated the gymnast. For the Olympics!

Later the gymnast limped to the awards platform with his teammates to receive the gold medal.

Now

By the age of ten when I saw my first Olympics I had fallen down many times off tricycles, bicycles, scooters, and roller skates. I had come home bloody and been bandaged by my mother, and every injury had healed perfectly, leaving only a little badge of distinction to compare with other children's scars. I had been sick for no more than three days at a time before recovering my whole strength. From reading, I knew about death, that it could happen even to a child and would happen to everyone eventually. But I didn't know, or I knew only in the most abstract way, that the body can also be hurt in irreversible ways short of death.

Shun Fujimoto, the Japanese gymnast, injured his knee further when he leapt from the rings that day in 1976, dislocating it and tearing ligaments as he hit the floor. He never competed again, and his knee still bothers him. Asked in later years whether he would do the same thing again in the same circumstances, Fujimoto said he would not. Middle-aged now, I approve his good sense as much I did his courage back in 1976. Too bad it's too late for the mature man to undo the damage done to the 26-year old hero. Too bad the young will always find ways, and reasons, to elude the wisdom of the middle-aged.

Oh, reader, nothing is more precious than your health and well-being! Certainly not a scrap of metal and a few television clips.

1972

The marathon was the final Olympic event, and the announcers made the most of it. They retold the story of the Greek messenger Pheidippides, who ran to Sparta from Athens seeking military aid in the war against the Persians. The Spartans declined on the grounds that their religious calendar didn't permit fighting until later in the month, so Pheidippides ran home—almost 300 miles round trip. He got to the front lines at the plain of Marathon in time to see the Greeks' decisive victory, then he ran back to Athens—26 miles—and reported the good news before he collapsed and died.

The marathon was the crowning glory of the Olympics, the most dramatic and intense event. It *was* the Olympics, in concentrated form. That settled it. I had to grow up to be a marathoner.

...and over the edge

At the onset of puberty several things happened more or less simultaneously: my skin erupted in pimples, I became interested in boys (*a* boy), my food appetites changed, and an intermittent menstrual flow began. Except for the skin, I viewed these developments in a mostly positive light.

Sexual feeling was familiar in one way, unfamiliar in another. Private experiments in earlier years had already taught me that my body could be stimulated in certain ways. But what went through my mind at such times was not sex in any usual sense. I focused on images of my own body: running alone, or climbing and leaping, or flying as it could in dreams, or placed into some dramatic tableau involving injustice, brave endurance, and perhaps at the end a rescue of some innocent person, usually a pretty girl. Recently I had worried a little about the unorthodox content of my fantasy life, in the same way that I worried occasionally about being almost the only 8th-grader in the PE showers who still had a hairless crotch: was I going to be normal?

So it was a relief to find out that I could "like" a boy. The new desire seemed to spring up overnight, fully formed, like a mushroom. Something that had already happened by the time I noticed it. *Oh*, I thought, I want to do this *with* someone. A specific someone. Richard was in the smart English class, the smart social studies class, and also Spanish, where he had given a talk about Aztecs that took up the whole class period, almost. I had bad luck in the assignment of topics and my own report—on the bullfighter El Cordobés—took less than ten minutes and my knees shook the whole time.

Richard was one-quarter Iroquois and three-quarters Austrian, or at least that's what he said. Kids had been known to invent romantic combinations sometimes. I wanted to believe him. In any case, he had smooth tan skin, and was tall like me, and had good looks and poise enough to keep out of the nerd category despite being smart. He wasn't popular by any stretch, but that was fine since my preference for intellectual elites was already unshakable. He suited me perfectly. Richard, Richard, Richard, I thought. Oh, Richard.

My fantasy life melted out of its old forms and flowed into the new as easily as wax. My feelings for Richard caused no hardship at first; I savored them though there was no question of actual reciprocation. Among my peers my deficiencies were by now officially established: I was a zit-faced, flat-chested, tongue-tied social freak. The boys had a term, "dog," for undesirable girls. It had been applied to me with some frequency—not as much as some girls, but enough that I knew I was on the other side of a line Richard wouldn't cross, nor any other boy worth aspiring to. Still, being accounted a dog didn't much affect my feelings about myself. The boys had been too sweeping in their evaluations, too many girls were called dogs who really weren't bad-looking at all. My face was not quite pretty perhaps, but nothing was wrong with it other than the skin. And my body was *good*, I knew that, with shapely long legs and a high waist as beautiful as anyone's. The mindless emphasis on breasts prevented anyone from really seeing my shape. I was still growing into my desirability. Later I would find myself among people who knew what to appreciate.

In fantasy I cast Richard and me up on a desert island, alone together. With no other distractions, no pressure of outside judgments, Richard would be free to turn to me and discover the full depths of our compatibility and passion. As I kissed my image in the bathroom mirror, touched my body at night, I knew that passion to be profound. Just feeling it was an accomplishment in itself, a significant milestone. Now I understood that the great fulfillment my life had always been aiming toward had something to do with sex.

My food appetites took new forms too, around the same time though not as abruptly as my fantasy life. Suddenly some of my embarrassing limitations were gone. Green beans, spinach with lemon juice, cherries, pecans, pickles, vinaigrette, mustard, Mexican food: many tastes were newly piquant and interesting. Previously they had been too strong-flavored to eat, almost dangerous, with the threat of subtler nauseating half-tones beneath the dominant notes. Meat too became easier to eat. If my family went out to dinner, I could order a grown-up hamburger with all the trimmings instead of only bland lettuce and tomato, and now I could usually finish most of it.

On one of my sister Anita's visits we went to a steak place. In the flickering candlelight I watched her with envious admiration. She was like me, a mystic Aquarius; she was unlike me, grown and beautiful, known to be beautiful, loved as a woman. Back in Austin she lived with her boyfriend. Therefore she and a man had sex. Often, presumably. I looked in her face for the evidence of deep secret pleasures, such as the reserved little smile she gave the waiter as she ordered. "Medium rare."

The waiter turned to me. "Medium…" I said. "Wait. I'm not sure." My father, afraid of germs, had always ordered well-done meat for me when I was little.

"Medium-rare meat is red and hot at the center; medium, pink at the center; and medium-well is brown at the center but retains more of its juices than well-done meat," the waiter said. "The longer a steak is cooked the drier it becomes."

The idea of pink meat made me squeamish. "I'll have medium-well, please," I told the waiter, then instantly suffered agonies of remorse for my cowardice. Maybe I could change. No, it was too late now, he had already gone on to the next person.

"Very, *very* well done," my father said.

The fluid on my sister's plate looked dark in this light but in reality must be red. "Do you want to try a bite?" she said.

I would have eaten anything from her plate. "Yes, please," I said. The wet tang of it was a revelation similar to the discovery that I was attracted to Richard: meat could taste good, could be something you wanted. I thought of the Greeks and their animal sacrifices. I thought of sex, which also would be a matter of juice and sharpness, like this. Blood too, perhaps, the first time. I was ready to pay that price. Red and hot at the center.

There were beans, baked potato, salad, and bread. I ate those things and left most of my own steak on my plate. I vowed I would never again order meat any other way but medium rare...

Now

...and I never have. A couple years ago I read in an expose memoir by a famous chef that many restaurants make a habit of serving their oldest, most questionable meats to patrons who order them well done, since this is the state that best disguises their lack of freshness.

the edge of puberty

Menstruation was anticlimactic after hearing about it for years and years in school. When my first time finally came it was a brown trickle. My periods were an erratic nuisance, coming at 3-week intervals for two months, then not at all for another two. I was glad to pass another milestone to sexual maturity, more or less on schedule, but the thing itself was nothing to write home about. Sometimes the blood looked like blood and other times like clumps of brown or maroon snot. This yucky sludge had not been mentioned in the

PE textbook, but I assumed there was nothing wrong with me. Why would there be?

The PE teacher began a study unit on body composition. Body types were: ectomorph, mesomorph, or endomorph. Those words were the scientific way to say bony, muscly, or fatty, respectively. Scientifically, one pound of fat equaled 3500 calories. Therefore, to lose weight, eat fewer calories or exercise more. All of this seemed obvious to me, though I relished the Greek words. For a week we had an assignment to write down everything we ate, all meals or snacks whether at home or someplace else, and calculate the calories using charts in the textbook. I was not faithful with my record-keeping at home, and many foods my mother cooked, like lentil soup, weren't in the charts anyway, so I ended up having to invent plausible entries the night before the assignment was due.

Next the teacher paired girls off to take each other's measurements and see whether we could "pinch an inch" anyplace. Plump Anna Capelli was my partner. We checked the circumference of each other's chest, waist, hips, thighs, and calves. We had to record these numbers on forms the teacher handed out, and beside them write our "goal" measurements and what we planned to do to achieve our goals. Anna copied down most of my body measurements as her "goal" column. This was a very clever strategy, I thought. I would have had no idea how to come up with appropriate goals if it had not happened to be the case that there was already little to no room for improvement in my own body. When I wrote down all my actual measurements a second time, as my goal, though, I was surprised that Anna gave me an argument, claiming she could pinch an inch on my calf. I was pretty certain that what she pinched was all muscle, but I could think of no way to say so that didn't sound conceited. And if there really *was* something wrong with my calf, then I had no idea what would make a good calf. Eventually the teacher supplied a compromise: I should plan to maintain the same circumference but "tone calf for tightness."

Lastly we measured each other's height and weight. By now I had crossed the five-foot and 100-pound boundaries. I recorded the figures (which I no longer remember exactly), then entered my actual weight on the sheet a second time as my goal weight. Anna was shorter than me so the teacher helped her look on a chart to find the right goal weight for that height. I reflected that it would have been simpler if Anna just took both my weight *and* my height as goals. But of course there was no blank on the sheet to record a goal height. Obviously the idea of having a goal height was ridiculous. Still, when I thought about it, I realized I had one.

Besides transforming the world, I had other secret goals, and one of them was to be six feet tall. The others were: to have sex, to be a genius, to win an Olympic gold medal in the marathon, and to live to be 140 years old, a greater age than anyone ever attained before.

What body type are you? said the last blank on the sheet. "Mesomorph," I wrote. Naturally. "I am an endomorph," Anna wrote, in small round letters.

Chapter 4

Is Any Sick Among You?

1975, Hurricane, Utah

In the summer as we visited my grandparents on their farm, my sister Anita had a full-blown psychotic episode. Obeying instructions from some other world, Anita ran around in circles on my grandparents' front lawn, occasionally speaking some quiet words. With the rest of the family, I stood and watched, feeling there was probably something I was supposed to be doing, but having no idea what. Talk to Anita, touch her? The prospect of either made my skin crawl, yet I can't truthfully say that I wanted not to see what was going on. I resented it whenever adults would whisk me away from the scene of action, or censor their conversational topics to protect my tender ears.

My mother went to Anita and took her arms, tried to make her stop. "No, no," Anita said, "I have to run, run, run!" She spoke gently, almost musically, not as if her feelings about her activity were really very urgent. But still she brushed my mother aside and kept running. She smiled at us all, not in pleasure but jocularly, ironically, as one does when juggling two social interactions at once, as if she couldn't leave the telephone but still tried to include us vicariously in that other dialogue.

My mother turned her back on Anita, which left her facing my direction. I saw that her eyes were full of tears she was blinking back. I saw too that she saw me and knew I saw her, and didn't care. I was feeling vaguely guilty over my inaction and quasi-voyeurship, but that meant nothing to my mother. She had no reproach or request to make, no reassurance to give, and in this moment she was completely indifferent whether I witnessed her distress and Anita's compulsion. She didn't much care whether she looked toward me instead of the trees and grass in the yard. I felt more profoundly insignificant than I ever had before.

My parents, my grandmother, and I talked it over and decided that I would remain for the summer in Utah when my parents, Anita, and Dan started on the return drive home to Arizona. After all, maybe I would rather be away from the center of excitement. The specific scene on the lawn had alarmed me in a personal way; my own obsessions seemed to echo it in some ways. If the perfectly admirable Anita could go crazy, out of the blue, nothing was safe. I brooded over it.

Was there a right way of thinking and living that would guarantee to keep you sane? Maybe it had been a mistake to play at believing in the Greek gods, or to think that Aquarians might bring completely new ways of perception to the world. Maybe it was dangerous to toy with ordinary reality.

"You're thirteen years old!" my grandmother said, beaming as if this fact by itself were enough to make anyone ecstatic. Her mouth curved higher on her left side than her right. She put an arm around my shoulders and with the other hand clasped my knee, giving me a series of increasingly exuberant squeezes and laughing in time with them. Her grip was pretty strong, I thought, for an old person. It wasn't unpleasant to be handled this way, though I wasn't getting as much satisfaction out of it as she was. She had wanted a heart-to-heart talk on our very first night alone together after my family's departure. I was already wondering whether I had made a terrible mistake.

"And you're getting so tall and graceful, with a strong, healthy young body. You're turning into a young woman, and I can already tell you'll be a beautiful one." I knew this was an exaggeration. Like my grandmother's, my features were a little out of true symmetry.

And there were the lurid pimples, red badge of social inferiority. But good hopes for my body were certainly justified.

"This is an important, exciting time of your life, the time when you're deciding what kind of person to be." Her relentlessly upbeat tone made me crabby: I certainly wasn't "deciding" to be a zit-face. And Anita had not decided to go insane. "With your remarkable mind, you certainly have the ability to lead an unusual life. You have to make choices now with your whole future life in mind. Over the next few years, you'll be making many changes as you turn into an adult woman—"

"I think I've made the most important change already," I said, thinking of my sexual epiphany.

"What do you think is the most important change?"

There was no way to say *I want to do it with a boy* to my grandmother, but there was nothing else I could bring forward that was of the same order of magnitude. "Oh, I don't really know," I said lamely. "I just have a feeling that the main change is… Uh…" I hoped for some inspiration, but nothing came and my grandmother was still waiting. "That I already have changed a lot. That's all. You know?"

"Do you mean menstruation? The physical changing of your body?"

"Yes," I said. "That's it." It was in the ballpark, anyway.

"That's exactly what I wanted to talk to you about tonight: maturity. Physical, emotional, spiritual maturity. Now that you're becoming a young woman, the choices that you make are more important than ever…." Grandma had the tone of a PE filmstrip, but it wasn't yet clear whether it was one about sex, or drugs, or the importance of self-respect. I waited for an opportunity to show her that I already knew whatever it was she was talking about. "What I want to tell you, is that young people can encounter temptations. What your peers are doing is very important for a teenager, I know, but a mature young person will know how to make her own wise decisions, to refuse to use her body in ways that aren't healthy —"

"Grandma, you don't have to worry about me. I would never, ever, even consider smoking cigarettes or using drugs or anything like that."

"Of course you wouldn't. You're far too smart for that. But do you know there are even some young people—people *not much older than you*—who are experimenting with *sex*?" She looked at me expectantly.

"Hmm," I said. "Isn't that something?" Grandma's attitudes on sex were not surprising, I thought. She was old and religious, and the new wisdom of the 1960s had passed her by. But it was odd the way she had inadvertently miscued me: for sex I would expect her to talk about immorality and God, not peers and health—no wonder I had guessed wrong! It was her mistake.

For the first few days I was tentative in my grandmother's house, on my best behavior. One of the things good behavior meant to me was to eat all of the foods my grandmother served, even the strange-smelling asparagus. It grew like a weed on my grandparents' property, but not a weed that ought to grow anywhere on earth; it was something alien, halfway between plant and animal, shaped like reaching tentacles or a sex organ. With my new expanded ability to eat, I could get asparagus down. But other foods were downright enjoyable: fresh raw peas or cherry tomatoes plucked and eaten straight from the vines, little red potatoes that my grandfather grew and my grandmother cooked. I made quite a show of my appetite for the potatoes, believing that my grandmother would see my appetite in the same way I did: evidence of virtue. She didn't have to know how recent a development this virtue was.

Childhood

When I was a very young child, I used to have the notion that eating meals was a chore you were supposed to do at set times, like washing your hands after going to the bathroom. I don't mean that I never wanted food. Dessert was generally attractive, and so were other special treats like cheese puffs or bacon. These were the extraordinary foods, only occasionally served, and then in limited portions which of course you ate all of. And there were ordinary things I would sometimes ask my mother for: cottage cheese with applesauce, raw carrots, buttered toast, fruit. Cheese was good only if sliced very, very thin: thick cheese overwhelmed my mouth with its heavy burden. Milk was a staple beverage which I willingly drank several times a day, though it was certainly possible to get tired of a glass of milk partway through. Baked potatoes or corn on the cob or fresh-baked bread were not exactly treat foods, but, for reasons not completely clear at the time, they weren't everyday, either. Those too were foods I was eager to eat. But my most insistent memories about eating in childhood are negative: food on my plate that I didn't want at all, or had wanted at first but didn't anymore.

"Just eat two more big bites," that was my parents' refrain. But even one bite is a great burden to a person who is full—and who better to judge when I was full than me? Besides, even if I could eat two more bites, some amount of food would still remain on the plate, and it would be thrown away anyway, so if it was all right to throw *that* food away, then how could it be wrong to go ahead and throw the other two horrible bites with it? I knew that my reasoning was flawless but my parents persisted in their monotonous and intellectually bankrupt argument: food costs money, don't waste it.

Something I read early on in a children's adventure book puzzled me: prisoners punished by being "put on bread and water" and given nothing else to eat or drink. But what was supposed to be so unpleasant about that? Bread was one of the least obnoxious things to have to eat. Of course in an ideal life there would be whatever treat you wanted on demand, but I didn't expect anything as outrageous as that and presumably people in jail didn't either. They weren't getting bread and water in place of milk and cookies, I reasoned; they were getting it in place of meat and vegetables. That was no loss at all!

It occurred to me that a foolproof technique would be to announce that I was full *two bites before* the moment when I really was. But alas, I couldn't make this ploy work for the same reason I couldn't put the right amount on my plate to begin with. I didn't know when I was going to run out of steam, and when I did it was all at once, a complete loss of stamina like a marathoner hitting the wall.

For the first three years after starting elementary school, I routinely threw away half the lunch my mother packed. Typically the bag would contain a peanut-butter sandwich (or else a hard-boiled egg), a little box of raisins (or else an apple), and a couple of cookies from a store-bought package. I knew I was misbehaving. But it was such a relief to be unobserved, to stop exactly when I wanted and be rid of the leftovers in a second. No one would ever find out.

After a while, neither the guilt nor the pleasure was acute anymore. Tossing out the raisins and half the sandwich was just what I always did at lunch. My mother asked me sometimes if I had eaten all of my lunch. It didn't occur to me that her motive could be practical, that she wanted to adjust her provisioning to my physical needs. I thought she was checking up on whether I was behaving decently out of her sight, just like asking if I had washed my hands. I wanted to be thought exemplary in all things, even though I knew I wasn't, so I always said yes.

One day my lunch bag was somehow misplaced, left at home I thought, and the kindergarten teacher gave me half of her sandwich, an outlandish construction of cold meat, mustard, and lettuce. *Meat wasn't supposed to be cold!* I was surprised to find myself able to eat this abnormal thing and more than slightly proud. It didn't occur to me that the teacher had made any sacrifice; I couldn't imagine anyone ever wanting more than half a sandwich for lunch.

But in fact my lunch bag wasn't back home; I'd left it in the station wagon which picked me up every morning, and the school principal delivered it to me herself before lunch was over. I was glad to see it, because I had missed the cookies. As soon as Mrs. Roan left again, I plucked them out of the bag, and put everything else straight into the garbage can. When I looked up I saw the kindergarten teacher staring at me fixedly. My stomach plunged as the floor fell out from under me. Trying to look casual, I turned and walked away, clenching my bladder tight. I avoided everyone's eyes.

I tried to persuade myself I had done nothing wrong. I had already done my duty by lunch, as well as usual, anyway—one half sandwich—and indeed better than usual, since the food was so peculiar. But I couldn't escape the sense of guilt. My sneaking self-indulgence had gotten buried underneath habit and privacy; now it was freshly exposed. I was terrified that the teacher would say something to my mother, and I spent the rest of the day rehearsing for cross-examination. But nothing more ever happened and I gradually relaxed again, throwing away half my mother's packed food as usual.

Eating or wasting my school lunches appeared to me only in the light of abstract morality; other than the need to cover my tracks, I saw no practical component. The teacher who gave me her food was, potentially, an agent of grim justice, and nothing more. I didn't see her as a person with needs, a person who might be hungry. I really didn't even know what hunger was, had no conscious experience of it. Not yet.

1975

My new eating capacity saved me from the recurring childhood humiliation of being burdened with food that I couldn't bear to finish, even though it might have been something I originally wanted and fixed for myself. Then I would either have to waste it publicly with all the disapproval that entailed, or sneak around looking for ways to throw it out undetected: pitching it into the "jungle" of desert brush behind our back fence, burying it deep in the garbage in the outside can, or running it down the disposal. Those days of petty crime were behind me now, and I could behave as though they had never been. Now I could eat with gusto from all the four food groups, the way we were urged to do in school, and I would grow even taller and stronger than I already was.

1982, 130 pounds

Age 20 is when I hit my lifetime minimum weight as an adult, though I didn't know it then, was still trying to get thinner. Trying to make sense of my vastly different physical incarnations (but I didn't feel like a different person!), I suggested to my mother that there was too much "moral pressure" about wasting food in my childhood.

"Just wait until you're paying for all the food yourself," she said.

"Jean thinks nobody should ever have asked her to try a bite of squash," she laughed at family gatherings over the next few years. Her air of good-natured humor: she would remain jovial through any amount of misguided criticism. And so I knew I had hurt her feelings very much.

1975, grandmother's house

At lunch on my third day there was one freakishly large potato in the bowl. I took it, but that turned out to be a mistake, since the ratio of skin to insides was all wrong. Skin was the best part of a potato. I managed to eat the whole thing anyway, and afterwards took two smaller potatoes I liked better. I refused the asparagus, though, feeling that I'd better begin to set a precedent I could live with long-term. Besides, my heroic work with the big potato entitled me to a little respite elsewhere. I had done plenty.

I was surprised when my grandmother advised me later that I shouldn't rely too much on "concentrated foods." This phrase had never come up before in my hearing, or in any book I'd seen or class I'd been in.

"What are 'concentrated foods'?"

"Well, you ate three potatoes at lunch, for instance. First you ate the biggest potato in the bowl, and then you had another one—I was surprised you wanted another one after that great big one—and *then* you ate *another* one." She opened her eyes wide to show me how outlandish my actions had been. I was bewildered. No one had ever suggested I ate too much. Obviously I was not the sort of person who ate too much.

"But the other two were just teeny-tiny ones…"

"But the first one was huge. And all three with butter."

I just stared. What *else* would you do with a potato, other than butter it?

"And you drank a quart of milk."

"I did not! A quart!? No way! I only had…" I tried to think how much fluid I had required to wash down the vast dry insides of the big potato.

"Three glasses. That's a quart."

"No it isn't," I said. My grandmother got out a quart measure and a dinner glass and showed me, filling the glass three times from the tap and pouring its contents into the larger container. The third glassful did, in fact, bring the fluid level almost to the top. "Okay, I guess it was about a quart. But—" No words were adequate to express my disorientation. What could possibly be wrong about drinking milk? Milk was my faithful old friend, one of the few areas in which I had always been above reproach, at least in terms of my public image. Milk-and-milk-products was a *food group*.

"All that milk is the reason you didn't eat any asparagus."

"It is *not*! I *hate* asparagus."

"But you ate asparagus yesterday and the day before."

"*That* doesn't count! That was only the first two days." I waved my hands: it was impossible to explain.

My grandmother smoothed her face over, visibly deciding to withdraw from the head-on approach. "You see, Jean," she said sweetly, "what I want to explain to you is this: every type of living creature has its own particular food that it's supposed to eat. Rabbits have their kind of food that they're supposed to eat, and it would be unhealthy and wrong for a rabbit to eat meat, and tigers have their food that they're supposed to eat, and it wouldn't be good for a tiger to eat vegetables—"

"Cut to the chase, Grandma."

"Human beings are meant to eat grains, or bread made from whole grains. That should be most of their diet, along with fresh fruit and vegetables. Milk and butter should be used sparingly." She pulled a spiral-bound book out of her shelf of cookbooks. I noticed that she had copies of Adele Davis and *Small Planet,* too, like my mother. "Look at this," she said. On the cover was a drawing of an ear of wheat and these words: *The Staff of Life.*

It would be at least a decade more before I saw in print discussions of the food pyramid, with its foundation of grains. And it would be even longer before the pyramid ousted the old four food groups, and came to seem self-evident in its turn, a timeless unchallengeable truth, at least until popular beliefs about good nutrition shifted again. In retrospect it seems an interesting irony that my grandmother, whom I thought so mistakenly backward in her sexual attitudes, should have been so much ahead of her time in her views about diet.

the turn of the 21st century

In the last thirty years or so, we've heard the story a thousand times about how the well-meaning middle-class American parents trained their children into an erroneous belief that virtue consisted in cleaning their plates. Gradually, the children learned to ignore or override the physical cues of satiety, thus paving the way for a habit of overeating later in life. Poor misguided parents! Poor emotionally-encumbered girls and boys!

It's an appealing story—certainly many people have found it persuasive—and perhaps in another generation, upbringings like mine will be a historical curiosity because of its cultural sway. But excuse me if I say this is not my story. I never learned to keep eating past fullness. Hitting the wall was for me too absolute and unmistakable a condition. And even though they caused me some stress at the time, I don't regret my parents' policies now. Later in life I had reason to be grateful for the image I had formed of myself so early on, as a person uninterested in food, not eager to eat.

On May 29, 1998, in the era of the "fatlash," when vested interests in the weight-loss industry fought back against any loosening up of the official "ideal weight" guidelines, the *Arizona Daily Star* printed an AP report on a new study which concluded 54% of Americans were overweight. Obesity researcher James O. Hill was quoted to the effect that although people's bodies prompt them to eat when they need food, there are no similar physiological mechanisms "to stop us from eating if there is a lot of food around."

Yeah, right, we're just born endlessly self-indulgent. Like the way we're programmed to fall asleep when we get tired, but then there's no internal system encouraging us to wake up again after we're rested. Or the way, although our bladders signal us when we need to urinate, there is no corresponding Empty signal, so it's easy for anyone to overpee without even noticing, caught up in the physically pleasurable sensations. And thirsty people, under normal circumstances, naturally continue drinking water until the cows come home, until they burst, unless they're very careful to exercise self-control.

What's wrong with you, Hill?

James O. Hilll was born in 1951. Odds are he grew up, like me, in a middle-class household where regular meals were provided, where nutrition was emphasized as the laudable goal of eating, where housewives all knew that a judicious combination of the four food groups, including fruit-and-vegetables (eat your vegetables), milk (drink your milk), and meat (finish your dinner before dessert) would make children grow up healthy and strong.... Those days aren't so distant that by the 90s they'd been wiped from the memory of every living adult. James O. Hill and most readers of that newspaper report must surely remember what it felt like to get full. To get (ugh!) the-hell-full, so full you not only don't want more, you actively and passionately wish to be excused from the table.

There *are* physiological mechanisms and cues to stop eating. Remember the warnings against snacking because it would "spoil your dinner"? I know, you haven't heard that one lately, but it was a commonplace just a few decades ago. Are the Americans of today suddenly a different species with a completely different physiology?

Well, perhaps there has been some kind of change, some damage.

1983, at my thinnest

I couldn't get full to save my life or even—more precious than life—my self-pride. I'd twitch restlessly, jaw clenched, waiting for it to be time for my next carefully planned and self-disciplined meal, unable to think of anything but food and unable to believe that I had ever found anything else remotely distracting…. It wasn't a question then of lacking the will to hold out. I had sufficient will to delay eating indefinitely and even for the far more difficult task of eating "moderately" and then stopping. But I had no power to make myself stop wanting food.

That was the hellish thing: there was no way out. My only choices were to give in to what I believed was depraved desire, or endure it endlessly.

Now

I feel afraid for kids who are growing up today. If I didn't have my memories of what it felt like to be full, I might never have escaped, never have figured out that appetite is just appetite, not neurosis or sin.

1975

Alone in my grandmother's house one day, I found another book tucked away in a linen closet. *Is Any Sick Among You?* I liked the biblical cadence of the phrase, and I opened the book. People's private reading material was often more interesting than what was right out on the shelf. For instance, my older brother Howard's secret copy of *The Sensuous Man* had been thoroughly engrossing, as well as offering practical information on female anatomy.

The first sentence read: "Aristotle said: 'Dear is Plato, but dearer still is truth.'" That was exactly how I felt! People in my family saw me as having an argumentative personality, when really it was just that it was so important to get things right. I read on.

The author of *Is Any Sick Among You?* had polio as a child and got cured miraculously. She suggested that pretty much all illness was caused by eating the wrong foods, "concentrated foods," which accumulated in the body and then started rotting. She had seen many cases of people being cured of tumors by a regimen of prayer, raw fruits and vegetables: the tumors just popped out without surgery because the raw food cleansed them. She herself had often fasted for 21 days at a time and knew of other people fasting for twice that long with no ill effects. Fasting and drinking a lot of water was an excellent way to clean out your body.

So this was where my grandmother got her idea of concentrated foods. But the pieces still didn't all fit together, since according to this author, grains counted as concentrated foods, whereas in the other book they were the staff of life. Also, weren't potatoes vegetables? So they should have been fine to eat and my grandmother was wrong to criticize. Something didn't add up somewhere, but I decided not to worry about it. Surely my newly quickened food appetite, like my sexual appetite, must be a good thing, and if my Grandma thought different she must be mistaken. The polio story was stirring, though. Wilma Rudolph, one of my childhood heroes, had also had polio, besides being desperately poor and subject to racial discrimination, but she overcame all adversity to become one of the greatest runners of all time.

Perhaps, I thought, some people really did get sick from eating wrong food over the years. That made sense: I had read many stories in which hardship plus determination led to later triumph, or wealth plus indulgence led to deserved deterioration. Perhaps the polio and cancer cures had actually happened when formerly greedy people fasted and cleansed their bodies, undoing the damage. And the prayer part was just coincidence, perhaps, a superstition, like being against sex. In any case, nothing was wrong with me and probably nothing ever would be. But I would file the information away just in case.

Chapter 5

My Body, Myself

the start of high school, 1975

My mother helped me choose new clothes for my freshman year, slightly dressier than what I was used to wearing: pants with creases, shirts with buttons. Some of the pants that fit me were size 12, but in some styles the 12 draped too loose and we bought those in a 10. One pair of size-10 pants was a light blue color similar to the color of much-faded blue jeans, but the fabric was finer and crisper than denim. They soon became my favorite pair, the ones I reached for Monday morning. In junior high school I had always left shirts untucked for comfort. Now I routinely tucked them, pleased by the long line of my body. I was in love with my body and remained so for the whole first year of high school and a good part of the second.

My breasts were perfect little cones, set high on my chest and pointing straight forward from my body. I knew they weren't the most popular shape and size—my own cupped hands could cover them with room to spare—but just the same I admired them endlessly. I gazed at myself with pleasure in the bathtub, and nude in my bed by candlelight. In the daytime breasts were more awkward, irritated by the shifting touches of almost any shirt, outraged by the confinement of a bra.

An experiment with tampons turned out badly when the plug got stuck behind a thick ribbon of flesh which, according to the diagram inside the tampon box, I shouldn't even have. I got the tampon loose eventually, but I worried about my body. It didn't match up quite right with the biology textbook either. But I remembered seeing another book. Out in the storage shed, where my parents had put more sets of bookshelves to hold the overflow from the house, I found it. *Our Bodies, Ourselves* was written especially for women by a women's collective. It had drawings of sex parts that looked more real than clinical diagrams: they included the crinkly folds and hair. "Hymen shapes can be very different in different women," I read, squatting on the concrete floor of the shed. On the same page there were six different pictures of hymens, and the fourth one looked like me: an oval ring with a vertical bar that went right across the middle, leaving smaller oval openings on both sides. So my body was okay! *I* was okay!

"Can I keep this?" I said to my mother.

"It's not mine. It must belong to Anita," she said. I took *Our Bodies, Ourselves* into my room and read it cover to cover. I embraced my body, studied it with renewed pleasure. Maybe I would be a gynecologist when I grew up.

In the winter there were more new clothes. My mother had me try on a thin sweater in a subtle tan color that was perfectly poised in the middle between too buttery (unsophisticated) and too cold (uninviting). There was an abstract pink and white pattern across the chest that struck an equally clean midpoint between flowery and thorny. Other pink accents echoed the pattern at the neck and the ends of the sleeves. I looked in the three-way mirror. My breasts pushed out the pink and white band just enough so you knew they were there. Would a girl in this sweater be attractive to a boy? I hesitated over the pink. Beginning in elementary school, as soon as I began to have a concept of social life, I had rejected all pink clothing as too soft for my vigorous intentions.

"It's elegant," I said. "But is it really me?" This was a standard line my father used as he pretended to wear obviously absurd things, a frisbee as a hat or a plastic tablecloth as a toga. But my mother took the words as though they were a straightforward question.

"It looks good on you," she said. "It could be you, one possible you. It isn't… frilly." I could see she was choosing her words carefully, afraid of accidentally spooking me, as if I were a skittish horse. "You don't have to be so… relentless all the time." If she had sounded even a little impatient, if she had looked directly at me instead of my image in the mirror, I might have shied away, and dug in my heels against her. I felt in myself the potential for resistance, but close alongside it there seemed to be a potential for collaboration.

"Okay, we can get it. It can be my unrelentless sweater."

Having relented once, I relented again. We picked up several long-sleeved shirts in decidedly non-unisex styles. I tried on one with pastel stripes in lavender, pink, and a blue that would match my favorite pants. My mother ran her hand meditatively along one sleeve, which flared out dramatically from the shoulder and gathered itself again to button at the cuff.

"There's a vest in my closet," she said, "that I haven't worn in a long time; it's a little tight on me, actually. You can have it to wear over these shirts."

"Okay," I said. "Thank you."

The vest was navy blue, made of a stretchy knit fabric whose constant soft pressure against my breasts was comfortable. It narrowed with my waist, showing it off precisely. I wore it to school, feeling it displayed my body to good advantage, though there was no evidence anyone was looking or cared. Richard was still in my Spanish class, sitting near me and my delicately pretty best friend Holly, talking more to Holly than to me. Richard formed—like a miniature sun—a center of heat and gravitational attraction. But I had also looked with interest at some of the boys on the cross-country team, and some teachers.

Our English class did a joint project with the senior drama class, to film a play we had written involving an unwed teen pregnancy, abandonment by the seducer, failed attempts to find an abortionist, family uproars and threats, and, finally, miscarriage brought on by a random punch to the stomach. I was to play the part of the pregnant girl's grandmother and on the day of the filming I wore my blue pants, the pastel shirt, and my mother's navy vest, covering the outfit with a bulky sweater that came down to my thighs.

One of the drama seniors put makeup on me. He looked like a grown man. I saw stubble on the underside of his chin. I wondered if he had a girlfriend and if they had sex. As I walked away from the makeup chair, he called out.

"And keep your sweater buttoned up, so you look like a grandmother, instead of a teenage hooker." I was elated. Someone besides me had finally recognized the sexual potential of my body.

Anita went in and out of various mental hospitals, and then for a while she lived with her father, my mother's ex-husband. Books and articles about mental illness began piling up in our house. My mother passed on to me a book called *Eden Express*, by Mark Vonnegut, the son of my favorite science fiction writer. Mark had been a hippie, living on a commune. He and his companions meant to retreat from the insanity of modern, industrial, consumerist, militarist society. But instead of achieving fulfillment, he lost his mind. Friends who thought schizophrenia was a sane response to an insane society tried to help him with meditation, or by working on Mark's sexual and social attitudes, but he got crazier and crazier until they gave up and turned him over to a mental hospital. Eventually he met a doctor who told him "schizophrenia is biochemical" and put him on vitamin therapy. And now he was a completely mentally healthy person, studying medicine, and the author of a book.

The last chapter, "Letter to Anita," was especially moving. My mother said it must be some other Anita, but still. I read it over and over. Mark comforted his Anita, telling her to be sure to eat and sleep in healthy ways, and protect herself from stress and not listen to other people's misguided theories about what kind of mistakes she must have made with her life. It was not Anita's fault, it was not because of anything she did. I wept over the book and felt my thoughts about insanity restructuring themselves. It was as though something was being built in my head, a framework, like the scaffolding of a building, but also organic, like a tree that branches on its own. Mental illness was not a metaphor, I saw; it was, literally, illness. The mind was one of the organs of the body. To think that psychosis was something you caused yourself, by wrong thinking, was as crazy a superstition as demon possession. Maybe I would grow up to be a biochemist and help people, like Mark Vonnegut's doctor helped him.

In 7th grade, I had gone out for the girls' track team, but the longest race—440 yards—was too short to satisfy my notions of prolonged heroism. In 8th grade I ran cross country, which back in the 1970s meant running almost exclusively with boys. At the end of that year the junior-high coach urged me to try out for sprinting events in high school. I considered this bad advice, a misunderstanding of my personality and vocation as a runner. In the spring of 9th grade I was on the girls' track team, turning in mediocre performances in the mile. In the fall of 10th grade I went out for cross country again. In between, in order to be eligible to run, I had to get a physical exam. I measured 5'6" tall—halfway to six feet—and 120 pounds.

Coach Stefan gave pep talks before every meet, and other times too, lounging around before or after practice, his arms and legs flung out expansively. Often he concluded with the observation that the winning team is the one that wants victory the most. I didn't see how this could be literally true. One of the few boys who consistently ran slower than I did was Robert, who had some physical problems which were apparent even when he was only walking: one leg seemed longer, and that knee and foot pointed off to the side. Besides, people said, there was a hole in his heart. But lame Robert continued to run, doggedly, day in, day out, always in last place. Did coach think his desire was feebler than that of everyone else on the team?

"90 percent of running is in the mind, am I right?" Coach said. No, I thought. I had dressed out in my sweats and I sat near him on the ground, but not too near, with my knees up by my chin and my arms wrapped around them. A few boys were ready early too, but plenty of them were still horsing around in the locker room. In the girls' locker room there would be no one but me until track season started again in the spring. Coach had a clipboard, ready to take roll. "90 percent in the mind—am I right, Jeanie?"

It gave me a jolt like a stab in the bladder when he turned suddenly to me. The sensation of needing to pee when suddenly confronted by an authority figure was familiar to me from childhood, but now there was some new component added to it. My father still called me Jeanie, but no one else did, and I didn't invite it. Coach taking this liberty caused a mix of excitement and irritation, like when something touched my breasts. "I guess," I said. I kept my face as blank as I could. Recently I had had a complicated dream in which a boy on the cross-country team had taken me to a hotel, but they wouldn't let him rent a room because he was underage. The boy wandered off and then somehow Coach Stefan was there, taking my arm, smiling confidently at the clerk, saying a few words about "my daughter," but not touching me like "daughter," down below the level of the check-in counter, his hand rubbing my thighs. He rented the room, and left me in it while he went to the drugstore, "you know for what," he said, and of course I woke up before he could get back. My sex dreams always petered out in one dead end or another.

"Way to go, Jeanie, definite as always," Coach said. Perhaps he talked in ways that seemed flirtatious because he wanted so much to seem at ease. Perhaps he would rather not have had the responsibility of dealing with a girl. These things did not occur to me. I thought his manner was that of an adult mocking a child, and I was offended. Besides it was dualistic thinking like Coach's ("it's all in your mind") that had hurt Mark Vonnegut, and could hurt my sister and other people too.

"If a person was sick, would you expect they could run a great race? Is being sick 90 percent in your mind? 100 percent of the mind is in the body. Like mental illness. A person can have hallucinations and think all kinds of crazy dangerous things in their mind, but really the place where it started could be something like a vitamin deficiency." The coach looked nonplussed; I had never said so many words at a time to him before. I was surprised too at the eloquence the growing thing in my mind had suddenly blossomed into.

"Right," he said, "right." He fiddled with the clipboard. "They're finding out more about that kind of thing all the time." He looked away from me toward the boys' locker room. "Let's hurry up, you clowns!"

Officially, philosophically, I rejected mind-body dualism, but still I had a feeling that somehow I should be able to transform myself into a great runner. Robert's limited potential was one thing, my life quite another. Between meets, at least, I returned to the feeling that my true running abilities lay dormant within me and I would tap into them yet by the right combination of will and circumstances. It did not seem reasonable that I might have only average athletic talent. Stories were full of people who had transcended limits by the force of their will and desire. Why not me?

In practice I was plagued by injuries and erratic performance. In junior high something had gone wrong with my left knee. Not terribly painful, it troubled me only during "lunges" in PE class, when all my weight was thrown forward onto it. Otherwise, the trouble was hardly noticeable, and I kept on working out, until one day something seemed to pop with a sudden release of pressure. The knee healed to the extent that the pain went away, but it had never been quite the same since. It clicked every time I bent it past 100 degrees, and seemed unsteady at times, as though it might buckle sideways.

Early in the cross-country season this year I had a little blister on the bottom of my foot at the beginning of practice, but I ran anyway, trying to step down on one side or the other, instead of flat in the middle of my foot. I could tell the blister was enlarging, and I was running a lousy time, too, but I didn't want Coach Stefan to think I was a quitter. When I finished the course I found I couldn't walk. When I took off my shoe, my sock was wet with blood. Coach called the trainer, who cut the sock off with scissors and bandaged the sore that stretched across my foot. "You have more guts than brains," the trainer said. Complacent about my brains, I figured the remark was a compliment.

Now I had a persistent ache in my right leg, the strong good leg that compensated for the bad knee on the other side. I had heard other people talking about shin splints but I wasn't sure if that was what I had. "It feels like a bruise in my bone, kind of," I told Coach Stefan, groping for an accurate way to describe a pain that felt deep even though my shin was right there on the surface, and was strongly localized yet not sharp in its edges, like an object felt through a pocket. "Run it out if you can," he said. "Take a day off if you can't." I tried to run it out.

When my right foot hit the ground the shin hurt, but not *that* much. It shouldn't interfere with my running as much as I was letting it. Why was I being such a wuss? It seemed to me that the problem was the fact that my own efforts produced the pain. The sensation itself wasn't so bad. If a doctor had to hurt my leg that amount for medical reasons, I could be brave. Or if Nazis or somebody had hold of me, trying to make me cooperate, I wouldn't be close to cracking if all they were doing was *that*. I would split myself in half, I decided, to be more efficient. One part of me just to run without noticing how my body responded. One part of me just to feel and endure without becoming involved in the effort.

The plan succeeded. I had a group of boys I usually tried to keep up with—and could on a good day—steady pacers who could click off seven-and-a-half-minute miles one after another. I stayed with my group and the running part of me held the pace while the feeling part of me acquiesced quietly to the hurting shin. Then abruptly something shifted. It was not that I ceased to feel the pain, not that at all, but it was gloriously transmuted. Pain was a fiery steed which I could mount and master. There was no need to split myself anymore: I let the two pieces of me be ecstatically reunited.

During the Age of Aquarius I had loved to read books about supernatural abilities, though I had grown skeptical since. Eastern mystics walking on fire, conquering pain by thought. Was this the way they did it? Experimentally, I let my right foot hit the ground even a little harder than it had to. The pain leaped higher and I on its back rose with it, in pleasure. So it was true. You could transcend bodily pain by willing it.

My race times mysteriously failed to improve, however.

Chapter 6

How it Started

125 pounds… sophomore year (1976 or 1977)

If I had known in advance what was about to begin in my life, the amount of suffering it would cause and the years it would consume, the way it would color every aspect of my self-image, the sheer amount of energy and attention it would cost me, I would certainly have paid more attention to how it started. But I assumed losing five pounds was a trivial project that would take a week or two to complete at most. And so there are many details I've forgotten about exactly when and how it happened.

I know that I had not yet turned 15. Coach Stefan had recently made a little speech about keeping thin—"The best distance runners are ten to fifteen pounds underweight, so watch what you eat"—and that stuck in my mind. There was also a particular red and blue shirt, my favorite then, because it was a thick knit that I felt made a bra unnecessary, and because it was a hand-me-down from Anita. At a certain point my mother advised me not to wear it anymore—"It doesn't look good where it curves around your bottom." But nobody criticized my body. Nobody suggested anything was wrong with me.

There had been no changes in the way I fed myself, responding to my appetite directly with almost no conscious attention. I don't remember whether cross-country had ended by then, or not. One might guess that a change in exercise levels would make a difference. But it's equally possible that the cross-country training had already added lean weight—more muscle and bone—to my body months before I noticed. This would also have been around the same time that my rocky periods stabilized, and that may be no coincidence, since scientific findings of recent years show that leptin, a hormone produced by fat, is required for sexual maturation. I can't pin any of that down for sure. All I know is that sometime, somehow, I became aware that I now weighed 125 pounds. And I decided to take myself back to 120.

I had no very high opinion of the girls I knew who dieted. They flipped through their food indexes at lunch, crowded around the mirrors in the bathroom, ostentatiously deploring their body parts, Oh, I'm so *fat*. Nothing was more irritating than a smooth-skinned, pretty-faced, big-chested girl whining about how difficult it was to lose weight. What about it was difficult? It was calories in, calories out, a simple equation that anyone could understand. All they had to do was stop eating so much. Those girls were right about one thing, though: parents were an obstacle. I could foresee what would happen if I let mine know I intended to lose weight. My father would insist that my body was beautiful just as it was; my mother would insist that my mental perspective was all wrong. They would both interfere. Of course my body was all *right*, but that wasn't the point: I wanted a body suitable for the very highest aspirations of sex and athleticism. Obviously these goals were strictly private.

From health class I knew the theory that everyone knew: it was only total calories that counted. In terms of pounds of fat, it made no difference how and where you cut calories. So it was ridiculous to piddle around with those charts, counting, hoping to make your food add up to just a tiny bit less than you needed every day, taking forever. I would eat a *lot* fewer calories and *know* I was making progress, fast. From the times in elementary school when I had pocketed my parents' lunch money I knew how little it bothered me to skip a meal. From *Is Any Sick Among You?* I knew people could fast for weeks at a time with no harm. If by chance there was some physical unpleasantness, I could tough it out, it wouldn't be any worse than shin splints. For maximum efficiency and privacy, I would eat just enough in front of my parents to give the impression of business as usual. And nothing at all when they weren't looking. My calorie intake would immediately go down to one third or less—there was no need to count—and my body would use up five pounds of fat as quickly as possible. The plan was foolproof, so I put it into action the same afternoon.

My mother, or occasionally my father, still provided some kind of family dinner on most evenings in the week. This time it was fishsticks, corn, and salad. I didn't like fishsticks anyway, so it was easy to be skimpy with them. I drank water instead of milk. The following day, unobserved, I ate nothing for breakfast or lunch. It wasn't hard. During lunch I had plenty of time to read my library book. Ordinarily I would have had a snack—fruit, or toast with peanut butter or cheese, probably some milk—when I got home from school. Now I drank only water from a jar in the fridge. I was unusually aware of the cold progress the water made through my throat and chest, a sensation that was interesting and not unpleasant until it reached my stomach, where it seemed to create a violent division between the stomach walls. It was as if two animals had been nestling cozily together, then were suddenly jerked apart and hosed down. Now there was a shrinking, quivering, and whining in my guts, an animal misery which I regarded with detached satisfaction. If this was hunger, good!—my plan was working.

At dinner I had a piece of good luck: my parents were going to a party. All I had to do was dawdle until they were gone, leaving behind them some cooked peas and a porkchop each for me and my brother.

I went into the kitchen and meat smell filled up my skull. Dan had already eaten his pork chop and was watching TV; mine lay alone in the pan on the top of the stove. I had no intention of eating it, but as I looked at it I could feel how easy it would be to give in, for a person of lesser will than mine. It was strange to want meat; even with my recent appetite change, meat was still far and away the least interesting of all the food groups. But I wanted this piece of meat so much that I could almost imagine sacrificing my entire plan for it. Almost.

Suddenly I could vividly imagine myself bringing the pork chop straight from the pan to my teeth, eating it right there, standing up, alone in the middle of the kitchen. Saliva ran into my mouth. I might really do it. For the first time in my life, I was torn by the inner conflict known to every dieter: there's a razor's edge you straddle, a moral crux almost as tangible as a geographical location, where the dropoff on one side is so steep, and so far down, that it seems little less than damnation. At my very first, innocent time at this brink, my indecision astonished me, because my choice had already been made, I was going to climb upward, the *other* direction, I *wanted* to, and it was going to be so easy, food meant nothing to me, how could there be a danger of my falling for a lousy *pork chop*? Mentally, I reeled at the verge, and mentally I yanked myself back, and then the danger was past. But I was shaken.

I forked the pork chop onto a plate like some radioactive object that had to be handled with tongs. There should be some ritual, to celebrate my victory and put myself beyond temptation: a sacrifice of burnt meats, like the Greeks. I picked my way into the undergrowth behind our backyard fence. Grass that had escaped from the lawn grew in knee-high, weedy-tough bursts in between desert plants made unusually plump and green by the water they siphoned off from our yard. I put my back to the fence and squatted behind a stiff desert broom, facing west into the sun. My unease about playing Greek had faded again: what could it hurt, if I knew it was a game? Actually, I thought, the important thing now was to generate as much fervor as I could: it was alarming how near I had already come to screwing up.

I tried to put myself in a reverent frame of mind. To which god would I sacrifice? A Mary Renault novel from the library had given me the idea that Apollo was the patron of long-distance runners, and the noble sun god was even now driving his flaming chariot to the end of his daily course. Shining Apollo stood for the triumph of the rational will over desires of the flesh, so he was a good choice. But Artemis, virgin huntress of the moon, drew me even more strongly for this purpose. I did not intend to keep myself literally virginal, of course, but I certainly meant to be perfect possessor and sole energetic mistress of my own body, like her. Artemis was an athlete. Statues of her usually had small firm breasts, like mine.

"Artemis," I prayed, "accept this sacrifice." The meat came off the bone easily; it was still slightly warm. "I hereby dedicate myself to your worship and vow that I will hold to my resolve." There was grease on my fingers; I had a sudden urge to lick them, which I resisted. I pulled up grass and buried the meat, then I took the bone back to put in the kitchen trash can. The beauty of the sacrifice was spoiled slightly by my discovery that I had forgotten the peas. In a second trip to the jungle I dumped them unceremoniously over the fence. They didn't tempt me.

On my mother's scale the needle wavered inconclusively: it was below 123 but perhaps not all the way down to 122 and a half. Call it 123 then. No corner-cutting. Even so, the plan was working faster than I expected.

In the morning my stomach was dormant. Strangely, it felt less light than it had the day before. A bad taste in my mouth was puzzling too—why should teeth ever get dirty when you were fasting? I brushed them. My father was still in the master bedroom, so I couldn't weigh myself again. Wary of chilled water, I drank from the tap, two glassfuls to promote the cleaning out of my body. Afterwards, I felt a little sick. To feel that my body was becoming more attractive, I put on my unrelenting sweater with its pink accents.

By sometime in the middle of the afternoon, I knew I would eat when I got home. I told myself I had not yet decided, that I was back on the razor's edge and might still win out over temptation, but I knew better. As I sat in my last class, waiting for the clock to move and the bell to ring, I tried to think, to plan. It would do no real harm to have toast and milk when I got home, because that was how I normally ate, and how I normally ate obviously had been only slightly in excess of what it should be. So if I ate lightly again at dinner, then resumed fasting, I would still be on track.

Getting off the bus, walking toward our house, I tried one last time to avoid the defeat that waited. Why did I have to eat? My stomach didn't hurt now; it wasn't even rumbling. Yet the desire for food gripped me with inexorable strength. My jaws ached with wanting to chew, a yearning as specific and local as the desire for sex. Sex, I thought, maybe sex could conquer food. I tried to conjure the desert island where Richard and I would be driven to shelter together from a tropical storm, but the images wouldn't hold together. I made peanut butter toast and poured a glass of milk.

The peanut butter exploded in richness; my mouth felt very wet around it. The milk was thick as cream, yet I drank it all easily. My comatose stomach revived instantly; it felt as though it were boiling around its contents. The sensation reminded me of "subtraction soup" from *Phantom Tollbooth*, a book from sixth grade: the more subtraction soup you eat, the hungrier you get. Now there was pain in my stomach. I ate a banana, and then some raisins. It had already been a double-sized snack, but still I wanted more. Finally, I made another piece of toast and poured more milk. As I ate the second toast, the food gradually calmed down into something more normal-tasting, and in the end I threw away the bread crust and poured out the last inch of milk.

At dinner a few hours later, once I had begun to eat, I ate heartily.

Obviously it was useless to weigh myself now. I would have to start over from scratch. I didn't understand what had gone wrong. Over the next several weeks, I repeatedly tried the plan again, and failed in more or less the same way every time.

My father got excited about a scientist in Oklahoma who was studying the effects of nutrition on all sorts of diseases, including schizophrenia. "He only uses vitamins, no drugs. Dr. Philpot's treated diabetics, too, and he's managed to get them off insulin—off insulin!—with no complications. If he's right, this is a real breakthrough." Like me, my father was a fan of learned theories. My mother on the other hand greeted new ideas with peasant skepticism, "And if he's wrong, he's a deluded crackpot." But she made no real opposition and Anita went to Oklahoma. Afterward Anita would come home to live with us and share my room. I was looking forward to it. She would be back to normal then; the two of us would be best friends.

The Philpot regimen started with a total fast: no food and no medications—water only—for a week. Then for several more weeks a patient would eat one new food every six hours and have a blood sample taken to see if their body was "sensitive" to it. Later they would eat according to the Rotation Plan, where every food was only allowed to be eaten on one day out of four. This prevented the bad effects of sensitivities from accumulating. I wanted very badly to believe in Dr. Philpot. Lots of times it took a while before average people, slaves to tradition, were persuaded by new scientific discoveries.

I wrote to Anita in Oklahoma, to cheer her on through the fasting and blood-drawing, "Hang in there, Neat!" I was going to write her name in special writing, using felt tip pens, and I left extra space for that. But once the card was already mailed, I realized I had forgotten to go back and fill that part in. "Hang in there, ____" was the message Anita was going to receive. My stupidity made me frustrated past the point of even being able to cry. I went out into the back yard and lay prone on the grass. I wished *I* could go to Oklahoma and fast. So far all my efforts to get to 120 pounds had failed, and now I couldn't even write a simple card properly. I wished the card back from the mail so I could do it over again and get it right.

The idea of wishing got me going on an old train of thought, one pursued periodically ever since I first started reading. Suppose I had three wishes for real? Fairy-tale characters so often chose stupid and self-destructive things. I had always been certain I could do better. My first wish was obvious: to be desirable, loved by Richard. Next I would wish to be able to fly—no, that was silly. To be a great runner. Third: Anita to be normal again? No… that was going to happen anyway. And these were *my* wishes. Third: To have not a single molecule of fat anywhere on my body.

In the body, besides being an energy reserve, fat is also a shock absorber and thermal insulator, and it participates by chemical signals in the hormonal regulation of appetite, metabolism, and reproductive function. Fatty myelin sheathes the axon of every neuron like the rubber that surrounds electrical wires. If my wish had been granted it would have meant instant death.

My father started doing the rotation diet while Anita was still away. "Tomorrow is day four," he announced. He turned over a sheet in a stapled bunch. "That means I get to have citrus. Hey hey!" He set the papers down on the kitchen counter, swung his hips and shoulders in a twisting dance step, then leaned over to look at them again. "And melons, walnuts, olives, huzzah!" He raised an arm over his head like a flamenco dancer and stamped his feet against the floor, snapping his fingers in rapidfire accompaniment, two on each hand, to create an effect of castanets—a trick which once had inspired me with worshipful awe. "Freshwater fish, and dates!"

"That's great, Dad. Whoopee for you. Live it up." It was touch and go whether I could tolerate my father's antics these days. Sometimes his sheer pleasure with himself still won me over.

"Freshwater fish, pah toodle-y wah," he said, fitting the words to a strong nursery-rhyme rhythm and wagging his head along with it. Of all his habits, this one was the most likely to trigger my contempt. How could he have so little self-consciousness? "You know, I've lost a couple pounds doing this rotation thing. But I haven't felt hungry." He adopted a male-model pose, gazing pensively sideways to show his profile. "Do you think I look svelter than the average 44-year-old gent?" It was ironic, but I knew he also meant it.

"I guess," I said. Why should my father take such an interest in his physique? My own body had to, had to be made as desirable as possible. That drive needed no explanation or articulation; it was visceral and could snatch me up as suddenly and fiercely as thoughts of sex. But nothing about those feelings was appropriate for my father. What difference did it make how old he was? "Actually, I never think about you that way at all, as being 44."

"Well, thank you, sweetheart," he said in full unironic warmth. I was embarrassed for him.

"Let me see that," I said, reaching casually for the pages. The Day 4 sheet listed individual melons (watermelon, honeydew, cantaloupe) under the category <u>Gourds</u>. Without meaning to, I found myself pronouncing the word aloud, "Gourds."

"'Gourds' is a good word, I agree," my father said. "I'm going to say it oftener. Gourds. Gourrrdzzz." He worked his mouth as if he were playing with chewing gum, rolling and stretching the word.

I didn't respond. According to the sheet, gourds also included squash, cucumber, zucchini (but wasn't that a squash too?), pumpkin, and casaba (whatever that was). Casaba made me think vaguely of

Africa. I turned to the front page. 'Spurge: cassava' caught my eye. "What's the difference between cassava and casaba?"

"Uh," my father said, "let me put my thinking cap on." He pretended to concentrate hard. "One of them comes from Africa, doesn't it?"

I couldn't help smiling. "That's what I was thinking, exactly." Many of the food categories had a poetic quality. Onion, garlic, leek, scallions, shallots were all members of Lily, and wheat, rice, oats, barley, buckwheat, corn were Grasses. "This looks interesting," I said. "I want to do it too."

Chapter 7

Subtraction Soup

headed toward 130 pounds

Incredibly, instead of thinner I became fatter. These days I weighed myself only after I had already gone some time without food, but now it took over a day fasting before I was as low as 125. As *low*. It was unbelievable.

Anita walked around the house and yard as slow as a zombie, staring straight ahead like a tightrope walker whose slightest sideways flicker could mean death. She could be awake at any hour of the night, though she stayed quiet, didn't even turn on a light, at the most slipping outside to smoke. It was incredible now that I could ever have thought her face beautiful. She had protruding cheekbones, nicotine-stained teeth, oily hair, an expression of strained attention even when she was only sitting and looking at nothing—this rigid face seemed almost like something created on purpose, like art that was supposed to disturb you, or even assault and punish you, like some "realistically" painted moment of crucifixion agony or the horrors of nuclear fallout. Muscles rippled in Anita's constantly clenched jaw although the rest of her body was emaciated. She bathed rarely and exuded a sour smell.

I had never yet successfully gone three days fasting. It was almost as though there were some natural limit at that point, like the sound barrier. Sometimes it was my mother's fault, of course, for calling me to dinner. But not every time. Often I had no one to blame but myself, getting up in the night of the second day, or coming home the afternoon of the third, and eating many things quickly out of the fridge, great handfuls of nuts and raisins, milk, cheese sliced thicker than I had used to even like and eaten plain with sips of milk, not even bothering with bread. Peanut butter with honey and more raisins stirred into it, eaten by the spoonful. More milk.

These shameful disasters felt like a betrayal of my real personality, but they were becoming more and more familiar.

How come Anita could manage not to eat and I couldn't? She didn't even want to, that was obvious. She wanted to smoke, and she did, letting huge clouds come boiling out of her nostrils as she exhaled. If she had wanted to eat, she would have. She was adrift, there was nothing anymore that she was trying to do. Not even live.

Without thinking of it in those terms exactly, I considered that Anita's wrecked life was no longer very much worth preserving, and I strongly suspected that she felt the same. Without thinking of it in words or clearly imagining what it was I wanted to happen, I began to wish her gone. The motion my mind made was like some piece of heavy machinery descending in instant, automatic finality, clamping down flat like a press against a page, or cutting down like a guillotine blade. Thunk. Gone. Away. Out of my life by whatever means, out of hers too if she wanted.

I had always had occasional difficulties with writing assignments, especially in English, where there were "no right or wrong answers," but other classes started troubling me too. In chemistry I learned that energy is usually released when chemical bonds form. But in biology the year before we had always talked about energy being stored in ATP molecules and released when the bond was *broken*. I made an A in both classes, but I was distressed that I couldn't reconcile them in my mind. The books I had trusted were beginning to disagree with each other. I had no name for this form of unhappiness and it didn't occur to me to discuss it with anyone.

In English we were assigned to make a three-minute "policy argument" in front of the class. Take a position on nuclear disarmament, for instance, the teacher said. But every issue I could think of—death penalty, abortion, socialized medicine, legalized drugs—had so many different angles that my mind flipflopped endlessly. And even if I could find a single consistent resting place for my thoughts, I could certainly never explain it in three minutes. Every day I tried to think my way through to some conclusion but the more different things I thought of the more hopeless it seemed to organize them. It felt as though the multiplying contents of my own mind would overwhelm and drown me. When I tried to stop thinking, I couldn't do that either, like Mickey Mouse unable to stop the enchanted broomstick in *The Sorcerer's Apprentice* from pouring even more water into the flooded chamber, and from resurrecting itself out of destroyed splinters into hundreds more broomsticks. People were supposed to laugh at the cartoon but if you were really in that situation there was nothing funny.

It occurred to me that I might be going insane. After all, insanity ran in my family. Hours could go by before these manic cycles of thought (which I called the Flood) would die down, leaving me in a blank numbed state (the Void) which was a relief by comparison but didn't allow me to get any homework done. I tried to explain the Flood and Void problem to my mother, only not using those words, which were private. But I couldn't make her understand how serious the situation was.

"It's not bad to *think*," she said. "It's a *good* thing to be a reflective person, somebody who can enjoy mulling things over. Be happy with yourself."

The English teacher did his best, too, trying to get a Socratic dialogue going, "to help you sort out your thoughts." Hah! If I couldn't do it, he would certainly never succeed. "What kinds of things are you interested in? What do you have strong feelings about?" Everything, I thought, but then again, nothing. "I don't know," I said. Resolutely, I gave the same answer to all his other questions until finally he gave up and let me take an F on the policy argument. I watched in scornful silence as the other kids did their simplistic presentations. One boy who argued in favor of adopting the metric system caused me a pang of regret. It hadn't occurred to me to concentrate on something so limited and straightforward.

In computer programming things were going downhill too. I had been very happy to get into it, an experimental class offered this year for the first time. Only good students were in there, most of them older than me. The two girls who sat by me—a junior and a senior—were friendly with me, and a boy they knew even sometimes talked to me. The teacher let us socialize freely anytime she wasn't lecturing, while we worked on our Basic programs or flowcharts, or waited for our turn to dial in to the university computer. It should have been wonderful, but somehow I had lost my usual classroom powers. I got a C on a quiz, and moved to a different seat at the front of the room, away from the chatting girls. "We are not the reason you got that C," the senior girl said. "I didn't say you were," I said. "I just think I need to concentrate more." But really they were the reason. What else could it be?

Even in math class, which had always been a blessed sanctuary away from confusion and trouble, all was not well. On a flood-y afternoon, I was distracted, and on a void-y afternoon, I was drowsy. Sun came into the window, making my eyes droop, and I couldn't really pay attention. It shouldn't matter. Math came easy. All I had to do was read through the chapter sometime before the test. In my notebook I drew a picture of how I felt: a lizard lying on a rock, blinking. But underneath the torpor I knew I didn't have a firm grasp of logarithms, and I was afraid. Maybe there really was something going seriously wrong with my mind?

It didn't occur to me that my sporadic fasting might be precipitating, or exacerbating, my flood-and-void cycles.

I almost wished that something drastically bad could happen to me. Teenagers in the young-adult novels I checked out from the library endured poverty, or ran afoul of violent gangs, or suffered from racial prejudice, or were sent to unkind foster parents. In a certain way, they were enviable. For them at least it was always clear how to channel their energies. In my life I was free to move in any direction at any time, and so everything I might do dissipated into nothing.

Part of the time I blamed myself, my character flaws; the school trouble and the fat, though unrelated, could both be seen as expressions of a fundamental lack of discipline. The rest of the time I blamed my circumstances. I was too rich, oppressed by my leisure, trapped in my middle-class family, surrounded by its groceries, which sooner or later would close in on me. If only I had had the luck to be born in a poor and struggling family, if I had to go out and work in the afternoons to help keep food on the table, then I would be much better off. On the other hand, I was deprived—robbed, even—of the solitude that had been mine before Anita came. Nights alone in my room, brooding over my naked breasts or reading, no one seeing or wondering about anything I did. Freedom from scrutiny, perhaps, was the missing ingredient without which my life had gone out of control. I could regulate myself if only I had my room and my life back.

It was my mother's fault, for buying food and cooking it. It was Anita's fault, for being there. If I were alone, I wouldn't eat the way I did. I believed all these things, and at the very same time I believed they were just excuses. Fat was always the fat person's fault, everyone knew that.

I tried to train myself into better discipline. In the bathtub, I grasped handfuls of flesh on the insides of my thighs or the underside of my buttocks and squeezed it at various angles and pressures, watching for the skin to dimple and reveal the disgusting fat underneath. I told myself that I was holding over a pound of fat in each hand. There were probably at least three pounds apiece spread around my legs—nobody would ever want to have sex with me! Deliberately, ruthlessly, I pushed myself to feel as much revulsion as I could; I intended for these emotions to transfer over to the act of eating.

It became harder for me to wake up in the morning and harder to sleep at night. In English I skipped other writing assignments that threatened my equanimity. In computer programming I changed my seat again, back to where I started, and considered myself lucky that the chatty girls were still willing to take me in. I needed them now, not just for friendship but so I could look at someone's work. It was all wrong, it was a travesty for me to be reduced to this groveling. In the past it had always been other people wanting to see my homework.

The math exam came around and although I had quickly read through the chapters it felt now as though my mind was moving in slow motion, drenched with something thick and sticky. I bent deeper over the test page as though the honey would drain from my head if only I held it at the right angle. I circled back to start problems over again, repeating the definitions I had absorbed—"e is the number whose natural log is 1"—and trying to reason my way forward from there to the solution. At the end of the hour I had left many questions untouched or half done, and when the test was handed back with a big red C at the top my first feeling was relief just to have passed it. Then the embarrassment in the teacher's face woke me up to my shame: *relieved* to get a *C*—in *math*! Something had to change. I stared out the window the rest of the afternoon, my mind churning with plans for making a great comeback in all my classes. I would go home and begin studying immediately. I hadn't eaten breakfast or lunch; I would keep that streak going too. I would study many hours every day for a week, which would occupy my mind so that the time would pass without my thinking about eating.

I carried all my textbooks home, but the sheer variety of different tasks I could choose to start on made me feel slightly panicky, incapable of doing anything particular. For an hour or two I dithered, opening and closing books and notebooks without being able to settle on anything. Finally I let myself relax into my current novel instead, a library book about Olympic athletes. Anita usually had the decency to leave me alone in the afternoons, but I was aware of her moving in and out of the house, smoking in the back yard and returning. I heard my mother come home and begin to fix dinner. The smell penetrated through my closed bedroom door.

I held out until pretty late, when everyone else was finished with dinner and scattered, my brother and mother to their bedrooms, my father and Anita to the living room. Then I reheated the stew my mother had made, filled a bowl and ate it at the kitchen table. The food was very, very good. The tomato sauce had a tang that perfectly complemented the slight textured sweetness of the brown rice, the vegetables blended unobtrusively into the background, and the chunks of meat were tender but still distinct, silken bundles that seemed to squeak across the surfaces of my teeth like a polishing cloth. I would have enjoyed the stew, if it weren't for the fact that eating was something to be ashamed of.

At the beginning I intended to have no more than one bowl but when I got to that point, it seemed unthinkable to stop eating. Still, I didn't believe it was the good taste of the stew that drew me back so strongly. It was just that I wasn't done yet. It seemed as though I were helpless to resist, and yet I knew perfectly well that nothing compelled me. Somehow I must be deliberately choosing to do and be this vile thing. But why? There was no reason at all. It was not because I wanted to. It was only because I wanted to.

After the second bowl, I could feel that my stomach held a fair amount of food, but still I wasn't done. I was full—wasn't I?—but I didn't feel full. In childhood I had *felt* more full when my stomach was less full than this. I remembered the strength of my desire to be free of unwanted food, even though back then I had childishly believed that a well-behaved person would eat it. Why couldn't I still have that feeling now—now when I understood what eating meant, now when I so much *wanted* to not want to eat? Why couldn't I look at the stew in the pot with the same loathing that I had for my fat? They were the *same thing*. Grimly I filled the bowl halfway again, and when I had eaten that, at last, I *felt* full. My stomach was unpleasantly stretched, swollen and heavy.

Suppose there really were a subtraction soup. Suppose you could buy it in cans at the grocery store and keep it in the kitchen, and it would act like an anti-food, relieving the discomfort when you had eaten too much, undoing the mistake. A person who was committed enough could eat subtraction soup to grow hungry again, back to the point where she started. Further, even. Or else, I thought, a Star Trek transporter device, implanted in my stomach, would have the same effect. Beam it away. But there was something I didn't like about the transporter idea. It seemed like cheating, though I couldn't say how it was really different from the soup. Actually, if you had the transporter, you could just transport the fat itself straight from your legs and bottom to the moon, or wherever. Now *that* was *definitely* cheating. Still, I thought, if I had a transporter I would probably do it anyway.

Everything I had done all day was bad. And the worst was that in hindsight I saw how easily I could have prevented this ruin. All my study time had been poured down the drain. Even if I had brought home only one textbook from school and looked at it for only an hour or two it would have been better than this. And now that I was full of stew, it was obvious that I could have stopped sooner. The way I felt now, I couldn't really imagine wanting to eat anything ever again. But I knew that I couldn't trust that feeling. Too many times I had planned not to eat and then come straight home to the feeding trough.

Throughout my sophomore year, my mind and body oscillated between two incompatible states. There was the restlessness, increasing to frenzy, of pre-satiety, the drive to eat that would not stop, would not stop until I gave in and ate, and even then would not stop partway, would not stop until I went all the way down the road to ruin. Then there was the torpor and shame of post-satiety, during which the feelings of the pre-satiety time seemed to be unmasked as complete delusion: I hadn't really been hungry, or at least not *that* hungry, or at least, I should certainly have been able to moderate my response. Clearly, my incompatible sets of feelings could not be taken at face value: before eating I felt had to eat, during eating I felt I had to continue; after eating I knew I had not had to. That couldn't be right: one side or the other simply had to be a mistake! It never occurred to me, not until many years later, to doubt the *after* feelings rather than the *before*. The shame in hindsight seemed proof of guilt, the moral anguish in preview seemed proof of a winnable struggle.

In the morning I stood at the high school bus stop, trying to be inconspicuous: my most reliable friends all rode other busses. I saw Anita, leaving the house on my mother's bicycle, picking her slow and deliberate way down the driveway, *don't turn this way*, but she did, heading toward the park in her unwashed hair looking like a mangy, runty, ugly stray cat, *don't see me*, and I kept my own eyes firmly elsewhere in order not to see any gesture of greeting she might make, *let nobody else see her*. Nobody here knew Anita was connected with me, as far as I knew, so even if someone did say something or laugh, I could stay uninvolved, pretend not to hear, as long as she stayed away, *don't cross the street*, and she didn't, although it would have been easier to cross there than higher up where the road widened. Maybe she feared that dangerous concentration of unpitying teenage eyes, maybe she meant to shield me from the taint of her something-gone-obviously-haywire, or maybe she was simply as oblivious as she seemed, her scope of attention narrowed as if she wore blinkers, *don't look this direction*, and though I didn't look at her either, I was acutely aware of her progress. Sometime before the point of her closest approach, when she would be only the width of the street away, I turned my back fully, stared into the dry desert gully behind the group of waiting kids while the second hand on my watch went around, lying to myself for safety, *she's right behind you*, waiting another full circuit, *she's still just barely past*, and halfway around again, and then I could face forward to the relief of Anita's back already far and going steadily farther away and no more danger of meeting her glance. *Go away.* My mind flashed down like a blade that cleanly divides one thing from another. *Do it.*

In the *Reader's Digest* I read an article about a man who had begun a diet by eating many hot fudge sundaes in a row, concentrating as he did so on the thought that poison was entering his body and spreading out through his blood. After that, he never wanted hot fudge again. Late one night, I attempted to give myself an aversion to peanut butter. I was excited as I sat down with the jar, planning to give myself—the rogue element in me, anyway, the glutton—an extremely unpleasant experience. Ideally, I thought, I would throw up by the end, so there would be no calorie cost to the training session, but even if that didn't happen, it would be worth it in the long run to hate peanut butter. I dug out a spoonful and put it in my mouth. Poison, I thought, poison spreading.

After I had eaten several spoonfuls, my mouth was dry. I had already decided not to drink. It was boring to wait while the chewed peanut butter softened in my mouth. I tried swallowing the lumps right away while they were still hard, and my discomfort increased immediately—good! Poison, I reminded myself. Garbage being lifted out by the shovelful in jagged-edged clumps, studded with broken glass.... I quickened the pace of the spoon, digging out another scoop at the same time as swallowing the last. I noted with pleasure how reluctant I was to accept each new bite. It was working. Eat garbage, I thought, poking the spoon deep into my mouth, thrusting as aggressively as if my body were a deadly enemy—it was, wasn't it? This was my chance to defeat it. Garbage at the dump, old newspaper fused by rain and sun into a solid mass, crusted on the outside, moist and shredding inside, rotting, insects breeding there, squirming maggots, crawling around, looking for meat, now going into my body.... I began to gag—that was good! But it was not enough yet, not quite. I had to make sure the revulsion would stick permanently. I continued to stick the spoon in until my throat rebelled past conscious control. Hanging over the kitchen sink, I choked and coughed as quietly as possible, letting peanut butter fall back out of my mouth. I congratulated myself on the unplanned naturalness of my physical reaction. Good, I said to my body, as to a contrite child, that's better, and tenderly I rinsed out my mouth.

For an experiment, I briefly entertained the thought of eating a few more spoonfuls, but was satisfied by the intensity of my desire not to. I went into the bathroom to see if I would now throw up. Unfortunately, the peanut butter seemed to be sitting quite comfortable. Maggots, I thought, but they remained an abstraction. There was no squirming; my stomach felt perfectly fine. It was really too bad.

To avoid having the evening end on a note of failure, I went out past the back fence into the jungle and put my finger down my throat. My throat coughed up my finger but below that point everything stayed put. I tried again, deeper. My stomach hopped a little, but nothing came out. It seemed that I could feel some safety valve closing deep in my body, holding back. I put two fingers in and shoved hard. I could feel my uvula dragging softly across my knuckles, and I bumped into something at the back of my throat before I corrected the angle. Just for an instant, there was nausea and my stomach opened, but by the time I bent over it had already closed again. Only a small amount of slightly liquefied peanut butter squirted up into my mouth, little changed since I had eaten it, only a bit sour. I spat it out and plunged my hand in twice more but got only the same little burp-ups. If I couldn't improve it would take all night to pump myself out, and meantime peanut butter was being digested. The peanut flavor in my mouth ought to have evoked nausea all by itself, now that I was aversion-trained, but I realized with disappointment that in fact it was relatively pleasant. Now I really had to find a way to feel sick.

My mother was a medical minimalist who never kept anything like Ipecac around the house. But it seemed to me I had read somewhere about mustard being used as an emetic. Inside, I filled a wine glass with warm water and stirred four tablespoons of mustard into it. I didn't know the correct recipe, but the main thing was to get enough of it into me. Too much wouldn't matter, since I'd be throwing it up anyway. I sniffed at the liquid. It actually smelled kind of appealing, which wasn't promising, but maybe the effects were internal. I drank the mustard water and felt depressingly refreshed. After ten more minutes of nothing, I knew mustard was a flop.

There was one last thing I could try. In childhood, when we twirled in circles for the pleasure of acceleration, and to make the world spin around our heads, I had often gone on to the point where nausea started before quitting. I could spin now, and just not stop short. I went outside again.

Even at the start, spinning didn't give me the pleasure I remembered, and I began to feel sick much sooner than I expected. I tried and failed to feel glad. Somehow I had forgotten what an exhausting, shameful feeling nausea was. I stopped spinning and lay on the ground for a short rest. Get up, I told myself, but I didn't, and when I felt the wave of sickness drawing back from my body it was an unspeakable relief. In a minute, I told myself, I would start again. It ought to be simple. It was no great effort, like running was. There was no good reason I couldn't make myself do this.

I got up and started my body turning but knew I wasn't going fast enough. I pushed harder, just enough to press against where the border of sickness began, like stretching a membrane, but not hard enough to burst through. I scolded myself for cowardice, then felt myself somehow sicker although I hadn't sped up, and sicker still although I was slowing down to nearly nothing. Then nausea blotted out my own will completely and my body flung itself onto the ground, reflexively fighting not to vomit. By the time I was aware of myself again it was too late: the gate was closed, the membrane intact. I was firmly outside of sickness and I couldn't bear to plunge myself into it again. Not because I was weak-willed, I told myself. Because it was a disgusting, wrong thing to do. It was cheating. I thought of decadent Romans and their vomitoria. Noble Greeks never threw up on purpose. Fasting was the decent way to become pure, and since the thought of food held no appeal now, I would succeed this time.

Two days later, hungry and trying not to eat, I put a spoonful of peanut butter into my mouth, hoping it would discourage me. But it tasted wholesome and desirable on my tongue, and the nuts felt good against my teeth. I went ahead and made a thickly spread sandwich of it, then another.

That spring, I made Cs in several of my classes. That was evidence, I thought, of my failure as a person. My body inched closer and closer to 130 pounds. That went beyond failure to sin and despair. Those are the things which consumed me at the time. Shortly afterwards, I had reason to turn my attention to another failing: the fact that I let my mentally ill sister see that her existence was a burden to me.

In retrospect, something that seemed relatively minor at the time has expanded in importance. After a few initial failures, I made no more serious attempts to throw up. My physical reflexes against it were a little too strong, my mental attraction to it a little too weak. Other women, having just a slightly different physical or emotional makeup, get hooked on subtraction soup's power to undo the past, correct the mistake, cover up the crime, of having eaten. As I think back over my life, I am profoundly grateful for whatever lucky combination of factors prevented me from becoming bulimic.

Me after half a year of secret weight loss attempts.

Anita before her time of troubles.

Letter to Anita
August, 2003
Dear Anita,

    The 26th anniversary of your suicide is this month, which means you will have been dead now for exactly as many years as you lived. Mom will buy flowers, as she always does, nothing elaborate, daisies or yellow chrysanthemums, simple and bright. The rest of us will let the date pass in silence. Half my lifetime ago—more, almost two-thirds. I regret that I can never know you as an adult. Not my only regret.

    The night after the day you died, I dreamed that you visited me in my sleep. You came to me in the bed that I was so eager to cede to you when you first moved in with us, before I came to resent you. That bed reverted to me when you moved into the University dorm toward the end of August. I don't suppose you ever intended to take that class you enrolled in. That was a fiction for our family's benefit, to get you through that one last summer in relative peace. Besides, it let you remove the site of violent death from our house. It was a careful plan, and courteous. I'm grateful.

In my dream we lay together and conversed, or touched, in some manner that did not depend on words or bodies. At times it seemed as though you lay next to me, and at other times that whatever you were now went through the surface of my body to suffuse me from within. Forgiveness flowed between us but that felt almost beside the point. Understood between us somehow was that no time needed to be spent, that it was already in the background. I am not a religious person, but I took some comfort from that dream.

I hoped to feel a similar sense of presence when we scattered your ashes on Mount Lemmon, but when the time came there was nothing. In fact, I was bored. As I took handfuls of the coarse, surprisingly heavy, salt-and-pepper grit of your body's minerals, I began indulging in a fantasy that I had the power to plunge hands into my own flesh, pluck out the fat from my bottom and thighs, and discard it just like this fine gravel. I knew I was secretly a terrible person who had all the wrong feelings; I was already planning my strategies for wasting away under cover of "grief." For the next several weeks no one would be likely to notice whether I was eating.

The cardboard box from the mortuary looked cheap and official at the same time. Mom shredded the box and started to scatter it too. Her fingers weren't strong enough to tear the taped-over label on top, so she threw it away whole. I picked it up and put it in my pocket, thinking vaguely that I wanted some kind of record. It had only been a week, but I'd already forgotten exactly which day you died, the name of the dorm you moved into, and I wanted to have the last piece of information about you preserved somewhere. Also, I wanted a relic to look at later; maybe I could use it, meditating over it to work up a more appropriate set of sad feelings.

Mom insisted that every scrap remain up there on the mountain. I couldn't explain why I wanted the label. It's littering, I said feebly. Mom was wild, shouting, "Considering all the beer cans and everything else people throw away here, I don't think this is anything to object to!" I was afraid and repulsed by her, the way I was by you in your sickness, Anita. With a sense of loss, I surrendered the label.

I had always coveted your purple sweatshirt. I know you knew that when you selected it as your farewell gift. So casual, so careful not to tip your hand. Nothing lavish, nothing that would raise alarm at the time, but a token that would be remembered and interpreted later.

"Hey, thanks, I always wanted this!"

"Yeah, you might as well have it," you said.

I guess that was a week or two before you did it.

There's another night I remember, from a few months earlier, just before my school year ended. You'd been reading that drugstore paperback—*Life After Life*—the stories of legally-dead people who revived afterwards. Yellow letters bright on the cover. Of course you were already thinking it over then.

It was late and I was tired. I had been working on something for school, I don't remember what, out in the living room alone. But for a change, this time I reached a point of feeling that the task had been accomplished. I had been on a kind of vacation from dieting and had eaten breakfast and lunch for several days in a row; I was not tormented by thoughts of food as I walked around the silent house.

All of a sudden I noticed that I didn't hate you any more. The burden of hatred had unobtrusively lifted off me, like fog clearing, sometime during the evening. An oasis, a remission.

That wasn't all. When I thought about it, it seemed plain I had never stopped loving you. I had believed I did, yes, but I saw now that I was simply mistaken. My mind was astonished at itself: obviously the chain of love stretched back unbroken right to childhood; how could I have been fooled by other feelings which were temporary and superficial? An identical sense of astonishment would revisit me for years to come, in dreams. More than a decade after your death, Anita, I continued to dream sometimes that you were still alive, that you had been away somewhere but now were coming back, and I was amazed—how could I have gotten so confused?—to think I had imagined you dead, when of course you had only been... where? The instant the question occurred to me, the memories would begin to form: you'd been out of the country, touring Europe, working in the Peace Corps, resting and being treated in a new progressive type of mental institution...

And I would turn to Mom to speak of my strange delusion, half-embarrassed to say anything, but too filled with the warmth of the moment not to, drenched in the intimacy, the light pouring in through airport windows as we waited for your plane, any minute now, to touch down. "You're not going to believe this— but somehow the craziest thought was in my head—"

The layered intensities of feeling, the incompatible beliefs we run through in succession, or hold simultaneously. The sense of revelation—No, that was an error, *this* is the truth—and fresher revelation beyond that—No, *this*.

On this particular late spring night, it was shiningly obvious to me that hating you had been sheer delusion, a thin film that peeled off in a second. Love lay underneath.

I turned off all the lights before I opened the bedroom door. I felt with my legs for the end of the low trundle bed and stood close up against it to ease the door shut behind me. Floor space was tight when the trundle bed was rolled out. Gently I set my books and folders on the floor beside the bed. I checked to see that my clock radio alarm was turned on, took my pants and shirt off, and crept into bed in my underwear.

You were not asleep. "Do you believe in life after death?" you said.

"No," I said, "I'm a materialist." But even as I spoke, I attempted to communicate love by pouring it directly into your mind, and it did not seem impossible that I might succeed. How did you know to talk to me on just this night and not before?

"Really? What about near-death experiences? All these people who say they went through a tunnel, and then saw light."

"Maybe that's just what it feels like to be dying. It must feel like something."

"I believe in it," you said.

I wish I had taken the opportunity to say I loved you, then, the last night when I felt it clear and strong, before I became enmeshed again in my secret drama.

I'm not religious. I believe nothing is left of you but recycled atoms, circulating now through air, water, earth, the trees growing on the mountain where we left you.

But I have always had a sneaking fondness for movies and books about life after death. I can't help picturing you with your personality restored, your sanity intact, dear friends around you who, perhaps, continue to be interested in the affairs of the living. You chat, peering and pointing down from a cloud in the cheesiest, most literal-minded afterlife that ever came out of Hollywood.

"Look, my kid sister is writing a book about her life."

"Oh, that's cool, are you in it?"

"Well, sort of. Mostly it's about how she thought she was too fat in high school. She's, like, 'Yeah, my sister shot herself. Now, here's what I ate and didn't eat that month.'"

I have no right to tell your story. The tragedy is too big, too arbitrary, for me to take on. And I don't even know it well enough to tell it, with all that I've forgotten or never knew at the time. Yet I have no right to airbrush you from my story. That sense of kinship pulsing between us, so horrifying at the time—I no longer wish to deny it. In writing about my own life, I don't mean to say my problems compare with your suffering. I am, as far as I can tell—and I attribute it to the vagaries of chance rather than any particular merit of mine—sane.

Do I have the right to set you aside, just when the stakes were the highest for you, to focus on the petty obsessions that absorbed my attention at the time? Forgive me, Anita, what else can I do? The disproportion is ludicrous, but for that very reason I believe there is a story worth pursuing. So many women and girls have done and thought the kind of things I did. So many spend whole lifetimes preoccupied with their successes and failures at achieving right eating and a good body.

I know that you do forgive me, would forgive me if you still existed, did forgive me, long since, before you died. I know that is what you meant to say by the gift of the purple sweatshirt.

Love from your little sister.

Chapter 8

Other People's Eyes

From 130 to 140 pounds

   For all the rest of high school, fat was the central mystery of my life. I still felt, most of the time, that I didn't have a fat personality, not really. Other fat people loved food, cared about it more than they did about their bodies, or how they looked to other people. I didn't. But what *had* happened to me? I had accidentally become fat, accidentally taken in more than the right number of calories, starting perhaps at puberty when my food tastes changed. Perhaps the very same potato my grandmother scolded me for had been the beginning. If only I could time travel, if I could talk to that naïve 13-year old girl, I could nip this whole thing in the bud, stop her before she ate the potato, explain that the skimpy, finicking ways she was embarrassed about were in reality something to be proud of. Hold on to that, I would tell her. Don't change.

   Obviously this heartache could have been prevented very simply. But still, why couldn't I fix the problem now by simply cutting back on calories one way or another? The only possible explanations were a weak will or gluttony, and yet I couldn't fully believe either, despite the irrefutable evidence on my own body. In earliest childhood it had always been easy for me to save my Halloween candy longer than Dan saved his, solely for the pleasure of being the one who had *more*. In elementary school it had been easy to skip lunch in order to pocket the money. In junior high it had been simple to resist a popsicle that cost only a dime. The cookie afternoon with Mona didn't mean anything, I told myself; that was evidence of immaturity, nothing more. But now that I was mature, now that I fully understood what was at stake, not a few coins here or there but *everything*, all pride, all hope for the future, the possibility of love, why couldn't I stop eating long enough to be thin? It was a paradox that could not be resolved no matter how often I thought it through.

I tried every method of weight loss I could think of, short of revealing my secret to my family. Just eating a slightly reduced amount at every meal sounded good in theory, but I couldn't seem to put it into practice. Up to the age of 14 I had kept perfectly thin by always simply eating whatever amounts I felt like. Now I had to stop myself somewhere before reaching that point, but before that point there were no landmarks to say how far away it was. There was no way to be certain you were eating little enough, except by significantly undershooting, making sure you were nowhere near satiety, which was tolerable at breakfast and lunch but became hard by afternoon. On evenings when my mother made dinner, it was practically impossible not to eat until I was all the way full. And then, after an episode like that, it was even more imperative to undershoot my appetite by a wider margin in the future, to make up for it.

It took longer now for me to get full. Had I somehow changed into a different kind of person? Once I had satisfied my appetites with a thoughtless faith in their rightness. Now they couldn't—I couldn't—be trusted anymore. It was very peculiar that a famously picky eater and secret food-waster like me had come to this state. It must, I thought, be some kind of temporary aberration.

There were days when I got up in the morning determined to redeem myself by fasting all day but came home in the afternoon and ate, then ate again at dinnertime, then again before bedtime, then got up in the morning to begin fasting again. Whole school weeks could go by this way. I tried making ritualized meals out of the smallest possible individual units of food: one egg, one tangerine, one slice of bread, or one cup of plain yogurt, but this worked no better and was more difficult than fasting. One of my books about aerobic training had charts giving calorie equivalents of food and exercise: one medium apple equals an eight-minute mile. I made vows to pay for everything I ate by running, but I didn't follow through. By the time I got hungry enough to feel the price was worth it, I was too frantic to wait until the exercise was done, but after eating any appreciable amount I was too sluggish to feel like working out. My debts mounted until I was hopelessly far behind.

In the *Reader's Digest* there was an article by a woman who lost weight by eating six times a day instead of three—the exact opposite of the advice we were given in health class to eliminate between-meal snacks. In a subsequent issue a man explained how you could lose weight by just keeping track of how many bites you took in a day and gradually reducing the number. I tried that for a few days but it was tedious and I had no faith in it: the man said the size of your bites and the types of food you ate would naturally even out, but I was afraid they wouldn't for me, now that I had become so strangely erratic. In the end fasting was the only method that seemed consistent and uncomplicated enough to keep doing. Sooner or later that was what I always came back to.

In the month or two after Anita's death I had broken the 3-day fasting barrier twice. But both times I had then spoiled my progress by eating. Lots. The virtue I accumulated by exercise and avoiding food was like a tiny pile of sand painstakingly gathered one grain at a time, washed away in instants by a torrent of indulgence. Slice after slice of the blueberry loaf, the casseroles, that my mother's colleagues had brought to the house in condolence.

For the first time, I began to buy food at school using my own money: hot pastrami sandwiches, pint cartons of milk, even candy-bars sometimes from the machines, though I had never cared about chocolate in the past. One hot pastrami cost the same as an entire tray lunch—55 cents. I would vow to save my lunch money for the whole week, but then by Wednesday, or Thursday at the latest, I ended up blowing it all and even dipping into my savings from babysitting. I'd never spent my own money for food! It didn't make any sense: I had to admit I was completely different, yet I was sure I was essentially the same person underneath.

In a book of jokes I read, Which matters more, a ham sandwich, or God? Answer: the sandwich, because nothing is better than God, and a ham sandwich is better than nothing.

A popsicle had not been worth as much as a dime. But a hot pastrami was worth more than 55 cents and my self-respect.

I had signed up for senior English instead of junior because I wanted to read Shakespeare. The teacher reminded me of Anita, though she didn't look much like her, really, especially not the gaunt Anita of recent memory. But she was a dark-haired woman between 25 and 30 and that was close enough. Ms. Bowland was slender without having any body part that could be called skinny or angular: she was elegant, graceful, smooth of surface. She was taller than Anita, tall the way I had once meant to be. Another terrible irony about my present condition was that I hadn't gotten any taller ever since first noticing my fat, as though growth in one direction had somehow been diverted into another. If only I could reverse that, will my body to stretch, to spend my excess fat in the drive to height!

Ms. Bowland told us she had been compared to Lynda Carter—Wonder Woman on TV. The comparison had merit, I thought, except that actually, Ms. Bowland was more beautiful: Wonder Woman was borderline fat, which Ms. Bowland was not, except perhaps just the slightest roundness in her face. She talked frequently about watching her weight and sometimes asked girl students if they had gained a few pounds. But she never said anything like that to me; my fat was still secret. That made it all the more imperative to eliminate it quickly, before anyone else had a chance to notice. I began constructing a fantasy in my mind about a tribe of amazons led by a tall and powerful woman chief.

Suddenly I was dating a boy, someone I had been vaguely aware of in analytic geometry though he always sat on the other side of the room, near the door. In driver's ed the year before, I remembered, during the discussion about higher insurance rates for boys, Bruce had forever sealed his reputation for weirdness by suggesting that perhaps for many males cars functioned as a penis symbol. The combination of brains and impossible geekiness was considered natural in high school, almost inevitable. But filling such a public role revolted me. I had never looked on Bruce with longing or even sympathy. I wanted to be connected with an intellectually superior person, yes, but not one other people thought ridiculous. Our similarities were a strike against Bruce.

Just the same, when I bumped into him alone one day after school, I did my best to seem intelligent and witty. After that first conversation, there was a first phone call, then a first date. I didn't see why the next step shouldn't be a first kiss, as long as it happened in private. And the next step after that ought to be sex. At least if he liked Freud, he must have sex on his mind.

The next time I was alone at home, I took off my clothes and looked at myself naked in the long hallway mirror, to see what Bruce would see, if and when. Despite my belief that fat was my most urgent shortcoming, I had no fear of nudity, in fact was still strangely confident that my body was capable of giving profound pleasure, once someone got over the initial hurdle of desiring it. I gazed at myself as I imagined Bruce's eyes might. I knew no one else thought me fat, and probably Bruce wouldn't either. What stood out to my peers at high school were my pimples, my braces, and a certain obtuseness about social convention. During sex, none of those things would matter. Very likely, my naked body might look beautiful to Bruce. If I hadn't already known that at 130 pounds I weighed ten pounds too much, I would find it lovely myself, I thought. Even now, I could, if I chose, bypass my own knowledge of those places on my legs and hips where the secret shame lay hidden, and get pleasure from contemplating my shape. My body would pass muster; it would present no obstacle.

In math class I took my seat near the window as always. I hoped Bruce would keep in his place too, not insist on talking during school. I longed for the next date to be made, but not under the eyes of our classmates. Wouldn't we appear as only too perfectly matched? Two social maladroits, farcically coming together just as if they couldn't tell the difference between themselves and really popular people. Just as if they didn't know how goofy they looked.

Bruce was tall and girlishly high-waisted. His limbs gangled; his face drooped like a Basset hound's. Unwisely, he had chosen to elaborate on this theme of willowy frailty by allowing his hair and fingernails to grow peculiarly long. The picture we would present to other people made me cold with anguish. Was Bruce looking at me? I kept my eyes forward. I willed him to call me on the phone.

After class, I waited a minute for Bruce to get out the door before I left my seat. The hallway was crowded when I got into it. I saw the back of Bruce's head poking up well above the swirl of other heads. It bobbed along, moving in the same direction I was going. I couldn't have overtaken Bruce now if I wanted to. The pleasure of watching without danger of being seen made me feel almost fond of him.

A curly-haired blond boy as tall as Bruce launched himself from one side of the hallway and shoved Bruce, hard. Bruce wobbled, then righted himself. The correct response declared itself to me viscerally: turn and punch him! But Bruce only shrugged sideways, and kept walking. I was as humiliated as if I had been the one pushed, and as angry with Bruce as I was with the other boy. Luckily, no one knew we had any connection. I pretended to take no special interest as my pace brought me up alongside the blond boy.

I knew him only by sight. He was not a jock or anyone remarkable as far as I knew. He was okay-looking: not really distinguished, but his face was better shaped than Bruce's. The blond and a comparatively runty boy who stood beside him grinned hugely, exhilarated. "I like messing with that dude," the tall boy said. A fresh wave of rage went over me, indiscriminately taking in the blond, the runt sidekick, Bruce, and somehow myself too. I didn't tell anyone what I had seen.

Bruce began giving me rides home from school. His parents were divorced, his father was often out of town for weeks at a time, and he had the use of a car, in which he did his own grocery shopping. He held my hand. When he brought me home after the second evening date, we sat on my parents' couch and he stroked my neck. I breathed harder, like a children's game of "warmer, colder," to show him he was on the right track.

"Your neck is very sensitive," he said.

"It isn't even my most sensitive part," I said. When he reached for my hand again, I tried to elude him, hoping he would be forced to set his own hand back down on my body.

The pants my mother bought me during this school year were in size 14, a fact she seemed not to notice. I had a new light green shirt with a gathered waist—still my best feature. To go with this shirt there was a pair of dark green pants with embroidered patterns down below the knees, almost like a brocade. I was ambivalent about this outfit: wasn't my body overdecorated? If I were a decent size, it would be fine, but as it was, I feared I was grotesque, like a jewel-encrusted, mentally and physically defective Goya infanta. I felt better about the simple pair of brushed cotton pants in the light, creamy yellow. Bruce complimented them: "You look nice." And of course there were always blue jeans.

After the third date, Bruce brought me back to his house. His father would be away for many days yet. Bruce poured me apple juice, since I didn't drink soda. "Sit," he said, patting his bed.

Was he making a dog joke? I glared at him. "That's not funny."

"What?" he said. "What did I say?"

Finally, finally, after all those years of delay, it was beginning. We took off our shirts and touched each other. I was surprised by the size of the muscles in Bruce's arms. He had seemed puny to me, but he wasn't frail at all, actually.

Bruce's hand, inching up in gradually lengthening strokes from my stomach to my breasts, didn't feel right. His touch was too dry somehow, it scraped against my mind the way certain sounds could, making me squirm. I tried to make the squirming seem like an erotic response. I was afraid to have those fingernails near my nipples, yet it was essential that we continue to make progress. After a while, Bruce reached his hand down into the yellow pants. "Is it all right?"

"Yes." It was happening. Why wasn't I excited? I had felt more the day on the couch when he touched my neck. Bruce unzipped his fly and released his erection. I knew all about this from sex ed and *The Sensuous Man*, and I took hold of it without hesitation.

The skin seemed so delicate. Perhaps my dry hand would be as unpleasant to him as his to me. It might even hurt him. My mouth would be more suitable, I thought. I had read about oral sex and done it in fantasy. But I couldn't just plunge my mouthful of orthodontic hardware onto him without discussion, and it seemed talking was out of the question now.

I couldn't properly concentrate on the sensations from Bruce's hand and also keep my own hand moving. Perhaps he had the same problem. He fumbled and gouged me with a fingernail. "Sorry."

"It's okay." He hadn't been in the right place anyway.

After a while, Bruce rezipped his pants. Relieved and disappointed, I sat up. He moved toward me for a kiss. I tilted my head sideways and let my mouth fall languorously open as actresses did in the movies. My braces would spoil the look of the gesture, but that couldn't be helped. We both had to make do.

"No," he said. "No, I don't want to do it that way." He held his face back from me until I closed my lips.

In English we read *Othello* and watched the movie. Ms. Bowland talked about how much reputation meant—"who steals my purse steals trash"—to Shakespeare and to us. When the class was skeptical, she said she would give us a different example, a former student who had been so embarrassed by a single incident that she ended up transferring to a different class. She hesitated tactfully as she began the story and I knew the student must have been fat.

"This girl was about 50 pounds overweight…." The number was a staggering one and I wondered if Ms. Bowland had chosen it arbitrarily. Was she really so expert that she could guess people's weight just by looking? I glanced covertly at the fattest girl in the room and wondered whether she was 50 pounds overweight. Ms. Bowland didn't look in that direction. She smiled ruefully as she told how the student's clothing had snagged on the desk as she was getting up. Then as she rocked and lurched, trying to free herself, the desk overturned.

"She was stuck," Ms. Bowland said. "Her skirt slid up and her legs waved—" she paused again, to avoid the rudeness of describing the fat legs in so many words. Instead she waved two fingers to show the helpless motion and the class laughed delightedly. I smiled, but I felt uncomfortable. It wasn't as though the girl didn't deserve it: *50 pounds*! She was in a whole different league, and yet… by rights I was one fifth that bad, although no one knew it but me. I snuck a peek again at Ms. Bowland's current fat student and saw that she was laughing as merrily as anyone else. So that proved it. Regular fat people *didn't* have the same kind of feelings. They *didn't* fully understand their shame. I vowed again to renounce food.

"Of course the whole class was laughing—they couldn't help themselves. I had to bite my lip myself. A couple of the strongest boys turned her desk right-side up, and then I let her go home. But I've often wondered whether it would have been better for her in the long run to make her stay and face it out right then."

Bruce invited me out for pizza on a day when I had been fasting.

"Oh, I can't tonight," I said. "What about tomorrow?" If I ate nothing during the day, I could earn it by tomorrow night.

"Well, okay," he said. "But tomorrow's not all-you-can-eat day."

"Good," I said. "All-you-can-eat is horrible, really. Don't you think the idea is disgusting?"

"No," he said. "Why?"

I couldn't explain. Wasn't it obvious?

Late at night I locked my bedroom door and took out the long-ago favorite pair of size-10 blue pants, from the time before my troubles started. I pulled them onto my legs as high as I could and bounced, trying to settle my body down into them. With difficulty, I buttoned them at the top. The fly was wide open, a gap of two inches or more between edges that stood straight up in an equilibrium of strains from different directions. With my left hand I grasped the edges and forced them closer together while I coerced the zipper with my right. I got it past the midpoint, and then it was up and I was in. Everything between my waist and thighs was squeezed into a compact immobile mass. This must be what a girdle felt like. Or a suit of armor: the pants seemed to be contributing as much as I was to keeping me vertical. Experimentally, I walked and was surprised to find that I could move more or less normally. The pants and my body were beginning to accommodate each other. I marched more vigorously and added some turns and kicks.

Just to prove I could, I bent at the waist and reached for the floor. I heard a tearing sound and felt a sudden change in the pressures on my body. It was a scene long familiar from movies. The fat person bending over or otherwise comically exerting himself, the almost voluptuous rending of the hopelessly inadequate garment, the spilling out of bulging flesh from intimate places—not shown on screen explicitly but implied—like Ms. Bowland's student. The joke was that for a person that fat the secret never had, never could, have been anything but public property, really.

It was monstrous, monstrous for me to have turned into a fat person. I felt along the back seam of the pants and found it intact all the way around to the fly. For a second I hoped it was all a mistake, but no. The seam of the zipper itself had given way along the right side of the fly and a frayed border of tape was clearly visible from the front, along with a winking white sliver of underwear.

"I don't want to take advantage of you," Bruce said. "There was this girl. At my last high school, before my dad moved here. I *used* her. I don't want to do that to you."

"You're *not*," I said. "You *wouldn't* be." Why was he so stupid? Why shouldn't we both take advantage of this opportunity to experience passion? How could it be *using* if I wanted to?

But Bruce's feelings were loftier and he cut our experiments short. Dear boy! I think now. He was holding out for love.

High school graduation, 1979.

Chapter 9

Science Fiction

Starting college at age 17 and size 18

Before my first semester at the university, my mother took me to the mall for new clothes. "We might need to go to a special store," she said matter-of-factly. I understood she meant a special store with clothes for fat people. By senior year my weight had crept up into the 140s and I began buying pants at the army surplus store downtown. When I started getting nearer to 150 pounds I stopped ever getting on any scales. My efforts to lose weight over the summer left me bigger than ever and now even the biggest army-surplus pants were too small. "But let's try the department stores first," my mother said. Abject and will-less, I let her lead me to the women's section of Sears, feeling myself as easily moved from one place to another as the puck on an air-hockey table. I deferred to my mother's judgment in the purchase of half a dozen shirts and pants. Size 18 was a new highwater mark that shocked me even in my dazed state: my pants size had overtaken my age! My worst fears were confirmed: I must be even more than 160 pounds by now. All the available pant styles in size 18 had elastic waists and stretchy fabric, humiliations I knew I didn't deserve to avoid.

I moved into the dormitories the first day they opened, a week before the first day of classes. There I ate nothing for five days, a new record. The new school pants my mother had bought me flapped baggily on my body.

It was so ironic, I thought, the way my willpower boundary expanded always just a little too late, trailing behind the expansion of my body, and my vices.

Back in the early days, when I weighed a mere 125, a five-day fast would have been more than enough to make me perfectly thin, yet I couldn't even go two. Now I was far fatter, which could only mean my self-control was worse on average, yet somehow I was able to fast longer.

At least I didn't have to wear the shameful stretch pants. I unpacked the army-surplus pants from last spring. I had brought with me to the dorm only the most recent stage of too-small clothing, planning however to return periodically to my parents' house for older clothes as I continued to shrink. The closet in my room back home still contained sections dedicated to all the different past phases of my body.

For many women, the effort to lose weight can be tantamount to a desire to return to an earlier version of themselves. At 18 I already felt that I had been debauched and ruined by my misspent life, my years of wrong eating. Changing my body would therefore be like traveling into my own past, to get things right this time. I pictured myself as an inventor with a time machine, needing to sneak into historical museums to outfit herself appropriately for each new expedition: traveling back to the 150s, then the 140s, then the 130s, then finally to 120, the golden age where I would junk the machine and stay.

Even a few months ago, I could never have imagined how bad I could get. That girl I had been at the very beginning, when I weighed only 125, would have been utterly horrified by me. And I could fully share her disgust and disbelief. But getting all the way back into her attitudes was as impossible now as wearing her old clothes. She was carefree, I suggested to myself. But I remembered perfectly well that I hadn't been. All right, then: she was naïve. If she had known what I knew about how low a person can sink, she would have been pleased with herself as she was. But, no, that wasn't right either, because 125 *was* still too fat.

If I had the time machine, I thought, what information could I give the 125-girl that would be of any help? I couldn't really think of what I would advise her to do differently, except to succeed at the fundamental tasks of eating less and exercising more. She should have studied more, too, but it stood to reason that if she couldn't maintain the simple disciplines of losing weight, then of course she didn't have the discipline for complex achievements either.

There was another direction for time-travel: forward. My future spread before me with no impediments now, no scrutiny from my parents, and I could do what I had to do to succeed. But the juxtaposition of myself now and myself at 14 made a strange pattern in my mind. Suppose—it was complete nonsense, really, but just for the sake of symmetry, suppose there could be a vantage point somewhere in the future from which a future self would look back on the very gross woman who had needed to wear size-18 stretch pants with feelings similar to the ones I had now toward the 125-girl. What would someone have to be, to see a great big 165-woman as young and relatively unsullied? The math was simple enough: she would weigh over 200 pounds.

200 pounds might as well be the edge of the galaxy. If a woman weighing more than 200 pounds came to me from the future, what would she tell me?

It was an absurd idea, just science fiction, but it chilled me.

Chapter 10

Sex

1979, shuttling between 150-155

"I dreamed there was a severed head in the cafeteria," I said. "Just, kind of, bouncing around, you know." Making conversation at work was a surprisingly easy pleasure. At work everyone had to be there, so fitting in socially was never an issue, and the serving and cleaning duties took the pressure off too: talk fitted in naturally around them. Being at work, in fact, is remarkably similar to the mental scenario I had once entertained about being marooned on a desert island with someone. Except without the sex.

Things were a little slow on the Saturday morning breakfast line and the other students crowded around me. They were generally eager to hear my comments about the customers or the permanent workers—supervisors—who roved around the university dining services, checking up on us.

"Whose head was it?" said a man I didn't know. I registered him vaguely: a few years older than most of us, black-haired, tall, with a slight belly, not too bad, and a face in which the rounded cheeks contrasted with a pinched nose.

"Edna's," somebody said. Edna was the breakfast supervisor with the British accent and prissy ways.

"No, it was nobody any of us knew. But! Edna *was* on duty, and so we were nervous." The menace of the head had not been of exactly a horror-movie quality—there was no feeling that one of us was about to become the next victim—but the head kept popping up inconveniently in the middle of the breakfast prep, nestling among the halved grapefruits, bleeding on the ice, and Edna was certain to blame us for it. It was too big and lumpy to hide under anything. Shut inside the walk-in fridge, it rolled around and thumped until we had to take it out again. Finally we wedged it in among the toasters, which were about the same size. There it stayed quiet, but Edna found it anyway when the lunch prep began.

"'Well, now *who* can have put *this* here?' I imitated her disdain and her **r**-dropping accent: 'here' came out as 'hee-uh'. " 'This doesn't belong *hee-uh*!' she said, just like the head was a misplaced tray of boxed cereals." Everybody laughed. The black-haired man introduced himself: Larry. He wasn't a Saturday regular but happened to be there covering a shift for someone else. On my next shift, Tuesday morning, Larry walked in and invited me to a Monty Python movie, *The Life of Brian*.

For the university's PE requirement, I had signed up for a class called Weight Control. On the first day I found I was one of the youngest and thinnest students, though not so thin that the teacher, Kathy, turned me away as she did a couple of other women: "This class is for women at least 25% over their ideal weight." I had been afraid that, at 152 pounds, I might not qualify, and I was glad that Kathy's standards for my body were no less stringent than mine. Half a dozen women in the class were middle-aged and enormous. The fattest of all was Georgia, who panted hard just walking slowly up the ramp to the classrooms in the gym. She seemed hardly human to me and I averted my eyes from her lumpy moustached face, the soft globs and rolls of flesh that made her sweaty, wheezing body look like mounds of melting ice cream. Georgia didn't come back for the second day of class, and the other older women tut-tutted. "She really could have used it." They were hardly in a position to cast aspersions, I thought. They were only a little bit less disgusting than Georgia. And I was only a bit less than they were.

Weight Control class was ditzy, not what I hoped for, though it's hard to say what I hoped for exactly, except to thin down faster and better than anyone ever had. Kathy lectured: One pound of fat equals 3500 calories, so to lose one pound per week, cut 500 calories per day from meals, or exercise enough to burn an extra 500 calories, or a combination. This was all just review from grade-school PE, and a waste of time. Besides other piddling, childish assignments, we were supposed to keep a food diary, and I was already falling behind.

Kathy frowned on skipping meals, so plausible diary entries had to be invented for every day I ate nothing. But on the other hand, if I broke a fast by eating a lot of food at once, I didn't like to write that down either, particularly because one large meal usually led to more of the same over the next few days. But by then there was *no choice* about fasting for at least a day or two, because the weekly class weigh-in would be coming up. Before I knew it, it would be necessary to fabricate an entire week's worth of sensible meals. But that couldn't go on forever—week after week of sensible meals in the diary, and yet I couldn't crack the 150 mark? Anyone would see immediately that my record was a fraud. I began leaving gaps in the diary, then "forgetting" it at home on days it was supposed to be turned in. If I could just control myself long enough to get down into the 140s, stop shuttling back and forth between 150 and 155, then I could clean up the record, retroactively construct the story of my rehabilitation.

On the first date with Larry I was shy, and he didn't kiss me goodnight. But there was a second date, then a third. In the Modern Languages theater, we watched something old and black-and-white from the English Department's Classic Series—Larry knew about movies. On screen, men in suits and hats moved about looking sturdy and serious. The women were absurdly curvaceous and stepped around with surprising quick confidence even in the unliberated clothing and shoes that confined them. Halfway through, Larry took my arm and stroked it, and I stopped trying to understand anything on the screen. My entire self flowed down into my arm and hand. It was as though he touched my whole naked body, as though layers of film had been removed from between my skin and the air. My flesh felt as exposed and delicate as a peeled grape.

In Weight Control we did calisthenics and Kathy exhorted us to be graceful. I couldn't believe she meant it sincerely. How could a fat body be graceful? Clearly, Kathy was trying to give us a falsely inflated sense of satisfaction with ourselves. Maybe that helped some people, but I would rather face the full truth. The thing to do with a fat body was to fix it as quickly as possible, not to coddle it or pretend it could give satisfaction. To move as though I believed I could be attractive seemed like participating in a gross parody. "Show by the way you hold your bodies that you take pride in yourselves" Kathy called out, in a cheerleader voice. The other women, even the fattest ones, softened their faces, curved their arms. They looked ridiculous. I deliberately moved my limbs even more roughly and mechanically.

Larry was in the Society for Creative Anachronism and made money selling armor to fighters. I went on a road trip with him to a "war" in Albuquerque. In Tucson Larry had been restrained because I was not yet 18. But apparently out of town that mattered less, and he was amorous. On the way home we stayed in a motel where the room had red carpeting, Playboy movies on closed-circuit TV, and a mirror on the ceiling. The mirror made me shy and I didn't look at it while we made love, but afterwards, I caught a sudden glimpse of the pattern our bodies made. I had already studied Larry's body closely before this: tall enough that he had to bend, or me to tilt, for kissing. Heavier than me, though not fat—except for the tiniest little forgivable bit of protruding stomach, cute really. His skin darker and tougher than mine. Larry was no dreamboat, perhaps, but I found his body attractive.

The surprising thing was my own body. From this angle it looked unfamiliar. Instead of seeing my regular fat self, I saw light, shade, lines, curves. My waist came in and my hips flared out like the curve of a guitar, and Larry's dark arm cut across the lighter background in a line between the narrowest and widest points. It was beautiful. It could be a photograph, a painting. I thought maybe the effect was accidental, a momentary optical illusion, but when I shifted and rolled onto my side, the new tableau was attractive too. Erotic love had transformed me, at least temporarily.

I did not connect these moments of pleasure with anything Kathy had to say in class.

Fantasies about Larry filled up my mind. We would marry, most likely. There would be children, a family. Clearly, I would have to be the one in charge of nutrition and household management, because Larry's habits were terrible. There were only three vegetables he would eat at all—asparagus, beets, and green beans—and to be acceptable the green beans had to be frozen, while beets or asparagus had to be canned. I told Larry he would love fresh green beans, but when I made them for him once, he didn't. It wouldn't be easy, then, for either of us. I'd have to clean up my own act, first—get thin—in order to set a good example for my family. And I knew I had less domestic experience even than the average 17-year old girl. But surely I would rise to the occasion, and Larry would follow my lead, for the sake of the baby we would have. I would shop for healthy food and cook it, keep everything organized. Larry would be grateful for his transformed life.

It was harder to go to class or do homework now, even when I wasn't actually with Larry. The surge of feeling when I knew I would be spending the night with him that day, or the next, made it easy not to eat, but only for a short time. It was weird that when I fasted I now hit the wall in only a day or two, weird that I was stuck at 150 pounds and could do no better, and weird that I could hardly ever get around to eating things like fruit or salad when I had loved those foods as a child. What was wrong with me? When I ate, it was only heavy foods I wanted: breakfast at the cafeteria with cheese omelet, bacon, hash browns; cheese enchiladas with sour cream for lunch; dinner out with Larry to a steak place, or at least hamburgers, or sausage pizza, and ice cream afterwards. All that meat. It didn't make sense: I never cared about meat.

All this was the opposite of what I expected to happen when someone loved me. I must have become a worse person over the course of the semester, more unreliable. There was no other explanation: 150 wasn't some kind of magic number. There was absolutely no reason I couldn't do again what I had done the week before school, and knock myself down to 135. One good week, and I could still turn the whole semester around. I was on shaky ground in linear algebra, had gotten a D on the mid-term. Chemistry lab and the drafting class were less drastic: I was behind on assignments, but I could do the work if I would just buckle down, put in some serious time. And do something about the Weight Control journal, of course.

Larry took a long weekend off to go to a medieval event and instead of going with him I stayed in town to study. He left me his apartment key so I'd have plenty of privacy. I planned to eat nothing and work continuously in this secluded place, like a monk.

You may possibly be wondering, why would anybody with any sense at all keep charging headlong against hunger in the same way over and over when it obviously wasn't working? It was because I was in the grip of a theory. The energy-balance model of fat storage and weight loss, which you probably learned in school the same as I did, proclaims that 3500 calories always "equal" one pound of fat, and that your body fat therefore amounts to a perfect tally of the total number of calories you've taken in by eating, minus all the energy you've expended by exercise and the basic maintenance of your physiology. In school, this model was given no name and I had no idea (probably my teachers didn't either) that there are competing scientific models. So it entered my mind simply as a self-evident truth. This is why I persisted in my original plan despite the fact that it mysteriously failed the first several hundred times. The story of my life with my body is very much a story of theories. My faith in expert theory permanently altered my relationship with my body by the time I was a teenager.

around 1970

When I was eight or nine, I came across a book on the psychology of child-raising in the shelf in the headboard of my parents' bed. Child-raising was a topic that interested me; I was eager to critique my parents' performance. I read the book, which was full of interesting ideas. The chapter on sex education was particularly fascinating.

The book explained that sooner or later every girl—especially if she had brothers, or depending on her father's degree of modesty—every girl was bound to notice a difference between her body and the male body: she was missing something. At this point she was likely to become upset, feeling that her own body was deformed or inferior, longing desperately to acquire a penis, perhaps supposing that she once had one which had been confiscated as a punishment.

The parents should reassure the anxious little girl and explain sex differences and reproduction to her in a simplified, upbeat way that emphasized just how indispensable a vagina was.

Before I learned to bathe myself, I had often been bathed with my younger brother Dan. My father, proud of his body, was also rather lax about nudity around the house when I was young. So I was already acquainted with some examples of the male organ and had an opinion about it. I thought it looked stupid. Every time I happened to see a penis, I felt complacent about the streamlined beauty and efficiency of my own crotch. A penis was an obvious liability, an obstruction that was likely to catch on things and be a constant nuisance. I could tell that Dan didn't share my views about the superiority of female anatomy; his glee in handling his "pee-er" was apparent whenever we got caught short and had to urinate outside in the desert that surrounded the new Tucson subdivision where we had just moved.

The fact that my own experience completely contradicted the Freudian theory did not cause me to reject the information outright. It was printed in a book! Books were always the ultimate authority. Look how my parents pulled out the encyclopedia or the dictionary to remind themselves of something, or when they disagreed. I was passionately devoted to book-learning, and had a strong confidence that I could work out the ramifications of theories I had read. If penis envy was known to be something girls usually felt, it seemed logical to conclude that the average little girl didn't have as much sense as I did.

Theories are so often theories about someone else, aren't they? Freud knew sibling rivalry first-hand, but not penis envy. I picture Freud, sitting in his armchair, smoking, speculating on the female experience, trying to imagine himself into a woman's frame of reference. What do women want, what do they really want…? Suppose I were a woman…. To begin with, I wouldn't have my…. Oh, God, how horrible! Poor, poor women—to be so stunted! Their lives must be haunted with an unending sense of loss….

Similar possibilities for error creep in, perhaps, when people who have never been fat, who haven't subjected themselves to systematic deprivation and felt the power of the cumulative hunger that results, set themselves up as obesity experts, speculating about the psychology of fat people. Hmm… they know they need to reduce and yet they persist in overeating. What could possibly explain this perversity? Perhaps they have a compulsion to fill up some deep-seated emotional gap.

1979, still in Larry's apartment

But why, if I was so willing to put expert opinion above my own experience, didn't I listen to what Kathy and a long line of grade-school PE teachers before her had said about the importance of not skipping meals, particularly breakfast?

2001

"Why didn't she go to a doctor for help?" said the doctor in my writing group, after reading an early chapter in this book.

My friends, there's a difference between faith in a theory and faith in *people*. Obviously I could interpret the theory for myself better than any of the *people* I knew.

1979, still obstinately fasting

Of course Kathy and every health-class textbook since the beginning of time said it was better to diet slowly and gently. But there that vague advice wasn't explained or justified in terms of the *theory* that a calorie is a calorie is a calorie under all circumstances and all there is to understand about fat tissue in the body is adding and subtracting.

I hadn't questioned that penis envy existed, but I knew it didn't apply to me.

I was willing to believe that doctors and PE teachers and my parents (if I had ever asked them) were quite right about what would be good for the average person.

But I wasn't average.

Here's another thing: by 1979 I had also learned that hunger, at least in some forms, has its pleasures. You can acquire a taste for it. I was becoming a connoisseur of hunger.

Friday morning at Larry's apartment the sensations were enjoyable, like the embodiment of resolve and improvement. It started with simple lightness inside the body, and a feeling of extra energy that could be tapped. Even when the actual hunger pangs started, they were not unpleasant; they felt like focused effort, like going into labor in a pregnancy where I would give birth to my new self. I began rereading the algebra book from the beginning and felt I was making progress.

By afternoon, though, my hunger high had peaked and the euphoria gave way to manic, sour restlessness, a hunger whose physical manifestations were felt primarily in the jaw and around the mouth. Not pain but worse than pain, a tightness and a pressure building to urgency, unignorable, like the pressure of needing to pee, the instinctive pressure to do what the body prompts. Before I had held the energy beam in my own hand and could shine it in whatever direction I liked; now it was an equally focused, even more powerful force aimed at me from the outside, dragging me away from my true center. I couldn't make any more headway with algebra; nothing had any reality to my mind except the thought of food. By 5:00 I knew I was going to eat.

I had brought no money to Larry's, so I went through Larry's kitchen. In the cupboard there were boxes of macaroni and cheese, pancake mix, and cans of asparagus and beets. In the freezer, green beans, frozen french fries, and hamburger. The refrigerator space was mostly filled with soda, big plastic bottles that Larry bought a crate at a time from a soda outlet place. Also part of a loaf of white bread, the tail end of a sharp cheddar cheese, some butter, and pancake syrup. A carton of milk that felt depressingly light. And an opened plastic tube of store-bought raw chocolate-chip cookie dough.

I used up the milk in making a box of macaroni, which I ate. It wasn't enough. If I ate Larry's cheese, it would all be gone, like the milk, and I would look selfish and greedy. Of the other things to eat, the only one that wouldn't take forever to prepare was the cookie dough.

Do I need to explain what happened next?

Over approximately the next hour I danced with the cookie dough the tango that I know you know. The first tiny sliver, and the next and the next. Then the frank, inch-thick slice that was supposed to put an end to the slivers once and for all, and then the other inch-thick slices that followed.

What the dough debacle meant in terms of Kathy's weigh-ins, I could force away from my attention somewhat. I had practiced that.

What was new was that Larry would find out the worst about me now, learn that I was no fit mother for his children. I gave up hope of studying and abandoned myself to despair.

Around 10:00 that night, my stomach was hissing and boiling, hungry again, but differently now. This was hunger of an unnatural color, a vile, polluted thing that was the result of my having already degraded myself earlier in the day. I called Domino's and had a pepperoni pizza delivered, paying by check. I ate half and fell heavily asleep. Late Saturday morning, I walked to Denny's and ate a grand slam breakfast, paying by check, tip included. I went back to Larry's very full and spent most of the day reading science fiction in bed. In the evening, I ate the other half of the pizza. I got up around noon on Sunday and started cleaning the kitchen. I was hungry, but not in a bad way now. It felt like delicate fingers just touching the insides of my stomach and guts, almost like the way sexual arousal felt in other parts of the body, the first light caressing tickle. I knew I could resist eating now, that the feeling would be tolerable and even pleasurable for most of the day. How come I couldn't feel this way all the time?

This whole episode confirmed yet again that any time I felt comfortable not eating, I had to take advantage of it. If I was going to be subject to random crazy outbreaks, like with the cookie dough, I had to make up for it, just to stay in the same place, let alone getting thinner. I thought about the next weigh-in for Kathy, and for the first time I wished I hadn't had such a good weight-loss week before the semester started. If I could have lost those same fifteen pounds during Kathy's class, I would be in line for an A now. What was so different about me, why couldn't I lose *another* fifteen?

Larry came back Sunday night with money in his pocket. He missed me and was happy with the way the kitchen looked. We went to dinner at a fairly upscale place called Smuggler's Inn, and I had the raw vegetable platter, as a penance. Larry asked if I got a lot of studying done. Not as much as I hoped, I said. That was the truth.

"But you're feeling better," Larry said.

"Yes," I lied.

After dinner, we went back to the apartment to make love. Now, the moment of maximum openness and tenderness, now was the time I planned to make my confession about the cookie dough. I had spent the day framing it in my mind, how I had to make it sound both casual and forthright. "Listen," I said. I tried to make my face look chagrined, but in a mild sort of way, such as a habitually moderate person would feel about a minor lapse. "I'm afraid I ate some of that cookie dough you had in the fridge. Quite a bit, actually."

"I thought you were anti-sugar," Larry said.

"I was under a lot of stress," I said. "Worried about my classes." Stress that leads to eating had been a major topic in Kathy's class, so I knew it would sound believable. And yet I was absolutely sure I wasn't telling the truth about what I did and why.

Now

Freud's cultural influence is still strong. A great many people regard the sexual drive as a powerful inner force, something not readily subject to our conscious control, something which will insistently seek an outlet for satisfaction even if we ourselves strive to thwart it, even if we believe that our desires are sinful. Not many people think of eating as an instinctual drive similar in intensity and complexity to the sex drive but different in kind. But why not? Why should eating have to go piggybacking on sex or social fulfillment or self-esteem? Eating doesn't have to be a substitute for anything. It has its own reality and its own necessity. If you think of animal life in the most abstract terms, the major requirement to keep it going is that a sufficient number of the creatures presently alive must produce another generation like themselves. Hence the existence of sex drive. But in the meanwhile those creatures also all have to keep themselves alive at least long enough to reproduce. Therefore eating is at least as important in nature as sex—more, on a daily basis—and it's just as likely to have complex sets of pre-programmed physically-based instincts that go along with it, to prompt us to do what nature requires. We can fight against our drives when we find them inconvenient but we can't simply will them out of existence. Isn't it odd that a culture that encourages me to regard my built-in sexual appetites as a natural force tells me the opposite about my food appetites?

In 1979 I had not yet had these thoughts. I didn't believe I was eating for any emotional reason, but I didn't yet have an alternative theory that made sense to me.

1979

In class Kathy had us sit in a circle to tell what made us happy. The other women mentioned things I considered sentimental: puppies, kittens, and sunsets. Flowers. Nature. No matter what anyone said, Kathy's response was the same, "That's great! That's super!" Her voice was fruity and warm. Was I the only one who found it cloying, patronizing? She advised the women to find pictures of puppies, kittens, or sunsets to put up on their bulletin boards, to remind themselves of what truly gives them pleasure, so they wouldn't be tempted to turn to food as a substitute.

My turn to say what made me happy would come last, and I wanted to choose something unusual. Something true, something arresting, to cut through the syrupy falseness. What *did* make me happy? Sex, I thought. I couldn't say that. But it would be the truest thing. I tried to think of something else that would sound more normal but still be interesting. A substitute for sex. Ha. If there was one thing I was sure of, it was that food wasn't a substitute for some other pleasure. I believed at the time, and I still believe now, that this was a fact I could know about myself as surely as I knew that I had never envied anyone's penis. Maybe for the puppies-and-sunsets fat women food was a substitute for something else, but not for me. Food was hell. I didn't want it, I didn't like it. I thought of it with loathing, even when I was eating it, even when I was eating quite a lot of very delicious food. For a moment, I worried again at the insoluble paradox: why couldn't I stop, then?

My mind had wandered and it was my turn to speak. "What makes you happy, Jean?"

I only had the one answer ready. Why not say it, why not? I meant to speak out confidently but I ended up mumbling. "Sex."

"Great!" Kathy said. "That's really super! So maybe you could type out some of your favorite quotes and put those on your bulletin board!" Baffled, I nodded. I glanced at the women near me but they withdrew behind their faces and I got no clues. Later an explanation occurred to me. Kathy thought I said "Shakespeare."

In the last week of classes I sat down with the food diary and a handful of different pens and pencils. It took me an hour to make up a week's worth of meals. The task was hopeless, endless. I threw away the diary and told Kathy I lost it.

I flunked Weight Control and several other classes. As soon as I turned 18, I moved in with Larry.

Chapter 11

Withdrawal

Spring 1980, even bigger than size 18
Edna called me over at work and I thought she was going to tell me it had been too long since I wiped off the tables.

"I've noticed that you've been getting really fat lately," she said. It was true. I had gotten bigger by increments ever since moving in with Larry. When I happened to catch a glimpse of myself in a bathroom mirror on campus, the sudden overview of my body would depress me all day. I perfected methods for parting my hair or putting in contact lenses without really seeing myself, though of course it was impossible not to feel the ungainliness of my body: the flesh on my stomach bunched and touched me in more insistent ways as I bent to tie my shoes; when I went into the library, the sides of the turnstile brushed my thighs in unwanted intimacy. My clothes tightened to the point of claustrophobia, loosened slightly as I maintained a diet of single-egg breakfasts, salad-and-TAB lunches, fruit-and-yogurt dinners for a few weeks, then tightened again with unbelievable speed when I bought cafeteria meals again at school and ate with Larry at night. The size-18 pants my mother bought me no longer fit. I had been wearing some of Larry's Sears stretch pants as a temporary measure until I could get hold of myself. His little potbelly was nothing compared to my mounds of fat, but somehow his height compensated for the extra circumference of my butt and legs; the fabric in the pants rearranged itself and came out even, more or less. Avoiding mirrors spared me the details.

Edna regarded me with motherly concern. Or grandmotherly, I thought, looking at her wrinkled neck. Clearly she had no malicious intentions. Her face looked philanthropic: she was here to help me better myself if only I would allow her. I had to fight to keep my body from automatically cringing, just as I did when men on the street said things to me. At the same time, Edna's presumption was so outrageous that it was bracing, liberating. It was only a matter of time before my mother came out with a similar remark. When that happened, I would be angry, like I was now, but it would be an impure anger, shot through with helplessness and shame, worse than seeing myself in a mirror. Edna had no rights over me and nothing she saw reflected on my real self. Not exactly. My body was available for anyone to see, and know that I must be doing *something* wrong. But the nature of my failure, or how I might repair my life—that was nothing anyone knew anything about, certainly not Edna. In my mouth, already formed, was the answer I had prepared regarding the dirty tables, and I decided it was perfect for delivering a stinging rebuke while being irreproachably polite.

"Thank you for calling that to my attention, ma'am. I'll take care of it right away."

Edna didn't realize she had just been put decisively in her place. "Yes, you should, you really should. You're just a young girl. You shouldn't be letting yourself go like that."

I tried to move my body over the little distance back to the bussing station in a way that would be simultaneously graceful, quick, and casually self-possessed, but I was very aware of the gap where my required white bussing apron failed to reach all the way around my bulging bottom. I felt Edna's eyes must be on it.

Only two women who worked in the Student Union were fatter than me. Angie was just disgusting, beyond the pale: a squat cylinder, wider across than one of the tray carts. Her white bussing shirt couldn't button around her and she wore it hanging loose over giant T-shirts whose armpits were dark with great splotches of sweat by afternoon when the end of her shift overlapped the beginning of mine. Obviously I was a more together person than Angie. Vickie was a more complicated case. She could almost be called pretty, if she weren't fat. Her red hair was long and thick beneath her regulation hairnet. Her eyes were a clear blue-green, but crowded somehow by her fat cheeks, squeezed ever so slightly narrower than they should have been. Her mouth was well-shaped and small—unless it only looked small in the vast expanse of her face. There was a hint of shine about her lips that might have come either from a cosmetic gloss, or maybe just her own perfect skin, which was thin and fair everywhere it showed, almost transparent. Really, she would be considered beautiful—if it were possible for a fat person to be beautiful.

Vickie behaved as though she didn't notice she was fat. She brought roller skates with her to work, letting them dangle casually from one plump hand as she punched out at the timeclock. "What are the skates for?" I said. "Commuting," she said, "and exercise." *Of course*, her tone implied, but without unpleasantness. Her confidence, her proprietary air, struck me as a form of cheating. This vague belief remained unchallenged in my mind; I never tried to pin it down closely, not even for the purpose of justifying it to myself. It just didn't seem quite right for Vickie, an obviously not-normal person, to lay claim to exercise and pleasure as normal parts of her life. Besides, on wheels she must look like a clown. I pictured Vickie rolling past fraternity row, gaped at by men and neighborhood children, and my flesh crawled. At the same time, an opposite picture attracted me: Vickie amazing onlookers with unexpected strength and skill, twirling as gracefully as the hippo ballerinas in *Fantasia*. A fat woman skating was admirable, almost. But the hippos remained a joke, despite their mastery, or even because of it.

On slow evenings, other student workers gravitated to where Vickie held court. She talked with animation about the cafeteria, the university, movies, her life. The time that she lived with a homosexual film critic was an important period in her past. I knew Brian Cressler's name from his regular movie column in the university newspaper. For me this established that Vickie had a glamorous connection to a published author, a commentator on the arts. But her opinion of Cressler was bad now. They had a falling out, according to Vickie, when she finally voiced her disapproval of the constant parade of men in and out of their house. "In high school we were inseparable," she said. "Neither of us dated then. I didn't understand that only fear held Brian back. I thought he was like me: selective." Selective! Instantly I suspected Vickie of striking a false pose. Or if she *was* sincere, then it was a startling delusion, to see herself as a belle surrounded by many potential lovers. Vickie would be lucky, I thought, if anyone at all selected *her*, ever.

When I was enrolled in Weight Control in PE, Larry had more than once boasted, "I was always willing to date women anywhere in between 100 and 300 pounds." This seemed like a pose as well. 300 was not meaningful, was only a random large number. Perhaps Angie weighed 300 pounds but it was outside the normal person's experience. During the Weight Control era, I knew my own weight because it was measured every Tuesday—155, 153, 156—fluctuating by a few pounds depending how well I fasted on the days prior to weighing in. I didn't know what I weighed now, but it must be significantly more. Larry had said nothing about the changes in my body, and I wondered if it was possible he hadn't noticed.

My own notions of acceptable weights were simultaneously more stringent, more complicated, and more nebulous than Larry's—or than the ones Larry claimed to have. I knew fiercely in my most secret heart that I, myself, was supposed to weigh no more than 120 pounds. How much an ordinary person with ordinary aspirations might allow herself to weigh, I couldn't judge precisely; a woman with my build was still relatively decent even up into the 140s, perhaps, as the weight charts suggested, but no higher. Above there, the more the weight, the greater the shame, until a maximum point was reached—where exactly, I couldn't say—after which no larger degree of shame was available and there was no reason to make any more distinctions. 300 pounds was beyond the pale, without question, but not more so than 200 pounds.

The morning after the Edna incident, I couldn't make myself get up for my early class. In the middle of the day I went to campus, but by two o'clock I was deeply drowsy again. Staying awake when I was supposed to could be difficult when I wasn't eating. But keeping up the momentum of my fast was the most important thing; the rest would fall into place later. Instead of going to chemistry, I let myself drift off on a library couch. A couple hours later, since it wasn't a cafeteria evening, I walked home again.

"How was school?" Larry said. He knew I needed to make As and Bs this semester to get off academic probation.

"It was okay," I said. I placed myself in his arms and rubbed against him. To be absorbed in Larry for a while would relieve the pressure of guilt from cutting class. Besides, I was wide awake now, and hungry. I would substitute sex for food.

"Do you have homework?" Larry said, straightening his arms and leaning away. Behind him at his desk was his own stack of textbooks—business, the most boring major in the world. I remembered when Larry had seemed exciting, the knowledgeable older man who would transform my life.

"Not really," I said. "Some reading, but I already did it at the library. Get in bed with me for a while."

"I brought home hamburgers, do you want one?"

"Yes." So quickly, all hope was lost. A haze of shame surrounded me and all my future and everything else in the room was dark except for the food bags.

We brought the food into bed, since it would take too long for us to clear off the kitchen table. Like the coffee table, Larry's work table, and every other flat surface in the apartment, it was piled high with a mixture of dirty dishes, tools, and the loose links of metal that Larry knit into chainmail. Sometimes I felt there was no room for me anywhere in the apartment except in bed. I tried to shake my gloom.

It's only one meal, I told myself. Hamburger, french fries, and milkshake, a perfectly reasonable amount, the same thing Larry was eating. All I had to do was feel satisfied with this for today, and resume my not-eating tomorrow. But the food felt like bloated, creeping sin in my stomach. The awful thing was that nothing was wrong with me. There were no mitigating traumas in my past, no psychological compulsions. I was perfectly free to choose, and I knew what I was supposed to do, but I did this.

"I better study," Larry said.

"Wait," I said. I caught his arm. "Spend an hour with me." I couldn't be left alone with these feelings. We pushed the empty paper bags onto the floor.

If I had not seemed gross to Larry in the 150s, perhaps I still didn't, even now. Just for a little while, I wanted to wallow in the comfort of laxer standards although they were wrong. "What do you like?" I said to him, fishing for an ardent declaration. He was unlikely to guess from slight hints what complex sorts of feeling were required from him, but my own taboos made it impossible to be any more explicit. "What turns you on?" I said, stroking his belly and thighs.

"That does," he said.

I wanted Larry to say his love for me was not contingent on my good behavior: it didn't matter if I couldn't keep house or pass my classes. It didn't matter that I was fatter, because he understood and loved the essence of my personality, though it was temporarily blocked and muffled by my own flesh. At the same time, I wanted him to express well-observed, highly specific satisfactions with my body exactly as it was. He could talk about my breasts, which were still small and firm. He could admire the curve where my hips flared away from my waist. It wasn't impossible that a man could find that voluptuous, even now. And he could think my eyes and lips beautiful, my thoughts and conversation fascinating. My lovemaking would be exquisite, and that would make up for my other failings.

"Your penis," I said, taking it in my hand. "It's all velvety outside, and all wiry underneath."

"Mmm," Larry said.

"It's like drinking coke," I said. "The fountain kind, I mean, not canned."

"Huh?"

"I mean the combination of textures, tension underneath softness." Soda was a recent vice; even a few months ago I still disliked its fizz. But I had discovered that the stimulant effect was powerful, if you drank enough. Temporarily it made life seem manageable.

"If you say so," Larry said.

"Could anything make you not love me?" I said.

"I don't know. I guess not. What do you mean?" Larry said.

Later I interrupted Larry's studying to send him to the 7-11 for chocolate easter eggs, his favorite candy and now mine too. He didn't want to go but I nagged until he understood that it was less trouble to give in. He had to; I needed more to eat and I didn't want to appear in public as a fat woman buying candy.

"How many do you want?" Larry said, snapping his eyes and his voice to show his righteous indignation. Eight, I thought. I tried to think what was the maximum number of eggs a decent human being might eat.

"Two," I said. "No, make it three. And a Dr. Pepper too, please." Larry was already going out the door. "Fountain, not canned" I called after him.

"I know, I know!"

Wired on caffeine and sugar, I couldn't get to sleep until very late, and the following morning I cut class again.

A few weeks before the end of the semester, rather than flunk, I made a complete withdrawal from all my classes.

I knew that in a language class I could make good grades without a great deal of effort, so I pre-enrolled in Russian, Latin, and Greek for the fall. I also moved out of Larry's apartment to see if I could get my life into better order elsewhere.

Chapter 12

Vickie

Early in 1981, bigger than ever

"But if you already knew he was gay—" I said. Food Services had reassigned me to work with Vickie on the daytime bussing shift. Now that Angie had graduated and gone, Vickie was the only woman fatter than me working at the Student Union. We returned often to the subject of Brian Cressler. I felt like a sophisticate, speaking easily of sex, pretending *gay* was part of my everyday vocabulary. It was difficult to think of a polite way to phrase my question. No doubt Cressler's homosexuality was a comfort to Vickie; she didn't have to blame herself, her body, as the reason for his rejection. But privately I felt that if Cressler had been heterosexual it could have made very little difference. "If you knew he wouldn't ever be… interested… why did you even want to live with him?" This was disingenuous. I was mouthing attitudes I thought people were supposed to have, but I knew that if the boy I'd worshiped from afar all through senior year of high school had wanted to live with me, I would have done so on any terms, and still would.

Dan Cloud—I always said his strange and poetic name to myself in full, to distinguish him from mere Dan, my brother. Dan Cloud had recently resurfaced in my fantasy life. Now that I was sure of Larry, it sometimes began to seem to me that my attraction to him had been only a temporary infatuation. I had always thought I could have been desirable to Dan Cloud, if only I were thin.

"Because I loved him," Vickie said simply. There it was again, the *of course* in her voice that was kind instead of scornful, open instead of defensive. When I felt someone misunderstood me—Larry, for instance, or my mother—I said *of course*, but snappishly, not in Vickie's way. Liquid filled up Vickie's eyes and I was caught between embarrassment and awe. I changed the subject to my own love life, feeling complacent. Perhaps Larry was not as desirable a boyfriend as I deserved, as I *wanted* to deserve, but at least we had sex.

Larry's father, a land speculator, had made a million dollars before Larry was born. He had four sons, and he put parcels of land in each of their names starting when they were just children. Now he had sold off a few pieces of Larry's land, and Larry got checks every month that were big enough to pay the rent on a nicer place, a three-bedroom house out near the airforce base. Larry quit his job and invited me to move in with him again.

"So that's why I haven't seen Larry around," Vickie said. "And here I thought maybe the gypsies had stolen him away."

"I thought having all that space would make a difference to how we lived, but now the house is just as crammed with Larry's stuff as the old apartment used to be."

Larry had gradually bought a number of gigantic tools for spinning, punching, and cutting sheet metal. In his workroom he turned out replicas of helmets, shields, and plate armor to sell at medieval fairs. Soon squares of metal and half-finished armor pieces had to be stored in other rooms as well. Needle-nosed pliers, rivets, and links of chain mail collected in every corner, like lint. At times I felt a nearly physical fear in the house, as though the stuff were some kind of psychic quicksand that sucked away my mind and will. Even the room that was supposed to be my study was piled to the ceiling with Larry's collections, science fiction paperbacks, stamp albums, early 20th century cartoon books. I blamed him, but at the same time I knew a better woman, someone less lazy and greedy, would be able to make our household work. Collectively the stuff perfectly symbolized my indolence and my own creeping flesh. "I feel like I'm drowning in stuff sometimes," I told Vickie.

"That's not good," Vickie said.

"But even worse is that I can't get him to talk to me. Not the way I want."

"Yeah, I've had trouble sustaining conversations with Larry," Vickie said.

"The weird part is that I think he actually really enjoys my talking, but in the way you'd appreciate birdsong or a babbling brook."

"Just pleasant background," Vickie said.

"Exactly! He lets it all flow over him and then he'll suddenly say something completely unrelated, and then he's surprised when that makes me mad. I don't know if it's really a good idea for us to get married." Larry himself wasn't pushing for marriage. It was Larry's parents, Southern Baptists, who didn't like the thought of us living in sin. My own parents had been reticent on the subject of Larry, but I knew they weren't eager for me to tie myself down before I had a college degree and some plans for my future. I had felt them being taken aback by Larry the first time I brought him to their house, 26 years old to my 18, with unbrushed teeth, saying "Davenport" instead of "couch." More recently I had felt my mother's quiet dismay at the condition of our house.

"Well, but there's all that money," Vickie said. "Probably you should marry him and then take him to the Grand Canyon for your honeymoon. 'Sweetheart, come look at this incredible view. Lean way, way over the rail so you can fully appreciate it.'"

Vickie got along better than I did with the older women who worked full-time at the cafeteria. Her voice changed when she talked to them, became less arch and bantering. Why didn't she want to talk only with witty, interesting people? It wasn't very selective of her, I thought. The cashier asked her about her diet, and I squirmed for her, but Vickie responded readily, as though this were merely another pleasant topic of conversation.

"I eat anything I want, but I just stop and think first, what do I really, really want? That way, you know, you don't keep on eating, trying to satisfy yourself."

The cashier nodded and smiled her approval. She was a tiny birdlike woman named Jewel. Even perched on her high stool, she was raised barely far enough to look Vickie in the eye. "But you don't eat cookies and cake, things like that?"

"Oh, no," Vickie said. "I try to eat almost all healthy things." She gestured with her hands as she spoke, and I noticed that the pink under her fingernails was the same as the color of her lips, an almost albino pink. Vickie's lips as she talked became a focus of my discomfort for some reason, either because of their unusual surface texture, a waxy shine like a grocery-store cucumber, or else because of that vulnerable, naked-looking pink. It was like seeing an animal innocently display its sex organs: a dog's penis, a baboon's rear end, something private exposed.

"How much weight have you lost so far?" the cashier said, and Vickie, instead of bristling, leaned forward to answer. I was curious about this point too, but I busied myself inside the bussing station, hating the thought of standing beside Vickie and probably being classified by Jewel in the same category, Tweedledee and Tweedledum. But after I had done every chore I could think of to do the two of them were still chatting away, and finally I drifted back out toward the edge of their conversation, where I could include myself for a minute and then reclaim Vickie.

"What do you eat on the average day?" Jewel was saying, and Vickie was listing wholesome things, rice, fish, salads. Jewel acknowledged my presence by turning her face toward me with a static smile. The story of virtue and transformation that Jewel was constructing with her questions was only half the real story, I thought, and not the interesting part. It seemed to me that I could suggest this in a light, humorous way, parodying Jewel's earnest dullness.

"And what did you eat when you were on the way up?" I said, and regretted it immediately. I hadn't expected an answer; my remark was to have been the punchline. But Vickie turned smoothly from Jewel to me, with the same open face.

"When I went on break I used to pick up a little box of milk from each of the upstairs cafeterias and drink those," she said, "and then most nights I would buy a pint of Häagen-Dazs." She considered for a moment, looking past me, her face detached and analytical. "There was a certain preference for—"

"Dairy products," I said along with her. "Yes, I noticed that." I had noticed it in my own life too, how milk and ice cream had become rich and urgent beyond what I remembered from childhood, more *necessary*. But I said nothing about that.

Deep inside my ear, something was excruciatingly wrong. All night I dreamed fitfully of a parasite growing behind my eardrum, a yellow worm radiating heat, a soft-bodied larva that was maturing into something scaly and huge. It rustled its wingstumps and pressed against the inside of my ear. When I kept whimpering, Larry called the Student Health emergency number and was told not to worry, that even if my eardrum did happen to rupture it would immediately hurt much less, and in any case, I should come first thing in the morning. My eardrum held through the night and the pressure was unrelieved.

Now in the lobby, waiting for my name to be called, my clogged head and stretched membranes bothered me less than the fact that I was about to be weighed. I had gotten fatter again, and Larry's Sears pants were so uncomfortable that I had bought two new larger pairs of khaki pants at the army surplus store, just until I could get hold of myself.

"Brath…" A woman in a labcoat with a big protruding bosom stood just inside the door leading backward from the lobby. "…Brath-white?"

"Here," I said. I relaxed slightly: the nurse was fat too. Not as fat as me, perhaps, but then she was short.

"Did I get the name right?"

"Close enough," I said, letting her walk me down the hall. As she positioned me on the scale, shame squirted into my stomach as if injected by syringe. The nurse slipped the large block of metal on the lower bar of the scale into the notch labeled 100. This wouldn't be enough, I knew, but it would be like testifying against myself to say so. The nurse tapped the smaller weight gently all the way across the top bar to the 50-pound end, then, with a slight grunt or sigh, pushed it all the way back to zero.

She moved the large weight forward to the 150 notch and reached again for the small tab. I tried to locate the proper place to focus my thoughts along the scale arm, to know where to will it to balance, but my mind slid, too. The low 160s—too unrealistic. I had been only a little less than that during Weight Control, and back then the size-18 pants from my mother were too big. Now two stages of clothing separated me from those pants. I felt the different eras of my clothing lying stacked on top of one another like archeological strata. Certainly each layer must be more than five pounds' worth. All right, I would be delighted with anything under 170, and content with… what?

At the far end of the scale arm, 200 pounds loomed. That ghastly horizon was appallingly less distant than it once had been. It was a boundary stark as the edge of the earth, though I knew people could and did sail across it—Angie must have, Vickie perhaps. It wasn't as though you would suddenly explode when you got to 200 pounds. But I wasn't in Angie and Vickie's league. Even if I weighed as much as 175, that would still be only halfway to hell.

The scale arm teetered, pain pulsed sharp and deep in my head, and the nurse tapped the tag backwards and forwards across the line of 180. So that was me. That was where and what I was now. The pit opened up ready to swallow me; the edge of the whirling waters lapped at my feet; I tried to show no outward reaction to the nurse, looking away from her fiddling fingers. Later, when I was alone, I could think and plan.

The nurse made an indecisive sound and I maintained my bland expression. She turned aside to write down the number, then straightened herself resolutely. "Now, I'm going to tell you the same thing I told my own daughter," she said. She looked again at the name on my chart, then directly at me. "Jean, you lose weight. Do it now, while you're young, because it only gets harder when you get older."

"Okay," I said. Did the stupid bitch think I just hadn't noticed I was fat? Did she think I just never gave it any thought? She was too fat herself to be dispensing advice. I wondered what the daughter looked like. I couldn't raise my eyes from the nurse's loathsome chest. Irrelevantly, my ear blazed on.

"It's not just about your looks," she said. She ran through the litany: high blood pressure, heart attack, diabetes, stroke. To everything she said, I answered okay. None of that had any significance. As though you needed a reason, as though being thin were a means to an end!

Looking for something to read on break at work, I shuffled through the mess of discarded newspapers at the bussing station. In among them was a black spiral notebook with a postcard taped to the front: Godzilla standing in front of a city skyline.

"Is this yours?" I said to Vickie.

"Yeah, it's my diary for PE."

"Which PE class are you taking?" I said, but I already knew. Below the Godzilla picture Vickie had written a caption, or title. The Thing That Ate New York City.

"It's called Weight Control," Vickie said. "It's a blend of exercise and exhortations, and you have to keep an eating diary."

"Could I look at it?"

"Sure."

I was aware of pleasurable sensations of tension in my body, a faster heartrate and breathing. This was like being a voyeur, lurking outside Vickie's bathroom to catch a glimpse of her body in the shower. My hands were awkward, trembly; I tried to make them turn pages casually. "Dear Thing," the entries read, instead of "Dear Diary." I kept my eyes moving, so I wouldn't seem to be rudely lingering over the details.

"Dear Thing, I went to the movies tonight, but I didn't order any popcorn!"

"Dear Thing, Weigh-in today, and I didn't lose any weight, but I'm not going to feel bad, because I know I was good all week."

The entries chirped along steadily, recording the discipline and enjoyment of Vickie's life. The different parts of her cooperated with each other, and the diary was like a conversation between them. For a second, I envied her passionately. But still, she was monstrously fat. Far more than me.

Just inside the front cover I could see the edge of the card I knew was Vickie's weekly weigh-in record. The sight of it brought my own failure back viscerally. My only real progress had occurred before the class began and had never shown on the card. After that came the time of erratic wavering where the advances just balanced out the setbacks, more or less, then the blank spots where I started skipping class, a few at first, then more and more until no turnaround was possible.

I wanted to sit down with Vickie's weight chart and study it closely. But the very object of greatest interest was exactly what I had to pass over the most lightly. I sneaked my left thumb and forefinger just inside the front cover of the notebook. As I swung the rest of the pages closed with my other hand, I created a gap, a tiny triangle of space that I could peek into for a split second. The most recent number stood out clearly above the blank spaces: 225. Above that every square was filled in. My eyes, tracking upward, retained vague impressions of higher numbers, 230s, 240s, but there wasn't time enough to see all the way to the top before I finished the gesture of swinging the book shut. "That's nice, thanks."

"No biggie."

On the bus ride home, I pondered the enigma of Vickie. It was horrifying and titillating to think of how fat she was: almost 50 pounds more than me—that's what she was *down* to. And Vickie herself seemed oblivious to the horror. She was content to chip away with a teaspoon at that mountain of fat, being good for weeks at a time with no result. How many months, years, would she have to go on, at that rate? Her slow progress was pathetic, and yet, looked at in a certain way, her long-term faithfulness was better than I could muster.

It was becoming harder and harder to keep thinking of myself as a fundamentally thin person in a state of temporary disorder. Fat people's bodies were said to contain thin people inside them, struggling to be free. But what if that was just sentimentality? Some fat people had to be fat all the way to their core—many, most of them—or you would see them change oftener than they did. It was intolerable to believe I was one of these incorrigibly diseased souls. But it was impossible never to suspect it, as years passed and I got bigger and bigger.

I had ways of turning aside from intolerable thoughts. Like the mirrors that lined the bathrooms I entered in the course of my daily life, I knew where these thoughts were located, and had practiced getting around them without looking, feeling for the edges of the dangerous zone. In a corner of my brain now, a conclusion formed and was acknowledged without full attention, a new detour, a bypass in the line of my thought: Vickie was superior to me. At life in general, at dieting in particular.

In any case, it was clear what I needed to do. If I was incapable of being gently good for months on end, like Vickie, the only choice was to be heroic for a shorter time. I thought of my fat under assault by pickaxes and earth-cutting engines, with teams of workmen toiling round the clock, a rescue operation to dig out my trapped and smothering core self, before it was too late. I needed to think about *me*, not Vickie. But the incredible unbudge-able fact of her was still lodged in that unexamined corner, and other thoughts continued unfurling wispily upward from the bulk. Vickie was irrelevant right now, I wasn't going to think about her, but still—How had such a disciplined person ever gotten so fat in the first place?

Now

Oh, Vickie, where are you now and what is your life like? You were the first person to show me that a fat woman can inhabit herself with grace and dignity and even pleasure.

Chapter 13

War

1981, even more than 180

Early in the summer Larry began planning for the Pennsic War, the largest annual event staged by the Society for Creative Anachronism, and the biggest opportunity to sell armor. He negotiated with an importer in San Francisco for as much rattan as his van could carry. (By SCA regulation, the shafts of any weapon used for actual combat could only be rattan, which shredded when it broke rather than splintering.) He ordered a button-making machine from a mail-order catalog and wrote the slogans which would be printed on the buttons: "Chaste… but seldom caught." "Do it in the woad." There were references to the second Star Wars movie, which had just come out: "Get off my back, Yoda." "Luke—give your father a hand." A friend of Larry's drew a tiny, hairy cartoon Viking that looked something like Bugs Bunny's Tasmanian Devil in a horned helmet. For this picture the caption was "I4DW3: Wine, Women, War." The humor was too broad, I said. At least, I said, make it "D3W." Larry was confident his version would appeal.

I had to have appropriate "society" clothes. Lady Gwendolyn the seamstress showed me reference books and discussed patterns, went with me to the fabric store where I chose dark blue velour, sky blue linen, satin ribbons. She measured around my waist and hips and took notes on a piece of paper with her mouth closed and her eyes evasive. I looked away from the paper too.

Larry knit chainmail and spun more helmets and shields. I xeroxed button slogans on different colored paper and cut out small circles around them, pleased with the orderliness of the folders and notebooks where I kept them all arranged. Larry pored over atlases and SCA flyers and plotted a driving route from Tucson to Pittsburgh that would take in the maximum possible number of lesser wars and medieval fairs on the way. We would spend nearly a month on the road going there, and then come flying home just as the first week of fall-semester classes started. In July I filled out the paperwork that would allow me to take a leave from the cafeteria and return to the job in September.

With a blank check signed by Larry, I went to Lady Gwendolyn's for the final fitting. She turned me toward the mirror. I knew what I was supposed to say. "It's beautiful," I murmured, blurring my gaze so I saw nothing but an enormous blue smudge. She demonstrated how to tie the ribbon, one straight line high up under my breasts, then two angling down in a triangle that framed my stomach. Even without looking, I felt a horrible exposure. "Doesn't that kind of… overemphasize my front?" I said.

"That was the fashion," Gwendolyn said. "After the plague years, pregnancy was a status symbol. Every marriageable girl wanted to suggest her fertility." Her hands touched my body, authoritatively putting pins in and taking them out, smoothing down the ribbon. I wanted to relax under her hands, felt it might be possible to travel so far into shame that you escaped on the other side. When Gwendolyn bent to the hem, I looked into the mirror. My breasts had become cushions and my face was round, round, when had that happened? My upper arms were fat too under the sleeves of the dress, and I had no real waist anymore. Could anyone have found this shape attractive, even in the fifteenth century?

The weekend before we left, Larry drove to San Francisco and picked up the rattan. It made a foundation two feet deep on the floor of the van. Around the edges I packed the other armor and things for sale, our clothes and our folding table and other gear, the button-making kit and receipt booklet. I built a nest of sleeping bags on top of the rattan. It gave me great pleasure to feel completely in control of this limited space, to have imposed order on it.

The last stop was to say goodbye to my parents. I wore the new velour dress to show them. "Don't wear the belt that way," my mother said.

"It was the fashion," I said. "Pregnancy turned men on."

"I don't care," my mother said. "You can't wear it like that." She took me into her bedroom and moved the ribbon so that the straight line of the triangle cut across the middle of my stomach. It was slightly less comfortable but made me feel more organized, better packaged. My mother's hands touched me as Gwendolyn's had, gently but impersonally. I stood still in front of her dresser mirror and let her arrange me. As she finished, her hands changed, patting and smoothing me in gestures that were closer to caressing. For a moment we looked together into the mirror. Now might be the time she would speak. I willed her not to, but at the same time felt what I had felt at Gwendolyn's: a tickling sensation in back of the rising fear, the possibility of some kind of release beyond it. "You see what I mean?" my mother said. Her hand fell away from me tentatively. "It looks much better this way."

"Yes," I said.

In Albuquerque, at the first war, I sat behind our table, surrounded by rolls of embroidered ribbon, leather pouches, and buttons: our wares. I was engrossed in my work, cutting out more I4DW3 circles—those buttons had been selling like hotcakes. When I looked up Dan Cloud, my high-school crush, stood in front of me, strong and handsome in a belted tunic, wearing a sword. I was in my blue linen dress but I felt that my real clothing was my fat, luridly covering me like a full-body tattoo, or like neon advertising that moved with me everywhere. I was keenly aware of the difference between my body as Dan Cloud had last seen it, and now. We looked at each other without speaking, my face flushed. Dan Cloud bowed in courtly fashion, I nodded, and he walked on. Was it possible he hadn't even recognized me?

After Albuquerque I ordered vegetable plates or the salad bar at every restaurant. I would keep away from concentrated foods. Larry ate meat and French fries, drank milk and soda, ordered hot fudge sundaes for dessert. The khaki pants loosened on me, and I wore Larry's pants again for a couple weeks when we were in the van. When we stopped for an SCA event or meeting, I used a safety pin to take in the slack of my ribbon. But then I became ravenous, fell off the wagon. I ate what Larry did and more, begging him to pull off the highway when I saw a Dairy Queen sign.

The blue velour dress.

At the Pennsic, we bumped into Linda. I knew about her already, from having quizzed Larry about previous girlfriends, how he felt about them, and reasons why I was more satisfying to him than any of them were.

"How are you?" Linda said. She rested her hand familiarly on Larry's shoulder. She was dressed in a coarse brown-colored cloth: her persona would be a woman who kept an inn, or something like that, a prosperous low-status position that gave her plenty of freedom to mingle widely. I felt how much easier it would be to wear clothes like hers than my dresses. Linda's face I judged to be more dumpy than mine; she was at least a decade older, and had moles. Her body was harder to decide about. She was taller than me and large-boned, busty. Even with my recently-inflated breasts, I was still a relatively flat-chested woman. Was Linda fat, or was she just "buxom"? Overall she was certainly less fat than me as I was now, but at my smallest back in the Weight Control semester I was thinner, I decided. So that did make her kind of fat.

"I'm glad to see you with somebody," Linda said. She turned to me: "Do you know that this gentleman spent most of the last war following *me* around? And then wrote letters for months afterwards." She rolled her eyes as though this were ludicrous.

"Well," I said, "let me know if you have any other castoffs I could use."

In our tent that night I urged Larry to review his romantic history again. The girls he had crushes on in high school but didn't get anywhere with. Linda, of course, who had been mildly interested, but less so than Larry. They cuddled but never went all the way. The crazy woman who propositioned him at two in the morning at 7-11 was not a girlfriend, but, at her request, he locked up and took her in the back of the store.

"That's it?" I said. "Linda, and a crazy stranger, is your whole experience with romance? Before me, I mean." I put my lips on the place where his ear joined his neck. I was afraid Larry would clam up now, but for once he seemed to want a conversation to go on.

"There was one other person," he said. A woman he knew as a friend, also relatively inexperienced, who proposed they try a few things with each other—oral sex, for instance—just to see what it was like. They did, but the next day she called off the experiment; sex without love didn't agree with her. "She had tears in her eyes," Larry said. He sounded awed by his memory.

"What did she look like?" I said to the bottom of Larry's ear. I pushed the earlobe from side to side with my nose. The woman in his story was like a mirror-reversed image of me: aggressive at the beginning and then shy later. I wondered what sort of body she had.

"I don't know," Larry said.

"Well, was she fat or thin?" I said.

"I was always willing to date women anywhere between 100 and 200 pounds," Larry said.

"I know," I said, "you told me that before." I didn't point out that Larry's weight range had suddenly shortened up by 100 pounds. It depressed me, even though I had always known his numbers weren't accurate. I couldn't be very far short of 200 now. Where did you meet her?" I said.

"Working at the cafeteria."

"*Our* cafeteria?"

"Um, yeah, I guess so."

I let this ridiculously uncooperative answer pass, because all my attention was focused on the next question. "Is it someone I *know*?"

I could see that Larry was trying to decide how to answer. But if the true answer were no there wouldn't be any reason to hesitate. I was surprised that Larry would think of concealing something this significant from me. He should feel I was the one person he could be completely open with about anything. But I didn't follow up the issue of Larry's shiftiness because, again, there was something more important on the horizon. Larry needed to understand that I *had* to know this. "I don't know—" he started to say.

"Larry." I straddled his torso and leaned over to look intently into his face, putting one hand flat against each of his temples. He had to see me. This wasn't a case that required me to argue or bargain or force the information out of him. Just to open up my own face for him to see that it was absolutely necessary for me to know.

"All right," he said, "it was Vickie."

Vickie! I peeled myself off Larry, energized, almost thrilled in a way I couldn't easily account for. Larry and Vickie both seemed more interesting with this drama in their past. I pictured her waxy lips going around his penis. It was a little surprising that Larry had kept this quiet, but it was *amazing* that Vickie did. I knew if the situation had been reversed, I would have told long ago. Each of them, I realized, had carefully protected the other one's privacy. From *me*.

As I thought it over, their mutual discretion seemed even more striking than the sexual contact itself, and required a larger revision of my previous mental model of all our relationships. I'd been assuming that although they'd known each other longer, I stood between Larry and Vickie like a gate, so that neither could have any significant information about the other except as it passed through me. It took only a few seconds to notice just how childish an assumption that had been. But anyway, I thought, Vickie was outside Larry's current official weight limits and neither of them knew it. Only I knew that.

I had begun wearing the linen dress unbelted. On the final day of the Pennsic, Linda *did* give me another castoff, a cloak she had made for herself. "Something for when it gets cold," she said. We broke camp and hit the road.

Larry drove all night and then handed off to me. I drove for several hours through a rolling green landscape. Traffic was light and I was growing more confident about shifting the gears. When Larry woke up the needle on the gas gauge was getting low, and he directed me to a truck stop where he fueled up again and we stopped for food, his breakfast. Both of us had steak and eggs, hash browns and pancakes. I felt grubby and the khaki pants were tight on me as a sausage skin. Larry took the wheel again when we got into the van.

He woke me up around 3:00 the next morning, at another truck stop. "You better take over," he said. "I keep imagining I see a kid on a bicycle at the side of the highway." I got out of the van and went to the bathroom. It was cold enough that I put on Linda's cloak. It looked silly in a truckstop, but looking silly didn't matter since we were out of town. Inside I bought coffee and No Doz pills, swallowing two of them immediately with the hot fluid. I felt no desire to eat. A pleasurable sense of necessity and destiny sat on my shoulders: difficult work awaited me. In the bathroom as I put my contacts in I looked directly at my face in the tinny mirror. The gritty reality of my pitted complexion and doughy shape mixed with the dented, scratched surface of the mirror, and both were part of what I had to do now.

Larry slept on what was left of the rattan. The level of our stuff was lower by a foot and a half than when we had set out. I pictured the contents of the van as a volume and felt how the volume had shrunk, becoming converted by our labor into money. The coffee began to take hold: my hands and feet were chilled and remote but perfectly controlled. All the power I needed was at my disposal, under my foot, but also inward, humming. My body was like the van—or could be—a thing driven and steered by my will. The white dashed line was easy to adhere to, the green highway signs were easy to understand. I didn't get bored, or waver, or become tired though hours went by. I saw with exalted clarity that my future could unroll just as steadily as this road; the volume of my body could also be forced to shrink.

Always before, I had counted on being able to hold onto the correct frame of mind long enough to get thin. And then that other person who I was at times, the gluttonous one, had undone all my efforts. This time, I would outwit her. If I didn't go back to the cafeteria job, she would have no money to buy food and wouldn't be able to sabotage me. As a side bonus, instead of wasting a lot of time going to movies or playing pinball, she would have to stay home. Then I would spend most of my time studying, or cleaning up the house. My grades would be outstanding. Right around the time I was thin again, Larry would have learned what a valuable housewife I was, and would be happy to start giving me a groceries allowance, submitting to my management in general. He would want to improve his life, inspired by my example of transformation, and then I would run our household the way it should be run. I would learn to cook nutritious things for us both and the baby we would have later. The plan was foolproof.

I looked up Vickie's schedule at the cafeteria and, with a complex mix of anticipation and nervousness, went to visit her during the slow part of the afternoon. One fear was that Vickie might have been getting steadily thinner as I was getting fatter. But much to my relief she looked the same. So whatever she was trying to do about herself these days, it wasn't working. "Hey," she said, "haven't seen you for a while."

"I bet you thought the gypsies had stolen me away," I said.

"Something like that." With a handful of paper napkins from the tray in front of her Vickie swiped globs of refried beans from a plate into the garbage can. I waited and watched her until she looked up at me.

"What do you think of Larry Lovejoy?" I said. The question so obviously portended something more, that I imagined—almost counted on—Vickie insisting on probing further before she answered. It was clear that she saw something was up, but she didn't pursue that. She let herself be steered by my words as though I were a teacher assigning a discussion question. Her eyes went up and back, looking into her mind, to come forward again with the most accurate and concise answer she could find. "I think he's a kind person with good intentions who when he was growing up somehow missed out on part of the socialization process." What's next, her face said.

"His parents are really pushing us to get married," I said.

"Ah," Vickie said. She tossed silverware into a bin, poured out the dregs of a glass of iced tea. "Are you going to?"

Probably, I thought. "I don't know," I said. "Do you think I should?" I expected Vickie to demur, to say that only I could make that decision, or else to ask me some diagnostic questions like Do you love him? although anything that conventional would be un-Vickie-like.

"Larry isn't someone I'd want to marry," she said.

One of my anticipated pleasures in coming here was discussing Larry's shortcomings as a mate; still, I didn't completely like for Vickie to say things that implied he wasn't a conquest worth making. "Larry was interested in you at one time," I said to Vickie, not making it sound like a question, but looking a question at her with my face.

"Yes," she said drily. "I do seem to recall an episode like that." She smiled and shimmied her head and upper body as if she were trying to shake Larry off of her.

"But you weren't interested."

"I want someone I can really talk to." Beggars can't be choosers, I thought. If Vickie thought Larry wasn't good enough for her, did she think he was good enough for me? Was I a less desirable woman than Vickie, who was big as a house?

Since getting home from the Pennsic, I had needed to get some even larger pants from the army surplus. It wasn't clear what had gone wrong with my plan. With no meals provided at home, Larry began going out to fast food places for breakfast, lunch, and dinner. I ate only in the evenings, when Larry took me somewhere, or brought take-out food home. Incredibly, I was still getting fatter under these conditions. Larry's body was about the same. Perhaps, because he was taller, he needed more calories than I did—but *that* many more? Occasionally I wondered what Larry thought I was doing for food during the day. But there was no resentment in my musing. I was fat, so, really I didn't deserve to eat at all, never mind three times a day.

By now, I thought, I might have reached 200 pounds. At least, I must be very, very near it. Who would ever love me again if I didn't take Larry? "If I don't marry Larry," I said, "what would I do instead?"

"Make a life for yourself," Vickie said.

By October even the new pants were tight. I had taken to wearing Larry's shirts since I didn't like the way mine stretched across my stomach. I was worried about winter; my coat and sweatshirts from last year wouldn't fit me now, that was certain. There was Linda's cloak, but it was too conspicuous for school. Something would have to be done—a shopping trip with my mother was the most likely scenario—but I put off thinking about it. Maybe something else would happen first.

I had been in limbo for many weeks, going foodless every day until evening without much discomfort, then, with Larry, ordering whatever I wanted for dinner: hamburgers and French fries, steak and baked potato loaded with butter and sour cream. Milk or soda to drink. Ice cream or chocolate after. Once in a great while, I tried ordering a vegetable plate instead, but then by the middle of the night I would be desperate to eat again and have to wheedle something out of Larry, send him out for chocolate and soda. He went, usually, but the disgust in his face was so plain then, that it seemed best to feed myself when I had the opportunity, rather than disturb the equilibrium I had found. But I didn't trust my body—on a day when I got the chance to eat more than once it seemed that I could feel it expanding again—and something in the back of my mind gathered itself for an upheaval.

The professor who taught Ancient Greek was young and attractive. Slender, intellectual, well-spoken, with a sensitive face, he was everything Larry wasn't. He was living the life I ought to have been living. I mooned over him during the day; at night, while eating, I screened out of my thoughts anything which might make me too aware of my shame. But I got in the habit of doing homework a bit more regularly, at least for Greek. Dr. Chamberlain swayed gracefully at the front of the classroom, pointed with an elegant finger to a tricky passage, smiled enigmatically. Dr. Chamberlain. Charles.

At Halloween my mother and father invited Larry and me over to carve pumpkins with my brothers and nieces. I disliked giving my family opportunities to see my body, but it was a relief to escape my own house for a while. My mother's house seemed like a miracle of order and space, light and cleanliness. Every cupboard had its own internal logic. Dishes were washed right after they were used, instead of right before. When we arrived in mid-afternoon, I couldn't help looking into the fridge, and then I couldn't help fixing a peanut-butter sandwich, eating raisins, drinking milk, although I knew what I must look like to my family. They didn't know I hadn't had breakfast or lunch.

"Would you run out and get some lightbulbs?" my mother said to my father.

"Do you want to go with me?" he said to me. I did.

In the hardware store, oddly, there was a display of shirts for sale. "Look," my father said, holding a tan corduroy shirt against his front. 2XL, said the tag. "I'm going to get me one of these splendid shirts. Do you want one?"

My father bought two shirts, and we put them on immediately. I felt the relief of being covered up. This would hold me for a while, at least.

My mother laughed when she saw our purchases. "I got you a couple shirts, too," she said. I went into her bedroom and she brought them from the closet: two Hawaiian shirts in bright colors. A solid red, and a blue with a print of palm trees. I tried on the blue one. "It looks good," my mother said.

Nothing could look good on me, really, but I understood what she meant. The shirt fit. I was decently concealed, and it wasn't about to split its seams. For some reason, the loud colors had an effect like armor: they seemed to deflect attention rather than attracting it. This would hold me for a little while too.

My mother and I stood in front of the mirror where we had been in the summer. Even though I was fatter now, I was less afraid she would speak. She too, I thought, must feel the necessity of not disturbing the equilibrium.

But no. She moved toward me and touched the shoulder of the shirt, adjusting its hang, then let her hands move down, smoothing it at my waist, such as my waist was these days. I could feel her thinking the same thing, and knowing it was my thought too. Let that be enough, then, I said to her in my mind. Her eyes looked for mine in the mirror, tried to hold them, but I put mine firmly elsewhere. "You know," she said. Gently, so gently. "You're getting huge."

"Yes, I know!" I said. I flung myself clear. "Of course! Jesus Christ! Did you think maybe I didn't?"

My mother turned aside abruptly and I knew it was to conceal tears.

My mother's house was a miracle of order and space.

Chapter 14

I Finally Manage to Stop Eating

November 1981. Considerably more than 200 pounds

Roughly ten days before Thanksgiving of 1981 I stopped eating. There was nothing to distinguish this fast from hundreds before, lasting from a few hours to five days. The fact that I was besotted with the Greek professor was not new, since I had had a crush on somebody or other since puberty. The feeling that this time would be different was not new either—didn't every diet or fast start that way? If there was a specific triggering event, it is something I no longer have the slightest recollection of. I didn't weigh myself, or choose a special date to start. There were no feelings or thoughts I hadn't had before, no outside advice, no new techniques. Nothing to suggest that I or my life had changed.

The only boundary between one era and the next was a casserole I had made from bulgur wheat, spinach, and cheese—my mother's recipe, one of three things I knew how to cook. Larry had reminded me of my promise to do more housework when I quit the cafeteria, and I had retaliated by making a dinner I knew he wouldn't touch with a ten-foot pole. Therefore I can deduce that my fast was not premeditated, because I must have been intending to eat all the casserole leftovers myself. But I never did.

Every evening for a week, when Larry went out for his usual fast-food dinner, I told him I wasn't hungry, or that I had to study. He didn't press me. The sixth foodless day passed, shattering my previous fasting limit. I suppressed pride in this accomplishment as premature; every broken record in the past had been followed by a gross failure of will within a day. There was no room for complacency, all my thoughts must be focused on driving myself forward. Nevertheless, I noticed my pleasure, glancing sideways at it. Morning and night I ritually brushed my teeth, lingering over the sensations of the brush on my gums and tongue, the taste of the toothpaste. My pants were decidedly loose and I tightened my belt by one hole. It really didn't seem that I was anywhere near to cracking this time. The sixth day was, if anything, easier than the ones before.

Thanksgiving week, suburbs of Phoenix, Arizona

Older than my mother and taller than me, Larry's mother had the massive look of marble statuary, heavily fleshed and thick-waisted, girdled to smooth contours where my fat jiggled or bulged. Because of her age, I did not classify Mrs. Lovejoy primarily as fat, but more as old-fashioned, the embodiment of antiquated ideas and appearances. Enlightened people understood that women's bodies, like men's, must be the real thing, firm from the core outward.

"In a minute now, Mother's going to have her juice," Mrs. Lovejoy said. "She drinks just a little glass of juice half an hour before every meal and it cuts down on her appetite. I'm going to drink a little juice too, would you like any?"

"No, thank you," I said. Mrs. Lovejoy was my enemy, to be resisted and outwitted.

Under normal circumstances when we visited Larry's parents we would be put into separate beds. But at Thanksgiving, with other sons and their wives in attendance, there wasn't enough space and his parents tacitly agreed not to notice when the two of us checked into a single room at the Motel 6 on Wednesday afternoon. Larry went out to make the rounds of the Phoenix used bookstores, leaving me a twenty-dollar bill for dinner at the Denny's next door. I bought a cup of coffee to break the twenty and studied the menu, planning what to say I had eaten and calculating what that should cost including tax and tip. Then I made a packet of bills and coins which would be Larry's change and divided that carefully from the money I would keep as my rightful earnings. I strode around the sidewalks for an hour, to use up dinnertime in case Larry came back early, then I paced in the motel room for another hour. The cream in the coffee had reanimated my stomach and it was roiling.

Sometime in my teens

Once on television I had seen a man who had lost a hundred pounds and now stayed thin by eating exactly the same carefully weighed portions of food every day, six ounces of boiled chicken at lunch, for instance. The interviewer expressed sympathy, and asked whether he didn't get hungry. The man began his answer before the interviewer had finished his sentence, as though he had to rush to forestall some danger. "Hunger pangs last only three to five minutes." He exaggerated the pronunciation of the final words in a sonorous manner halfway between belligerent and evangelical. "Three to five minutes," he repeated.

Nothing had been said about how often the pangs could recur, or whether two of them ever ran back to back, or anything about other less fleeting physical sensations that went along with hunger.

Thanksgiving 1981, Motel 6

For me the pain component of hunger had never been the hardest part to tolerate, especially if I could keep moving at the same time. It felt healthy, like the soreness of muscles after a hard workout. It was the sign of progress. I enjoyed myself until nighttime when Larry returned.

Larry had found Peter Arno and Charles Addams collections he was missing, and was pleased with himself. I stayed awake far past his bedtime, until Wednesday became Thursday. Nighttime was always the hardest to get through in a fast. My jaw could not rest comfortable no matter how often I repositioned it. Hunger was not localized to my stomach: it was a hollow metal tube that impaled my entire body from the muscles in my limbs all the way up to the strange industrial tang in my mouth. I had already brushed my teeth once, but I got out of bed at 3:00 a.m. and brushed them again. By the time I got up the next morning, Larry had gone out and eaten so it was natural for me to be alone again for breakfast. I was comfortable again in my sluggish body, as though hunger slept when I did, and wakened later.

I got coffee again at Denny's. On an empty stomach the caffeine took hold quickly. Hunger rose again, strong bright morning hunger like a spirited horse that would do my will for as long as I could stay on top of it. There were no contractions or gurgling now, just a keenness. Now the hollowness radiated light and pleasure, drew me forward to adventure, steeled against hardship. Outside, the sunlight seemed more than usually beautiful. Small sounds gave me pleasure in their texture—a bird, the scrape of my feet against parking lot grit—everything seemed rich with meaning and purpose.

The smells of baking at the Lovejoy house were a problem. I closed myself into the bathroom. There was a scale between the toilet and the bathtub, but I didn't even consider getting on it. It wasn't time for that. Intellectually I knew I weighed—or *had* weighed—more than 200 pounds, but it would still be devastating to see that number. I had to preserve the delicate psychological balance that was enabling me to maintain my regimen.

To pass through these dangerous days away from home, I was playing a game, pretending to be a spy on a mission, deep behind enemy lines, communicating in secret with the mission commander when I got the chance. I radioed in my report about the difficulty of withstanding the food smells. I had no particular line of dialogue in mind in advance, and was surprised at what popped into my head next.

"Don't worry about your feelings," the commander said. "Stick to the plan and minimize the damage, that's what counts. You always knew you'd have to eat *something* today." The voice was sane, comforting, intelligent. It didn't count as hallucinating, I thought, because the other personality was still me, only the better part of me, judicious, separated from my immediate impulses. Someone who saw the total picture and supervised from a higher perspective. I thought about the Latin roots of *supervisor*. An over-seer, literally. The other connotations fit too: someone to obey. Obedience made it unnecessary to master desire.

Now

When I say that nothing changed when I went anorexic—if you'll allow me that term—in November of 1981, I don't mean there were literally no differences at all that led to an outcome different from the previous five or six years: this particular assault on my fat began with about 10 days of no eating rather than my previous maximum of five, for instance. What I mean—and this is the difficulty of writing accurately about real life—is that there was no easily isolated, easily narrated difference, nothing of the sort you would find in a novel about a fat person, or the usual social-psychological nonfiction account of obesity either. I'd been maturing intellectually the whole time, of course; as my attention span gradually increased, my ability to carry on long-term projects improved even when the projects themselves were no more wisely chosen. And in 1981 I was in an almost ideal environment to behave anorexically: an essentially foodless house, with an inarticulate mate who had watched his mate become obese over the past year. So of course nobody said anything until I was well underway. And, as I finally began to have a real history of success to look back on, my abilities also improved not just to stay on an obsessive course but to return to it after a limited lapse. All of these things were factors. None of them is the kind of reason people are looking for in a story, or a theory. Nothing changed qualitatively in my relationships to food, exercise, or my body. All the differences were slight shifts of proportion.

Thanksgiving dinner, Lovejoy residence

I helped myself to small portions from every plate or bowl that was passed to me. My body responded instantly to the food, like an animal lunging forward against its leash, but my grip was implacable and brought it up short. I took tiny bites and chewed them a long time, smiling and smiling. It was strategically crucial that I still have plenty on my plate by the time other people were starting to take seconds. The taste of the food was intense, and my sight and hearing seemed heightened too.

Larry refused every vegetable but asparagus and potatoes and his mother protested—"when are you going to start eating right?"—but he held firm. "You better be taking vitamins for a deficient diet, then," she said.

"I am, I am."

"When will the wedding be?" Larry's mother asked.

"Next summer, I guess" Larry said vaguely. "After I graduate."

The Lovejoy men ate silently, the women made remarks. Larry's mother began talking about the key to marriage being compromise; fights could begin about anything, she said, even what color of toothpicks to have. She had given me the exact same speech the day before. "…one wants red and the other wants yellow you compromise and get orange." There was dead silence around the table afterwards. Once Larry and I get married and have children, I thought, what will our family life be like? It had never occurred to me before to think of having a child older than a baby.

It was a relief to move into the living room, away from the food. My body was unsatisfied but it stopped clamoring for more, relaxed and curled around what it had been given like a dog with its bone, gnawing, quietly but intensely occupied. Lines of force seemed to connect the immobilized men to the television set. They crackled with latent energy, while other, more active energies were employed by the women in the kitchen. I decided I didn't have to join the women if I pretended to watch what the men were watching. I began to feel pleasantly torpid.

Suddenly, Larry's mother stepped out into the middle of the circle, oblivious to the lines she snapped, the electrical interference she caused. "Now, *who's* ready for a piece of *pie*?"

I had to plead fullness three times before I was left alone. Around the room, the plates of pie made small fierce dots of desire that I had to pretend not to notice. My body and mind were fully alert again. The sounds of chewing and the clink of forks surrounded me. Mrs. Lovejoy began conversations that smothered quickly.

"We're trying to watch TV, Mom," a brother said.

The morning after Thanksgiving, I tightened my belt to its last notch. My fast had been broken—through no fault of mine—but I was all right, climbing straight back into the saddle, undaunted. My strength of will was a palpable presence inside me as I got into the van with Larry. At the Lovejoys' I would say I had just finished a large breakfast and couldn't eat anything yet. If I couldn't get out of a later meal, I would handle it the same as I had Thanksgiving. In my mind was the feeling of vanquishing an opponent, but it was unclear whether that was food in the abstract or Mrs. Lovejoy more specifically.

"We're not planning any sit-down meals at all today," she said. "There are plenty of leftovers and people can eat whatever they want, whenever they want. But they have to get up and get it for themselves. Nobody's going to wait on them or pay any attention."

The day went slowly. I drifted back and forth from living room to kitchen, pretending to be interested in sports on TV, pretending to listen to the women talk about people I didn't know. In the random milling about, nobody would notice me if I kept moving. I filled a glass with water, drank, refilled it, drank again, pretended to study. At 3:00 in the afternoon, when I drifted through the kitchen, Larry's mother offered to make me a turkey sandwich. She waved her hands toward ingredients she had laid out on plates on the kitchen table.

"No thank you," I said. I sighed like a person who is still recovering from the last hearty round of turkey. "Later maybe."

She rounded on me, suddenly accusing. "Well, now *you* haven't eaten anything all *day*." It took me by surprise that she had bothered to notice, and seemed like cheating, since she said that she wouldn't.

"Oh," I said, "I had a really big breakfast." It was meant to be a confident assertion of self-determination, but it came out like a lame excuse.

"*That's* not enough," she said. The nasal old-lady voice might have sounded petulant, a childish whine, except that she took her authority so much for granted. She was not concerned about me, I thought, or not only that. She was offended. To her, my not eating was a dereliction which she had every right to expose and correct. My blood boiled up. How dare she try to control me? She was a liar and manipulator and wasn't even ashamed.

Smiling fixedly, silently, I put a slice of bread on a plate.

"There's white bread or brown," she said, more conciliatory. The "brown" bread had a few oats sprinkled on the crust, and was a light tan color, but it wasn't *real* whole wheat, whatever it claimed on the wrapper: the consistency was as soft as white bread. Just the kind of flimsy, insincere bread she *would* buy, I thought. I took my time choosing a few strips of turkey to put on the bread, then covered them with another slice of bread.

"Don't you want some mayonnaise?"

"No thank you," I said sweetly. I kept my eyes away from her. I had never before been so angry without attempting to convey my feelings to the offending party. This was combat, but it was undercover.

"How about cranberry sauce?"

"Oh, no thank you. I really prefer it just like this." I looked at her and smiled the spy smile. She didn't matter, she was nothing. Meanwhile, over it all, the larger voice spoke: It's all right, you figured you'd have to eat twice today, so you're still ahead.

Larry went straight to bed when we got back to Tucson. I walked quietly around the rest of the house, savoring my control of my life. In the kitchen I looked into the fridge at the bulgur-wheat casserole, a relic from the distant past, before I began fasting.

Under the plastic wrap the casserole looked normal, but it was slowly rotting. Really, all food everywhere was rotting, the overseer pointed out.

In my study I sat down at the desk. My stomach felt slightly bloated, as if, forced in the last two days to stretch itself twice, it had lost elasticity and was still holding the shape of the turkey sandwich now, though the food itself was long digested. I knew this slack feeling from the bygone era, from a hundred broken fasts, the morning-after feeling of non-empty hunger, unclean as the black curds at the end of a menstrual flow, heavy as failure. Empty hunger asserted itself sharply, sometimes painfully, but with the cleanness of free-flowing blood. Bloated hunger insisted deeply, with the patience of congested despair. So many times, hopelessly, I had eaten again to relieve it. This time I would not. My certainty was like a portcullis slamming down; I would not and I knew I would not. But how could I know that? What was different about me now? The overseer warned me away from these thoughts, not in words but in a shorthand pulse like the clearing of a throat. There were things I shouldn't think about yet. My mind had to stay focused.

Now

Famously, anorexia involves delusions, but they are, or at least can be, willed delusions. (If I may call myself anorexic, if I may assume my experience generalizes to other anorexics.) The anorexic is continually rededicating herself, re-embracing propositions of dubious soundness or even obvious unsoundness *on purpose*, as a means to her larger end. The forces ranked against her, which include her own appetite, are powerful and cunning indeed, and to triumph over them, some degree of untruthfulness may sometimes be necessary. The anorexic is thus simultaneously the demagogue, and the credulous public, and the slandered *target*, of a massive propaganda campaign. She is both the besotted followers and the charismatic megalomaniac at the head of her own religious cult. Never mind common sense (sin)—banish doubt (sin) and rise to glory!

On the web these days, one can find "pro-ana" websites where young women exchange tips on maintaining their discipline in the face of hunger and their families, how to avoid getting sent to the hospital, and so forth. On the chatboards there are always wistful postings from women you might call wannabes. How did you do it, they ask the true anas, the successful ones. How did you push yourself up over the threshold where I keep stumbling?

These wannarexics show that many women are willing to trade away mental health for the sake of losing weight. At least for a while: presumably most are thinking that an eating disorder can be adopted temporarily, a diet aid that is taken only as long as necessary to reach thinness and then dropped again painlessly with no side effects.

So what does separate a true ana from a wannabe? In my opinion, nothing categorical, only differences of degree.

December 1981, down to 198

Every day I forced myself to get up early enough to ride to school with Larry in the van. The mornings were cold, but over my clothes I wore only the corduroy shirt my father had bought. The old sweaters belonged to an archeological stratum I had not yet dug down to. The discomfort would further strengthen my will. In Greek we learned another tense, the perfect. *Luo, luso, eluon, lelukuia*, I said to myself as I paced around my room in the evenings. *Lelukuia*. My lips came together in a kissing motion around the vowels. *Lelukuia*: I have released.

Dr. Chamberlain quoted Plato with reverence. He used the word "beautiful" in a way most men didn't, about lines of poetry or philosophy. The boys who were studying Greek in order to be ministers brought up questions about Bible passages and he listened to them respectfully, lengthening his spine and raising his chin as he thought. He seemed to descend again as he looked back to the student, nodding in acknowledgement—just a one-inch movement, but it looked as courtly as bowing. "That's interesting," he said, even to obviously irrelevant remarks. His restraint was mirrored by the elegant slimness of his body. I had seen him at the Student Union with his young pretty wife.

I looked in the course catalog to see where and when Dr. Chamberlain's other classes were held, then stationed myself where I could see him walk to and from Latin 101. I wasn't supposing that becoming thin would make Dr. Chamberlain fall in love with me. That wasn't the point. The goal was to *deserve* love in general, from the type of person I wanted to be. Besides, if I let myself go deep into desire, Dr. Chamberlain could be a lens to focus my will, to burn away my fat. Like the overseer, he was a useful tool.

From the second floor of the U-shaped Psychology Building I could look down to the classroom where Dr. Chamberlain taught. The window in his doorway was narrow, like an archer's niche, and I could see only a sliver of desk into which his forearm sometimes protruded. When he moved to the blackboard, his body appeared for a flickering second, turning as he walked, graceful and sensitive as a candle flame. That was all. If I watched the entire hour, I might see the movement to the board half a dozen times. But in any case it was another hour gone from the day, an hour I wasn't eating, an hour to the good. The long waiting and the unpredictability made even the forearm sexy, and the spin of his hips around the desk was erotic.

Afternoons now gave me even more trouble than nighttime. Once Dr. Chamberlain's classes were over for the day, there was no reason to be one place rather than another. A bad feeling came over me, reminiscent of the way it used to feel when I was about to flunk a class, a swirling paradox of fear, guilt, and weariness—irresistible forces meeting immovable objects. It seemed that powerful opposites rushed to meet in my body and I would be able neither to contain nor escape them. Fear would build up in me, almost to panic.

I was annoyed with myself when I couldn't dispel the senseless anxiety. In reality I wasn't flunking anything, and I wasn't eating. Therefore, nothing was *wrong*. Why did I feel so bad? I couldn't read or study. There was nothing else I wanted to do. I walked endlessly through a gray landscape of neither night nor day. How could I possibly get through the burden of time? This is intolerable, I thought. But it must be tolerated, the overseer said, reasonably. What other choice is there? All you have to do is use up each next day without eating; you don't have to worry about your feelings.

Ten days had passed since I'd been forced to eat at the Lovejoys', and it had been about three weeks since I had voluntarily eaten anything except for the milk I put in my coffee. It was time to weigh myself, a test more significant than any of my finals, and a holiday more religious than anyone else's Christmas. Late in the afternoon, gold light poured into and through me as I approached the women's locker room like a pilgrim, from the east. Inside it was deserted, as I had hoped. I removed my pants and shoes.

Disappointment and relief were intricately mixed when the scale arm balanced at 198. I'd been unable to help fantasizing that the number would be low, even perhaps as low as 180, my last known number on the way up. The overseer pointed out that I shouldn't have been counting my chickens, that I was justly punished for my presumption. But at least I was below 200, and what a close call that had been! Suppose I'd come even a day sooner?

Behind these two immediate feelings was a subtler regret for the lost pounds I would never know about. Someday I might want to know exactly how far into hell I had descended and returned from.

The overseer let me know that I wouldn't be allowed to weigh myself any oftener than once a week.

The bulgur-wheat casserole didn't look so very bad. I had imagined slime, terrible smells, and planned to make the most of them. There was a constellation of bluish-white spots on the surface of the baked cheese, but they were discrete, tidy. I leaned over the glass dish and inhaled deeply. Yes, faintly, it was there, the rotten corruption which you would never, ever, willingly accept inside yourself. But rising up right alongside it, and stronger, were the smells of the original ingredients and it was impossible to deny they were desirable. The wholesome, stolid wheat smell was covered, decorated, by a layer of exaggerated richness, as though the cheese were a dense gold paint. The spinach was heightened past its normal vegetable stature into a fruit-like sweetness. The smells could be braided together into one, or separated out and felt as counterpoints. It reminded me of a description I had read in *Looking for Mr. Goodbar* about listening to a symphony while high on marijuana.

This would still be edible, I thought, if you picked around the mold. The idea could be entertained abstractly, in the way a person standing on an upper-floor balcony might think, not of jumping, but of the idea of jumping, the detached knowledge that people in extremis did, sometimes, leap. Yes, a starving person might eat this casserole. But that was nothing to do with me and I was in no danger. I scooped the casserole into a plastic garbage bag and took it out to the dumpster, where I made sure to breathe deeply. All food ended the same way eventually, in garbage or sewage.

187 pounds

I dreamed of food every night now. Restaurant buffets at which I piled my plate with macaroni and ate right where I stood, grocery stores where without any intention of paying I unwrapped candy and ate it in the aisles, opened milk and drank it out of the bottle. I took no pains to conceal myself, either: the dream world had its own set of morals and risks, different from the everyday ones, and no one ever accosted me. Alone, embracing my own damnation, I ate and ate without becoming satisfied until I woke up, jaws aching. The shame took long minutes to dissipate even after I was fully conscious, and the temptation to get up and eat in reality was strong, since it seemed I had already succumbed. But you didn't actually *do* it, the overseer said, with the exasperated affection of someone fighting a friend's self-destructive impulse. It was only a *dream*.

Dr. Chamberlain was gone, out of sight, not to reappear until spring semester in January, unimaginably far off. Shrewdly, I had saved up something for this bleak interval with no occupation. The day after finals was the tenth day since I had weighed myself. I made a special trip to the locker room and learned I was 187 pounds. On the bus home, I made calculations. Losing a pound a day, I should weigh 145 by my birthday and be almost finished by Valentine's Day. The overseer made a show of squelching these uppity thoughts, and I made a show of meekly submitting.

Christmas

I lost control at my parents' house on Christmas, eating disgraceful quantities of holiday food—cheese, crackers, nuts, and fruitcake. But I managed to get back on the wagon by the day after. Even the smaller khaki pants were loose on me now; I was clearly getting somewhere. The virtue I had already excavated from myself was like a mound of earth too big to be washed away by a trickle of rain.

The feeling of anything passing through my digestive system now was rare and strange; in the day after this binge, long-unused muscles stretched themselves with luxurious slowness. I sat on the toilet in almost erotic penitence as I waited to be delivered of the consequences of my lapse. The skin around my anus cringed away from the harsh scraping, as though normally callused places had grown soft. I willed myself to relax and embrace all the sensations of my body returning to its pure emptiness.

When I weighed myself just a couple days after Christmas, I was 179 pounds.

Chapter 15

The Year of Not Eating

1982, the new year

Larry dropped me at my parents' house. Before dinner I pored over my mother's photo albums, trying to discover the exact time at which I had become fat. There weren't so many pictures from the relevant period, age fourteen, since that was also the time when it became clear that Anita's problem wasn't going to be quickly solved. I looked at a family picture my father had taken the following summer, at Bryce Canyon in Utah. Anita stared gauntly forward; my mother stood with one hip advanced to the camera. My brother Dan had gone into his growth spurt, and looked thinner than at any time before or since, long straight lines everywhere except for the slightly soft waist he always had. My own waist was hard and flat; I was leaner than either my mother or brother, but it wasn't good enough. Sometimes, I knew, women looked at their younger, thinner selves with an indulgent eye, decided they hadn't been so bad after all. I wouldn't make that mistake. At the time this picture was taken the seeds of my disgrace had already been sown. I knew what to look for and my eye could detect the subtle curve of hip that shouldn't be there. Five pounds overweight, maybe even eight, smiling for the sake of convention but knowing myself flawed under my clothes.

Summer 1977. I'm "fat." Anita will kill herself in August.

I flipped backward through the albums. Twelve, not full grown yet. Thirteen, yes, fine, but I hadn't had my first period. It didn't count. The summer Anita went crazy, I was at my grandmother's, no pictures from then. Fourteenth birthday, seated at a table, hips out of sight. Impossible to tell. It was sometime that fall or winter that I had first noticed my fat. Somewhere there had to be a last thin picture. I needed to see what I looked like in a state of grace, what it was to have a body that had attained its full height and was sexually mature, but definitely not yet fat. I couldn't find an unequivocal picture.

It was warm enough that my family sat down to eat in the backyard. I ate a chicken wing and allowed a breast to remain on my plate as a decoy. Then I ate salad and vegetables until my stomach was tight, but I had no sense of satiety. The chicken breast continued to radiate deadly seductive waves. Time to carry out my mission. I carried my plate into the kitchen and stood lookout duty through the window as my hands quickly pulled chicken meat off the bone. The garbage disposal was too great a risk. From my pocket I got out the tinfoil I had prepared in advance, and made a packet of the meat. This was the moment of greatest danger: if anyone moved toward the back door, I would have to make a run for it. No one moved. I blotted the grease from my hands with a paper towel, walked into the bedroom where my casually unzipped backpack lay ready, and slid the foil packet into a plastic bag inside the inner pocket. I zipped both zippers and shut the bag into the closet and shut the door of the room behind me. My heart beat hard. The whole adventure had taken less than two minutes. I got a beer from the fridge, picked up the plate with the bones and went back outside.

Alcohol made it easier to ignore the sounds and smells of other people eating.

"Where do you want to get married?" my mother said. "Do you want to do it here?"

"I don't know," I said. "I haven't really thought about it yet."

My mother delayed her response, holding her eyes on me steadily. "Why haven't you thought about it?" It was her psychologist's look, leading; I was supposed to notice a significant pattern in my own omissions. In reality I was preoccupied with something much more important than any relationship, but of course my mother couldn't know that.

"I guess because I've been thinking about other things," I said.

"What other things?"

"Well, school," I said. Was there anything else I could cite? The simple truth was that long-range planning was impossible, because being fat or thin altered the foundation on which everything else rested. While that hung in abeyance, no decisions could be made, no future even imagined. Thinness was the horizon point I was working towards, and nothing could be seen beyond it, naturally, but for all practical purposes, day to day I couldn't even see that far. Not eating was a labor so demanding that it required every lesser consideration to be sacrificed or deferred, even thoughts about the eventual reward of thinness. To succeed, I had to hide my goals even from myself. But my mother would insist on some kind of response. "I never told you about Thanksgiving with Larry's family. His mother is so awful—"

"She's not *awful*," my mother said, with her usual quick sympathy for anyone I found myself in opposition to. "Don't talk that way."

I had been going to say "but the way they treat her is worse," but since my mother hadn't waited to see whether my thoughts were balanced and compassionate, she didn't deserve to hear them in full. "Did *you* enjoy her conversation?" I said.

"Yes," my mother said. Her eyes slid away from mine. "The only problem is her hearing. She can't really enjoy other people's input. But her stories are interesting, she's had an interesting life. You can listen to her, and be nice. She'll be your mother-in-law for a long time."

"Well…. Maybe."

"You're having second thoughts," my mother said.

"Maybe." It was impossible to think now. None of this was the point. Urgent messages were coming from the overseer, a repetitive pulsing loop like Morse code: no changes now. There must be no change. It was impossible to look so far ahead, and was not the point. Change nothing! Say nothing!

"Don't marry for money," my mother said. "It's one of the hardest ways in the world to earn it."

"Okay, I won't."

"What are you going to do?"

"Just wait for now, okay?"

"Wait for what?" my mother said.

I shook my head. "Just wait."

When Larry picked me up again, he wanted to stop for soda on our way home. "Do you want anything?"

"I had plenty at my parents'."

While Larry was inside the 7-11, I flung the chicken packet into the farthest corner of the parking lot.

the time the math let me down

Since I'd weighed 179 at the last weighing, I planned to wait two weeks before going back to the locker room, so I could break a ten-pound mark each time. But after a week I couldn't hold out anymore, couldn't fill the empty days without it. The overseer warned me sternly in advance not to have immodest expectations. Yes, yes, I promised. I would be somewhere in the low 170s this time, and break the boundary next week, plunge deep into the 160s. That was better, really: it would feel less precarious than dangling at the far edge of each ten pounds.

177.

Something was wrong. A mistake. I got off the scale and put the metal indicators back to zero, then climbed gingerly on it again. With the big weight on 150 I tapped the little weight ever so lightly. I tried approaching from below and from above, but it balanced in the same place each time. 177. It was impossible.

Shame overcame me. But I had eaten nothing to speak of, just the one dinner. Vegetables were nothing, no calories or almost none. I had never been in the habit of counting calories, but I knew that much. Some beer, a chicken wing—those were more costly. I *could* have done better, skipped the alcohol, thrown away both pieces of chicken. But still, surely everything taken together couldn't have amounted to even as much as half a day's worth of calories for a person who was eating normally. People ate much more than a chicken wing in a meal. Even if I assumed that somehow beer was so rich that I had drunk a whole day's calories, I still should be only one-seventh worse than last week. I didn't know the basic numbers but I knew it was numbers that mattered, and the math wasn't working out. Something was wrong.

Instead of getting on the bus I walked along the street, sunk into myself, wrestling with disbelief and fear. A bus passed me, its interior lit up in the early winter dark. Something was very wrong. What if I was hurting myself? That's only hunger talking, the overseer said, you know it distorts your thoughts. But it was weird, I said. Maybe I should do something. Like what? the overseer sneered. Go to a doctor? Talk to your parents? You know what would happen then.

It was heartbreaking to feel the horizon of the future recede still further from me. How long would it take at this rate? I can't, I said.

Yes you can, said the overseer, you can hold out as long as it takes. Look, it's already been more than five weeks and fifty pounds.

Dimly I tried to penetrate the curtain that covered all thoughts of the future. When I was thin, would I only be able to eat a couple of chicken wings per day? It doesn't *matter*, the overseer said. Look, think it through. Which is better, going on, just like this, or staying fat? This, I said. Indefinitely? the overseer said.

I took a moment to consider it. A lifetime just like this, or be fat. Yes. This. If those were the choices.

There you are, then, the overseer said.

I sat down at the bus stop to wait. Maybe I should buy a calorie-counter book and try to figure out more precisely what was going on. No, don't, the overseer said, because in the first place there's no point in messing with that. All you have to do is aim as close to zero intake as you possibly can. If you do that, no other course of action could be more effective than what you're already doing. That being the case, why take a chance on getting upset again?

I had to admit the reasoning was flawless.

Now

Not eating, or eating very small amounts, or even eating consistently just slightly less than what you're hungry for, is back-breaking work, a labor from which you never dare turn away long, certainly not long enough to fully rest, because the hole refills itself even as you dig. It's understandable to me that famous women who have lost weight—Oprah Winfrey and Carnie Wilson—tend to cite it as their life's greatest accomplishment. If you measure achievements only by the dedication required to bring them about, it's perfectly accurate. Holding myself to this task was the most difficult thing I had ever done, or ever will do. I don't know what hardships or success may lie ahead in my life still, but I can safely say that.

My school transcripts show that I completed Greek, Russian, and linguistics classes in the spring of 1982. But in my own memory there are only a few bare, unconnected fragments about school, my teachers, or the other people in my life. My secret inner world, my food transactions, and my game (or whatever it was) with the overseer absorbed my attention to the exclusion of anything going on outside me.

There is little to say now about this near-gap in my memory, this blurred, fragmentary, missing time. And yet I remember enough to know that this time passed more slowly, and in greater suffering, than any other time in my life.

the blurred time, dropping to 150

I discovered that food rituals could protect me somewhat from the danger of bingeing. The overseer and I would decide what a day's allotment of food should be and I ate only that every day. For a couple of weeks it was orange juice and two strips of bacon every morning, nothing more. Then a single tortilla with refried beans and lettuce at lunchtime, nothing more. Then one muffin every afternoon, spun out through a half-hour's gnawing. Nothing more, nothing more, nothing more. The rigor and clarity of these limits pleased me, made me feel secure. It was better not to eat food in the evening, because by then I wanted it too much and couldn't be sure of being able to stop. Occasionally I binged anyway. Occasionally I went back to total fasting for several days or a week. The rate of my weight loss was fairly steady at a pound or two a week.

For one week I bought a certain fried pastry every morning on campus, along with coffee and a half-pint carton of milk. Thinner on average than a doughnut but bigger across, and only approximately round, these fritters were greasy, crisp, brown, and lumpy. They resembled flattened, deep-fried cowpies. Clear sugar glaze coated them like shellac, squeaking against my teeth as I ate. Rich veins of this glaze, and recently-congealed shortening, ran like ore between dryer clumps of dough. It was important to bite so that the proportions remained constant between the fluffy, doughy mounds and the luxuriously dense and gritty canyons between. The crunchy, fat-drenched outer edges had to be managed carefully too, since although they were the best part it was too painful to eat out the middle and then be left at the end with only tiny fragments of great richness.

I saved the coffee for afterwards, keeping it in reserve against the sense of loss which inexorably came no matter how carefully I ate the fritter. Milky coffee scoured the sweetness from my mouth and comforted my stomach with its warm weight. Coffee was a sermon on the pleasures of bitter strength, and after my palate had absorbed that lesson in full, an extra swallow of the milk was sweet by contrast. Afterwards, before my mouth could turn sour, I brushed my teeth with the toothbrush I carried in my backpack. There would be nothing more then but water for the rest of the day.

One day I bought and ate a second fritter, and after that they were irretrievably tainted and could no longer be used as virtuous items of food ritual, even though I lost a pound as usual that week, suffering no tangible setback for my sins.

At some point I left Larry and moved back in with my parents. At the time I assumed that Larry was glad to see the last of me. There had been, I thought, nothing to make me desirable as a mate: I neither kept house, nor paid bills, nor soothed him with a sweet disposition, nor looked even halfway good. So I was very surprised a few years later when a mutual acquaintance told me that Larry said I had broken his heart.

"You know," my mother said, the day before I moved, "you shouldn't have some romantic idea about how wonderful everything will be when you start living back here again."

"I don't," I said.

"You're thinking about what you want to get away from over there, and you're not remembering how much you used to want to get away from here."

"I remember vividly," I said.

"Or you think this time is going to be different. But it's not. The same things you chafed at before, you're going to chafe at again, just as much."

"I know," I said. "Why are you such an expert on what I think? Why are you telling me this right now, anyway?"

"I don't know," my mother said. The next day she brought home a present for me, a white coffee mug with a brown interior and a brown circle round the middle where the mug's thick body drew in like a belted waist. Another single brown accent above the waist looked faintly Asian in its spareness. It was only a grocery store mug, but it touched me.

The following day my mother forced me to go back to Larry's house and retrieve the copper-bottomed pots and pans she had bought for us as a housewarming gift. I argued for letting Larry keep them as a consolation prize, but she was adamant. I gave in though of course I wasn't going to be doing any cooking.

Now

I still have the pans and the mug, and I'm glad I do.

150-something and dropping fast

Living in my body now was like standing on the threshold of a second puberty, on the verge of some great change. Motion which had been imperceptibly slow at first was now rapid, practically visible to the eye. Particularly while running I felt that some great consummation was almost at hand, some unimaginable creature about to emerge from the chrysalis of my body. At the very least, I would be back to where I had started, and take up again that destiny which had always been intended for me. Before I became so strangely entrammeled in fat.

My face was coming into sharp focus. My breasts were almost as small and firm as they had been at 13. My waist had returned. It was almost time to weigh myself again. The rule these days was to wait until I thought I was at least five pounds thinner than the last time before making another pilgrimage to the women's locker room. I was getting pretty good at estimating five pounds.

I ate quite a bit these days. Once or twice a day, at least, I ate fruit or vegetables, and several times a week something more substantial—"concentrated food"—in my grandmother's terms. My weight loss not only had not slowed but actually speeded up a little, as though running shook the fat off my body directly. It was strange, because according to the charts in my aerobics book the calorie totals burned by running were not really all that high, less than 100 per mile at my current speed. But I would think about that later. Now was not the time for questioning my progress.

The overseer had receded, or rather, I had reabsorbed most of its functions myself. I could command myself now without the need for childish tricks.

Running up the final hill on my way home, I had no reserves left. But I refused to slow down. My will was a ratchet. I didn't have to ease off just because of fatigue or pain. I should even be able to speed up. If I were running for my life, I could certainly push just a little harder. And, really, my life was at stake, wasn't it? The overseer hovered somewhere behind me, in the back of my head or over my left shoulder, available if I needed to draw on it again. My vision switched off and for a few moments I saw only gray, then I was on the downslope of the hill and my eyes cleared again. I stopped at the end of the street where the sign said STOP and checked my watch. I had beaten my previous best.

130 pounds

My mother denied having done anything with my high school clothes. "You took them with you when you moved into the dorm," she said.

"No I didn't."

"Yes you did."

"I only took—" I knew I had only taken the layer which was then the most recent layer of past clothes, the blue jeans and army pants from senior year in high school, that fit my body at around 150 pounds. These were what I was wearing now. But I couldn't explain to my mother about the archeological strata. "I took just a few things and I brought all those back with me."

"You don't know what all you had or what became of it after all the moving around you did."

"You mean *you* don't know. *I* know exactly what I did and didn't take. Back in 1979, I mean, when I started college." It was true that I had abandoned at Larry's the largest pants from the later, fattest epochs, in accordance with the ratchet principle: forward only, never back. But of course I would never have left behind any clothing that was too *small* for me. It was weird that my mother even considered this a possible explanation; abandoning overlarge clothes made sense, but what woman would do something so insane as disposing of clothes she might fit into again some day?

"Well everything you left in this house is still here," my mother said.

"Except for the things that aren't. I guess the mystery will never be solved." The lost clothing crowded into my mind again, in its ranks from the lemon pants all the way back to the torn blue pair. The unrelenting sweater gone! How could it be? But it was.

"Everything you left here is still here," my mother said with finality. It was clear she would brook no more argument, regardless of the facts. Nothing could withstand my mother's domestic authority when she chose to exert it. At Larry's I had assumed the grungy pots and pans had passed beyond the point of ever being truly clean again, but once they were back under my mother's roof she had somehow managed to scour the crust off them.

"Okay, okay" I said. "Never mind."

I weighed 130 pounds and it was not clear whether I was done yet. I had weighed 130 for weeks and weeks. At least once a day I ran 5 or 6 miles. Three times a day I ate as much as my stomach could hold, almost exclusively fruits and vegetables. About two meals out of three were supplemented with something else as a main dish: a sandwich, cheese, eggs, or something my mother cooked, or something I bought at school. I got no fatter, I got no thinner. My running times went no lower. I could hold an eight-minute per mile pace for my entire workout, but I did not improve. Why not? In high school cross country, when my will had not been as strong and my training not as intense or faithful, I had often run four miles at a 7:30 pace. What was wrong? Was I still just about to break through some final barrier, or should I consider that I had now reached my goal?

Where I was now certainly didn't look like the destination I'd been bound for. 120, not 130, was the number I was supposed to weigh. Though when I looked in the mirror, parts of me—my face and arms—seemed actually thinner than they had been at 13. My breasts and waist looked the same to my eye as they had when I loved my body the most. But my hips and legs were still rounder and fuller than they should be. Weren't they? I made a circle out of my hands, thumb to thumb and pinkie to pinkie, and used it to measure each of my calves. My hands slid over the curve, but just barely. I had to push my fingers together hard to keep the circle from opening. On campus as I strode into the gym I could see my legs reflected in the glass door, watch the working of the muscles under the skin. Were my legs actually acceptable right now? The blue pants might have cleared up the question.

My best workouts were an approach toward ecstasy. Some sort of great consummation seemed almost within reach, something that would fully involve, and fully delight, all my physical and mental faculties. A payoff worthy of the long sacrifices I had made.

In jogging class we were taught to take our pulse during exercise. Supposedly the desirable range for aerobic exercise was 60-85 percent of your maximum, which for me at age 20 was supposedly 200 beats/minute. 85% of maximum didn't sound like very hard work to me. In terms of the standard grading scale, you needed 90 percent for an A; 85 percent was only a B. We all ran a mile together and then the instructor walked us through a sample pulse count. I put my hand up to my neck along with everyone else.

In the student union bathroom, another girl emerged from a stall as I was washing my hands and stood beside me at the mirror. The relief of being one of the thinnest women in the bathroom, on the bus, in a classroom, was intense. The world had become easier to move through, not just physically—though of course I could squeeze through tighter spaces—but morally. A mirror was no longer a window into hell. If I was meeting my friend Lauren and her friend Nick, I could stand up comfortably in the crowded cafeteria and look around. I could stand as long and look as freely as I liked. I had a right to be there. The eyes of strangers didn't oppress me.

In the bathroom, I looked sidelong at the other girl. Long limp blonde hair, bluejeans. She looked slightly familiar, like a customer from the cafeteria, perhaps, though I didn't remember her specifically. Her legs tapered down to thinness, but both her stomach and her rear end stuck out. Her shoulders and arms were big—a strong big rather than only puffy—and her face was a square heavy, rather than round. She wasn't huge, overall, perhaps about the size I had been when I moved in with Larry the first time, though the fat was differently arranged. Bodies were hard to compare, really.

I averted my gaze when the girl turned, but she caught the tail end of it. "Hello," she said. She looked at me.

I didn't have to cringe. I was free, I was free. "Hello," I said.

The girl flicked her eyes politely to one side and drew a breath, preparing to say something more. It could only be one thing. It seemed impossible that a stranger would raise the subject of my fat, but what else was there about me that a stranger could know or be interested in?

"Listen—I'm sorry, but—You really lost a shitload of weight…. How did you do it?"

Her words were exactly accurate and they pleased me more than anyone else's praise or tact: I had been delivered from shit, from wallowing in my own shit. And the girl's question wasn't rhetorical, either. She really hoped I might have something useful to tell her.

Suddenly I strongly desired to help this slightly familiar person with her alien shape and her unknown life. After all I had been through, I must have acquired wisdom, or at least practical knowledge. I thought of all the things I had done in the last year and tried to think which of them would be most helpful, easiest to package into a simple set of sound principles. "For a long time I ate pretty much the same thing every day. Like, for lunch, I'd go to the Mexican cafeteria, and get one of their bean tostadas and just, you know, after that I'd stop. Just something pretty small, and stop when it's done. And then after a couple weeks, I'd switch to something different, but still little."

"Didn't you get hungry?"

"Well, yeah." I shrugged. What could you expect?

"What do you eat now? Is it hard keeping it off?"

"No. Well, I guess, yeah." There were problems with my meal system. On a day last week I had packed dry-roasted peanuts as an item in my lunch, but the smell of them, plus the nagging sensation in my jaw, pressed at me continually until finally I unpacked and ate them though it was only two hours since breakfast. And every so often I bought extra food at school. After eating my bag lunch, I might go and buy the enchilada plate in the Mexican cafeteria. And I had invented a brand-new vice, as well: a pair of cookies from the Student Union bakery could be glued together into a sandwich with the cream cheese which was available in chilled two-ounce packets from the Student Union deli. But I had gained no weight from these occasional lapses. If I botched up one day, it was simple enough to be abstemious the next day, and run twice.

Keeping it off. Did that phrase apply? But the original transformation was not yet complete. Or, yes, maybe I was thin enough, or almost thin enough, but I was still training myself to live right. Sometime in the future, soon, my life would arrive at its final form, and when it did, it wouldn't be a struggle to maintain. It wasn't clear yet exactly how the future would be different from the present, but it would.

To the girl I said, "I mean, I guess it's not easy. I eat a lot, but still more vegetables and fruit than anything else. And I exercise." Running was the key. As long as I could run, I never had to be afraid of fat. So I was safe forever, because I would just keep on running. That was simple. In the back of my mind, though, I worried about my knees. Lately, three or four miles into a run there would be a peculiar feeling of pressure at the outside edges of each kneecap that intensified as I went on. Probably it was nothing.

"I really have to hand it to you," the girl said. "You lost a *shitload*."

During finals I missed a few of my regular runs, so I cut back on eating. It gave my knees some relief also. I took a single banana from home as my day's allotment and ate it sitting at the bus stop as I reviewed verb forms. I had forgotten how good the physical sensation of clean emptiness could feel. I had forgotten the pleasure, visual and mental, of feeling transparent enough to be pierced and suffused by light. I would not forget again, I promised myself. I would take this opportunity to break through the status quo of 130, and then I really would be changed forever.

On the bus, I surveyed the other women, looking to see which were fatter or thinner than me.

In Greek and jogging I made A's, in math and Russian B's. "What do you want for Christmas?" my mother said.

"A car," I said.

"No, try again," she said.

"Oh, well, in that case, what I really dream of is some new socks."

"I was thinking maybe a new wardrobe," my mother said. We went to the mall.

We looked at an abbreviated knit shirt in grass green: the edge came down only as far my waist. White denim pants to go with it. I had never owned white pants before. "I'm not sure about this midriff thing," I said to my mother. "You don't think it's too daring?"

"You look good in it," my mother said. "Why don't you branch out a little, try a different look?" She had me try on a shirt with a metallic sheen. Light hit the fabric from different angles and the color wouldn't stay constant, varying from a light brown to a dull luster like something made from aluminum. Instead of a normal collar, it had a ruffle around the neck which extended out almost as far as the shoulders, like a scalloped plate of fabric. I thought of Elizabethan courtiers.

"Really?" I said. "Wear this big foofy ruff thing?"

She nodded. "Really."

There was a white shirt in a delicate fabric with vertical and horizontal stitched lines that divided it into puckering compartments almost like bubble wrap.

"A bra with this shirt would certainly not be optional," I said.

"Nope," my mother said.

There were tan pants and black pants and subtly peach-colored pants with pleated fronts, pleats that stayed flat where they lay on top of my flesh. There was a striped vest in fleshy tones: salmon, melon, and a subdued peach that picked up the color of the peach pants.

"Try on the vest over that shirt," my mother said.

"The ruffy metallic shirt? Really?" I said. "You don't think it's too much? Clownish?"

"Not at all," my mother said. "It looks great. You're just not used to wearing anything feminine."

We bought them all. Most of the pants were size 12, but in the white pants the 10 fit better. So despite the difference on the scale I really was back to where I started. In one sense. In PE class we had discussed muscle weight. Maybe that was the explanation, or maybe I still had fat calves, extra pounds in places that didn't affect the fit of the pants.

The green shirt and white pants from Xmas 1982.

Chapter 16

Why Do They Want To?

1983, shuttling between 130-136

The ultimate consummation toward which my life was aimed was not sex after all, I knew because I had a new boyfriend.

Sex with Nick was good, but not orders of magnitude better than what I had known with Larry, despite the fact that Nick was thin and attractive and I was… well, I wasn't fat, anyway. If anything, the intensity of feeling now was less than what it had been in the early days with Larry. Sex was fine; I wanted it, but it simply wasn't *big* enough to match the labor and suffering I had put in, was still putting in, to shape my body. So the climactic event my body sometimes seemed to be anticipating as I pushed to my limits during my best workouts was not sexual fulfillment. What was it, then?

Maybe there was nothing really. Not everything people imagined actually existed.

By taking my pulse in the middle of a run, I discovered a curious fact: my fastest running times did not correspond to my fastest heartrates. On days when I broke records, or came near my best times, feeling my body moving fast and effectively, my pulse during a 10-second count was rarely over 27 or 28 before I started my final sprint. But on a day when I knew myself to be making a poor time by the clock, when my body felt heavy and lazy, when it seemed plain that I was not making my best effort—on a bad workout day, if I stopped and checked my pulse, it was rarely below 29. So if heartrate was a measure of how hard you were trying, I was actually trying harder on the days I was less successful.

I had always imagined the physical challenge of running as some kind of hurdle or penetrable barrier that a determined person could leap over or break through; in high school I had often reproached myself for shying away too early from the effort.

The feelings now were still the same: when I pushed, I felt myself approaching a barrier which it seemed must yield if I continued to push. But by now I had convincing evidence that I was not quitting too soon. I could run into pain, I could run all the way into that gray zone where vision failed, but I could not make my heart go any faster than 32 beats in 10 seconds. There was no other side of that barrier. It was simply my physical limit.

Maybe I always *had* been giving my best effort, even though it hadn't felt that way.

If there was no great breakthrough about to happen in my athletic performance, perhaps there was no breakthrough into bliss waiting for me, either. No type of satisfaction that I had ever experienced in real life did justice to the enormity of what I had anticipated, imagined. All those days I had fasted, all those miles I logged, what could ever equal them? Of course, exertion, like virtue, could be its own reward. There were pleasures in working out, and enduring hunger. But those austere satisfactions were not, in themselves, what I had envisioned, they were not the thing I had pursued.

Sex was not enough. I would never be a great athlete. Perhaps I would still have some kind of breakthrough and become a great student, but it didn't seem likely, and school wasn't a great satisfaction, though no alternative career I could think of seemed more desirable. My father had helped me get a few Russian translating assignments from a company he worked for, and I had made a little money, but that wasn't what I wanted to do with my life.

What was my goal now? I pondered the question off and on as I ran. During a good run, it still seemed as though something intense and unimaginable lay just ahead. But what? Did I want to run so hard, like Pheidippides, that my heart burst in one great unrepeatable orgasm?

I no longer felt that my daily deposits of virtue were gathering interest in a bank somewhere. Obviously, the longer you delayed gratification, the bigger payoff you should expect. That was the whole point of self-discipline. Taking self-discipline to its logical extreme, gratification delayed infinitely should yield an infinite reward. But in the absence of an afterlife you would never collect, of course. What, within my own lifetime, could be the reward intense enough to be worth what I invested? I could think of nothing.

Not being fat. But I already had that. All compliments were far in the past now; everyone took my body for granted. And I had still never gotten below 130 pounds! Those slow, suffering months of foodlessness had been an awful time, of course, but in one way, it had been better than now, because I was making progress and I knew it.

The tightness in my knees ripened gradually into a soreness which grew more and more painful until even walking hurt. Doctors examined me and gave advice: they prescribed ibuprofen, a new anti-inflammatory drug which helped only temporarily; they sang the praises of ice and stretching, neither of which made any difference no matter how religiously I followed the instructions. Other than that, they had nothing to suggest except that I cut back on running.

But the second I eased off, fat began to collect on my body. The flat pleats in my good pants stood up and began to move apart from each other.

With my Russian money I bought a bicycle and a swimsuit. Using the charts in the back of my aerobics books, I calculated the amount of swimming and biking that ought to calorically replace a running workout of 5 miles in 40 minutes. Biking and swimming took up far more time than running, and it was necessary to drop a few university classes in order to get everything done. And it was hard to get my heartrate up high enough, especially in the pool, where it seemed a paltry 25 was the absolute maximum count no matter what I did. Despite my careful calculations, the effect on my body was just not the same as running. I was up to 136 pounds.

All right, I would cut back on eating. I knew how to do that.

Nick called: "Do you want to come over tomorrow night?"

It was a godsend. I had managed to diet back down to a little over 130 pounds, but the position was more unstable than it had been when I could run properly; the least little glitch bumped me back upward. "What if I came tonight instead?" I said. It would solve the problem of what to do with myself this evening, other than eating.

"What if you came tonight *in addition*?"

"No," I said automatically.

"Why not?" Nick said. "Why *not*?"

By tomorrow night my knees might be rested up enough to run again, and if they weren't I would have to do a massive swim or bike ride instead. Certainly I couldn't let two nights go by without working out. "I just don't think I should do both, you know? I have translating, and school stuff to do."

"Oh, fine," he said. "Come now, then. See you soon."

At Jack in the Box they were just changing over from breakfast to lunch, but they let Nick and me order eggs, bacon, hash browns, and coffee. The food was good, but the amount was not enough. I had to have more. I shifted restlessly on the plastic bench of our booth. It was urgent, an emergency like needing to go to the bathroom in the middle of class. Could I make an excuse, get away and eat? Or could I get control of myself?

According to the concepts I then lived by, I was not *hungry*, since I had just eaten a standard adult-sized breakfast, and since I didn't currently feel the pain or gurgling in my guts which I could have confidently labeled hunger even if it came after eating something. Yet the state I was in had been familiar to me for years as the not-enough feeling. It was far, far harder to resist than a simple state of fasting hunger.

"What's wrong?" Nick said. Scraps of egg and even bacon remained on his styrofoam plate; I had cleaned mine completely. Nick wasn't controlling himself, I realized, breaking off sooner than he wanted to: the amount he had eaten satisfied him. He just didn't have the not-enough feeling. Neither had I once, I remembered. Not before tenth grade. What had happened to me?

"I think…" I groped for something plausible to say. People around me were carrying trays with lunch items on them. "I'm not going to have time to get lunch today, so I think I better eat something more now." There. The best, most comfortable solution was to go ahead and eat to satiety now, then refrain from eating the rest of the day.

Nick's eyes widened as I came back to the table with a ham and cheese sandwich, French fries, and milk. He and I never talked about the time when I had been fat. He was too polite to bring it up, and I didn't either. What would there be to say? He had known me then, but of course, he would never have dated me. "It's only the things that I would have eaten for lunch, if I were going to have lunch," I explained. I could see Nick suppressing his reaction.

I ate the food and then fasted for a day and a half. The following morning was Saturday, and I took a two-hour bike ride. My shorts felt too tight on my thighs—but maybe, I thought, the fabric was just pulled out of position. In the bathroom at home, I began undressing. I was soaked with sweat, and I laid on the floor to struggle out of the shorts. My thighs looked huge from this angle, but to get a good perspective I needed the mirror. I stood up.

"Wait"—someone seemed to say from just behind my head.

Time passed.

After a while, I felt that something was pressing unpleasantly hard against my cheek and lip, but it was too much trouble to do anything about that. Time passed.

Great weights sat on my head, my back, and my legs. I felt vaguely that there was some chore I was supposed to be doing, but perhaps on the whole I would just put it off for later. The pressure against my face receded, then returned, more insistently. I lifted my head and turned the other cheek. I opened my eyes and saw the baseboards where the bathroom wall met the bathroom floor. It came to me that I had been unconscious.

Slowly I picked myself up. In the mirror, there was a red blotch across one cheek, extending to the red of my lips. I didn't seem to be injured otherwise. It was odd how matter-of-fact I felt. Fainting should be something alarming, shouldn't it? I felt quite calm, only very tired.

It was weird to have no feelings about this. My body felt quite solid, not at all tentative despite its lapse into unconsciousness. Carefully I picked up my clothes from the bathroom floor. By my watch it was almost noon. As I opened the bathroom door I shivered in the cooler air of the hallway. Carefully I went to my room and got in bed, where I slept.

In the library card catalogue, in the SUBJECT section, I looked up OBESITY and checked out several books. Packing them into my backpack, I felt happy. I couldn't have done this before, couldn't have borne to be seen reading what everyone would assume was a book on diet advice. It was not just being able to go places and do things and wear clothes that I couldn't have before. As a thin (or anyway a not-fat) person, I was also free to think things I couldn't before. I read the books.

In one article, full of scientific figures and footnotes, there was a description of metabolic changes in people who were on severe calorie-restricted diets. After a few weeks, their basal metabolic rates had shifted so that it took fewer calories for their bodies to maintain themselves. I was astonished. If metabolism could change, then fat didn't work the way I always thought it did, the way every PE or biology teacher I'd had my whole life said it did.

It was sickening. Right at the time I was reassuring myself that eating almost nothing was the most efficient possible way to lose weight, I had been lowering my metabolism and making it slower.

It was funny, it was a science-fiction idea, but....

Suppose you lived on a bizarro-planet where people had the goal of making themselves as fat as possible as quickly as possible, this metabolic shift business would be exactly the way to do it. You would restrict yourself long enough to make your body shift, then eat. Restrict again, eat again, restrict again, eat again.

In other words, pretty much what I had done all through high school and the first three semesters of college. Perhaps there were other people who wanted to lose weight who had done similar things. Getting fatter and fatter the whole time.

I returned the obesity books to the library, but my mind kept whirling around the new ideas, trying to regroup.

My knees were worse, I wasn't exercising well, and satiety after meals became even more fleeting. My studies in obesity research had multiplied the areas of confusion instead of clearing them up. I was as tired of thinking about eating in abstract terms as I was of obsessing about my next meal, but I couldn't put either out of my mind. Eat to live, I told myself, don't live to eat. But in between meals I knew all I was doing was waiting for time to pass.

At 7:00, my mother called me to dinner, along with my father and brother, to eat some of the chicken and rice she had made. "No, thanks," I said. "I've noticed that I wake up feeling kind of cruddy in the morning if I eat anything after about 6:00 at night." I had eaten a sandwich earlier, and though I wanted more I was not going to have more.

"Oh, really?" my mother said. "6:00, huh?"

"Right," I said. "6:00." I pretended not to notice my mother's sarcasm, maintained the tone of someone providing neutral information. How dare she doubt what I said about myself? It was true! All those years in high school, eating at night and waking up to the morning after.

"Well, all I can say is," my mother began. Her obstinate face enraged me. She acted as if I were rewriting history to thwart her somehow, when *she* was the one trying to interfere with *me*! "There sure must have been a whole lot of times—"

"That's right!" I said, speaking with her, over the top of her. She was disgusting, my whole family was disgusting, and they wanted to drag me down to their level. "A whole lot of times!"

"—when you 'felt cruddy' in the morning."

In the night I woke up desperate to eat, but after the exchange with my mother that was impossible, obviously. I would have to hold out until morning. In the morning, I told myself, you can have some of anything you like. If you just wait until then.

What I wanted was one of those fritters from the Park Street cafeteria on campus. The idea soothed me slightly. I visualized myself getting up in the morning, bathing and putting on some of my narrow pleated pants, packing my school books, riding the bus, and arriving at last on campus, eating the fritter there in the cafeteria with my coffee and milk, and looking over a textbook as I ate and drank, the perfect picture of a trim, successful woman. Someone in charge of her life, someone with the pride of self-control. And besides, I told myself, you can get up as early as you want to, no time limit.

Was this, then, the great fulfillment toward which my life aimed? To eat a pastry every once in a great while? I thought of Nick, but the fritter moved me more. It was disgusting to feel this way. Eat to live, not live to eat. But without the promise of the fritter I didn't see how I would get through the night.

As soon as it was light I got out of bed and put my school things together. I laid out the white shirt and peach-colored pants. In the bath I washed myself with ritual thoroughness; it was necessary to prove I respected my body. On the bus, I looked at other people who were fatter than me or less well-groomed. How could they have so little pride? How could they stand even to look at themselves, let alone go out in public?

At Park Street it was the same, bleary-eyed sloppy people, chomping away like cows in a field. I bought my fritter and coffee and sat down, postponing the moment of beginning so as to postpone the moment of coming to the end, reveling too in the power of my will. If I decided to, even now I could get up and walk away from this food. Unlike the people around me, I could control my actions perfectly; that proved my problem was not a character defect. All I needed was to find the correct technique and I would be able to escape this terrible desire to eat. To live always in a state of wishing for the next meal was intolerable.

Was there any combination at all that I had never tried? Suppose I ate very small amounts, but also very frequently. Suppose I always knew that I was going to get something more to eat within two hours at the most, wouldn't desire relax its grip then? If the idea of a fritter could get me through the night, then the certainty of something else always coming up quite soon, should be able to get me through… through any number of days.

I ate the fritter and drank the coffee and felt perfectly content. This was the solution at last, then. Two hours later, the stirrings in my stomach, right on schedule, seemed to prove that I was on the right track. I walked over to the Student Union and carefully considered the options, finally ordering a single scrambled egg. I sat down and lingered over it as long as I could. Before I was half finished with the egg, I knew I was in deep trouble.

It was not enough, not enough. It would take a great deal more in order to be enough. I pictured the sour-cream enchilada plate, the rows of cookies in the bakery, the cream cheese I could buy to make a cookie sandwich. Two more hours, I told myself, and you can choose another thing, anything you like. I could walk away the time until then, or go to the university pool. I could do it.

The fact that I could do it was not the point. The new plan was supposed to release me, take me beyond this suffering. I walked the length of the Fiddlee Fig cafeteria and back, unsure what to do next. It was the breakfast rush time, just after 9:00. I looked at the crowded mass of eaters in the room, their jaws moving up and down, distorting their faces. They were perfectly satisfied! Oblivious to how disgusting they looked. Living to eat—how could they stand themselves? I refused to be like them. And I had the will not to be.

The room of people seemed to tilt itself toward me so that I looked down on them from above. In a dreamy clarity, I watched forks moving up and down in what seemed an orchestrated rhythm, in the same way that cicadas' songs seemed coordinated, not the output of individuals at all but an aggregate expression of one underlying force.

Eating to live was not really different from living to eat, I saw. Food was life, life was food, and both were disgusting. All these people ate food which if it didn't turn into disgusting fat would turn into disgusting shit, and they did it willingly, happily, solely in order to keep themselves alive, solely in order to cycle back around and eat and excrete even more food, endlessly. But why did they want to do any of it? Why did they want to keep themselves alive? There was nothing to do that was worth the effort, and nothing valuable about a life spent waiting for the time before the next meal to pass.

Chapter 17

I Finally Manage To Stop Not Eating

1983

I didn't kill myself.

Now

Duh, since you can see my picture on the cover, a middle-aged woman. Suicide would have been a logical next step after figuring out that life was endless, pointless drudgery, and I did think about it, at least in the abstract, but despite a year's starvation and problem knees I was still pretty robust physically. And I was young, with that abundance of energy that no young person even fully recognizes in herself until it begins to dwindle. I think my fundamental bodily robustness prevented me from approaching the idea of suicide very closely, just as it had once prevented my efforts to throw up.

If this book were a novel, something would have to occur soon after the climax: either a tragedy, or else a new insight which brings lasting change. But I am writing about what actually happened, and in fact…

1983

I piddled around in the same way for the rest of the year, breaking up with Nick, starting up with Chris. A passionate crush on a third, completely unavailable man (a homosexual) distracted my attention from the intellectual puzzles of eating and fat, and refocused my will to live, for a while at least.

What happened next is not very dramatic: I read some more books and gradually my thinking changed.

I can't pinpoint the time I first decided to diet, but I know exactly when I decided to stop: December 1983. Chris and I had broken up, unable to agree whether monogamy was a hygienic necessity in the era of AIDS. Moping through Antigone Bookstore on Fourth Avenue, in the hippie part of town, by chance I picked up a teen anorexia novel. I knew about anorexia from newspapers and magazines, but I had never read an account told from the perspective of the anorexic person. The girl in the story shared a shocking number of my private thoughts. She also intended to mold herself into a superior person in secret. She also tried to train herself to be disgusted by food. She even had an overseer, though she called hers the Dictator.

Over the last two years my parents had shown me that they thought I had some sort of problem about eating—my father tried to coax and wheedle me into what he considered more wholesome attitudes, my mother to shove me into them with sarcasm and anger—but of course they both were wrong. Unlike an anorexic, I was completely rational, doing no more than what was necessary to keep fat from engulfing me. Still, the girl in the book resembled me remarkably. Perhaps I had been anorexic, or something like it, for a while in 1982? Or even before? But no, the idea of a fat person being anorexic was ridiculous. Yet there was no clear boundary between one time and another, not even that first Thanksgiving. Other than the fact that I finally *succeeded*, there was no real difference from what I had always been trying to do since age 14.

And then, if I did have an eating disorder, when exactly had I recovered? That was not clear either. The next day I went back to Antigone's and scoured the same section for more books.

Now

I hope you can bear with me, because not much is going to happen in this chapter. It's hard to write in an interesting way about what happens only in the mind, reading and thinking. But these ideas are important, so please try to stick it out.

December 1983, learning setpoint theory

I had heard all my life and up until 1983 believed implicitly the idea that fat is a simple equation of calories in minus calories out. It's a simple and compelling picture of how things work, and its truth seems so self-evident that most people are unaware that it's only one of several competing scientific models. A rival category of models are the homeostatic or "defended-weight" or "setpoint" models. According to them, body fat, somewhat like body temperature, attempts to stay at the same level even though external conditions change. In an excessively cold environment, mechanisms in your body cause you to shiver and warm up; excessively hot, you sweat and cool down. Similarly, your body adjusts to meet the conditions of a variable food supply, by adjusting metabolism and appetite. Yes, if you're subjected to extreme enough conditions for a long enough time, your body can't compensate enough, and you will freeze/overheat/lose weight/gain weight, but if these adverse external conditions don't actually kill you outright, your body will always be *trying* to return to that just-right zone (from its perspective), centered between too much and too little.

Now

Here's another analogy that may be helpful. Many of us are in the habit of using exercise to train our hearts or skeletal muscles: you consistently put a moderate stress on the body, and over time the reaction of the body is not that it becomes cumulatively worn down by the stress, but rather that it finds ways to compensate and overcompensate, leaving you stronger than when you started. Most exercisers are able to find, by trial and error, a level of workout intensity that eventually makes them stronger. We are used to this idea and find it unremarkable, but really it's rather amazing what bodies can do.

The exercise effect is something that applies to living creatures only. Look: you wouldn't try to take a rope and make it stronger by hanging successively heavier weights from it. You wouldn't try to strengthen a piece of fabric or leather by subjecting it to friction, but it doesn't surprise you when the leather that covers your own hands develops calluses as you use it. The live animal skin behaves very differently from the dead animal skin.

People who believe in the calorie equations of the energy-balance model in its most extreme form are treating the body as though it were something dead, that can only respond by moving in the same direction as the stress, rather than reacting against it. But bodies are live tissue. People who go on diets, in effect, very often end up exercising their bodies, training them to become fatter and fatter.

Among proponents of the setpoint model, there are controversies about how and when—and how *firmly*—the setpoint gets set. Some have compared the setpoint to a thermostat; others have suggested that a ratchet makes a better metaphor: certainly large numbers of people who've tried (including me for most of my life) have found it far easier to end up heavier than where they started than ever to lose weight permanently.

1983

The setpoint model made sense out of everything that had puzzled me about my life with my body for the previous seven or eight years. It explained how I could be gaining weight on one meal per day (while Larry ate three!), and how I could eat nothing for a week yet lose less than a pound: the calorie-math could let you down because metabolism could be depressed under starvation conditions. And my weight-loss rate could speed up again later even though I ate much more, because running boosted my metabolism back up. And there was the always-puzzling fact that my fasting barrier expanded as I got heavier. For instance, that first semester in college, I lost 10 or 15 pounds in five days of fasting, but afterwards I couldn't even make myself crack the two-day barrier. This made sense if my setpoint had ratcheted up to around 165 by then: my body might be willing to be anywhere within 10 percent of that target, but far more reluctant to be further away from it than that, sounding desperate alarms at the edge of the danger zone. The fatter I was, the further away the body's idea of the danger zone was. I had thought of the fasting "barrier" only in metaphorical terms, considering it simply the point where my will happened to give out. But it could be a real physiological event, calibrated to how much fat was still available.

None of these experiences, common to dieters, are explained under the energy-balance model, where every pound of fat is identical and there is no reason why one pound should be any more "stubborn" than another.

The setpoint model was a guiding light in my life for the next twenty years.

Now

Eventually, for obvious reasons (see the cover!), I had to revise my thinking about setpoint, but of the two main *types* of model, it makes a better first approximation than the idea that a calorie is a calorie is a calorie no matter what. There are ways to modify the setpoint idea to take into account the complexities observed in real life, but there is no meaningful way to modify the idea that 3500 calories works out to one pound under all circumstances and no other factors come into play.

"There are some conditions under which 3500 calories equals one pound"? But that by itself explains nothing, and any actual theoretical work must then be accomplished by whatever other models it's supplemented with—such as an account of the body's regulatory systems.

Or how about this: "*Usually*, 3500 calories equals one pound, and yes, we realize there are exceptions, but we can simply assume that they're rare and insignificant, because the energy balance equation makes correct predictions in the overwhelming majority of cases." But in fact, laboratory testing has demonstrated otherwise. In addition to the individuals whose metabolisms have gone into supersaver mode who lose less than predicted (evidence for this goes back as far as World War II), there have been many experiments where groups of volunteers fed additional calories beyond their maintenance level gain less than predicted, even gain zero. *Most* people gain less than the amount the model predicts. Refusing to revise your hypothesis in the face of experimental evidence to the contrary means you have allowed it to turn into a dogma.

1983, my mental revolution

I've said that I didn't have any one sudden life-changing insight, the way people do in novels. But there was a night during the 1983 Christmas holiday when the weeks of reading and thinking I'd been doing came to a head. The books I had by my bed at the time were *Dieter's Dilemma: Eating Less and Weighing More*, and *shadow on a tightrope: writings by women about fat oppression*—two books, incidentally, which I would still recommend as relevant for anyone interested in the subject of obesity and weight-loss attempts in America.

In a month I would turn 22. I was between semesters and between boyfriends, though I did have a powerful crush on the calculus teacher from the first summer session. I couldn't seem to make myself stop courting his friendship even though I knew it was going nowhere. What was my life for? What should I do next?

Everyone else was shut behind a door and the whole quiet house was dark except for my one lamp. *shadow on a tightrope* had been stirring me intensely. It was a collection of articles and poems by various women, including a fair number of politically radical lesbians. The ranting some of them did about capitalism or "the patriarchy" made me uneasy, because it meant that the parts which discussed important scientific research would probably never even be seen or taken seriously by the average reader. I put the book down and tried to work through the concepts for myself.

The idea that you can lose weight by "simply" eating less than the amount your body needs to maintain itself had a big flaw. If you think about it, an organism capable of not noticing anything wrong when its own living tissue was being used up without replacement would be pretty poorly designed. It would be like being capable of falling asleep with an arm sticking into the fire—insensitivity like that would save you a little inconvenience and discomfort in the short term, but be disastrous in the long run. All animal bodies have built-in safety features to prevent such negligence, and humans are no exception. Why should we assume anyone's body will be content to be made thin, or kept thin, without putting up a powerful resistance?

It was clear to me now that all my efforts to lose weight over the years had actually made me fatter, driving my setpoint upwards. Which meant…

Overeating had not been my real problem, not even in the times I felt worst about myself. The shift in my reactions toward food happened because I had been subjected to long periods of artificial famine.

Our culture takes it for granted that many people mistakenly believe themselves hungry when they aren't. The possibility that people could also mistakenly believe themselves *not* hungry when they *were* had never entered my mind, though it's a logical enough possibility to consider, if hunger is the sort of thing you can make a mistake about. Finally, finally, now that more than two years had passed since that first Thanksgiving fast, and all attempts to will myself permanently indifferent to food had failed, I thought about it. Tension in the jaw, a heightened sense of smell, restlessness accompanied by constant thoughts of food (whether or not food was present), overwhelming desire to continue eating though some food had already been consumed—what were those things, if they weren't physical signals to eat? Where did these pressures originate, if not in the body? What should they be called, if not hunger?

I was not guilty of gluttony, and I never had been. Tears leaked out of my eyes and I blotted them with my quilt. I breathed carefully through my mouth to avoid snuffling. Not guilty.

I had made terrible mistakes and harmed myself, perhaps permanently. I couldn't undo the past, but at least I could stop making the same mistakes. All right, I would never again starve myself based on what I weighed. In fact, I wouldn't weigh myself at all. I would be guided only by the promptings of my own body, eating enough not to be constantly hungry, stopping when I felt full. My body would find its own equilibrium from there. If the theory was correct, as soon as I released control I would naturally return to my body's setpoint. But after all my changes in the last seven years, what would that point be? Presumably more than the 130-something I weighed now, but how much more? All the way up to my peak, over 200 pounds? Please let it not be that….

My reading had informed me that 90-something percent of all people who lose weight regain at least as much as they lost. If I wasn't in the lucky few percent, I would just have to live with that. If I could come into harmony with my appetite, eat healthy things, and exercise, I would be doing the best I could do. If I happened to end up fat again under those conditions it would be no reason for shame. Instead of futilely trying to sculpt my body, I would change my eyes instead.

I picked up *shadow on a tightrope* and read some more. The editors might be right about fat, I believed they were, but they were still doomed to be dismissed as crackpots by virtually every mainstream reader. Nothing I could do about that either.

The most awful and ironic thing was that precisely my strength of will, the fierceness of my self-denial, had led me to disrupt my setpoint and become fat. Throughout my teenage years, while I had been believing myself gluttonous, I had actually been essentially anorexic, if you defined anorexia as a set of food-phobic and fat-phobic attitudes and behaviors, rather than as a certain degree of thinness.

Fat people could be anorexic. Dieting could make a person fat. And so...

Maybe I wasn't unusual. I had always assumed myself to be very different from the average fat person, but, like so many of my assumptions, that could be wrong. What if I wasn't that exceptional after all?

Vickie—of course *she* was blameless. Vickie knew how to make a life for herself, and she did. She was going to be my model for the future. I thought of other fat women I knew by sight. A fat teacher I'd had in junior high school, my guidance counselor at the university—women I had always considered weak. What did I know about them? I knew that they went faithfully to work every day determined to do a good job, that they were capable of holding themselves in check in deference to students' well-being. How likely was it that in their private eating lives they were completely addicted to thoughtless self-indulgence? I searched for a more extreme example. Okay: Georgia—the fattest of all the fat women in Weight Control, who wheezed on her way up the ramp, monstrous, hardly-human Georgia who had made an object of pleasurable condescension for women big enough to draw public attention themselves as fat freaks—what about Georgia? About her, I knew absolutely nothing except her shape. Yet actually hers was the easiest case of all. It was idiotic to suppose that Georgia was unaware what impression she made on other people or that she was indifferent to contempt. Under the kind of pressure and shame Georgia had endured, there was no chance at all that she hadn't devoted years of her life to strenuous efforts to thin down. Getting fatter each time.

My story was not exceptional at all. It was the norm. Every fat person should be presumed innocent. I put down the book and cried quietly into the quilt. My personal tragedy had to be multiplied by the number of fat people in the country.

Reader, my narcissistic heart grew three sizes that night.

Chapter 18

Activism

Me in rollerblading gear.

1987

As I bicycled home from the Student Rec Center, no one mooed at me. Mooers in general seemed to have become somewhat more rare than they'd been in the olden days when I was a fat teenager, despite the fact that I was now even bigger than that, and went outside much more frequently. I didn't know whether it was because I projected more confidence these days, or because a woman over 25 just didn't attract the same kind of attention, or what. Oh, I still got a half-dozen or so moos per month, usually from men traveling in pairs or groups. It could happen biking or walking, but roller blading was the spectacle that delighted them most, understandably enough.

I had just finished a good workout, and I was proud of the way I felt and imagined myself to look, speeding exuberantly, fatly along under my own muscle power. Surely anyone could see how thoroughly at home I was in my body. The iron-pumping men who nodded respectfully to me in the weight room could see that I was like them, couldn't they? My workouts, like theirs, were profound exertions that altered my state of consciousness. Like them, I was in a trained state, had tested and gradually shifted the limits of my physical capacity over months and years until I'd pushed them as far as they could go. My body might not look like theirs, I might not be able to move it as quickly through water or over the ground, but my *relationship* with my body was no different from any dedicated athlete's.

I still had a slight endorphin buzz. Energy and pleasure surely must be emanating directly from my body like a halo. I put the bike away and went to the rack of apartment mailboxes. I am, I thought, a walking advertisement for fat pride.

"You look tired!" An old woman's voice called out merrily from a second-floor window off to my right. *What?* I kept my eyes grimly focused on the mailboxes. She didn't even know me, so what was she doing talking to me at all, let alone saying something so imbecilic? I had no more obligation to respond to her than I did to one of the mooers.

"You look tired!" she said again, a bit louder. There was no malice here. She understood her sociable impulse as irreproachable, commendable even.

In 1984, before meeting my husband Paul, I had comforted myself through a heartbreak with a wickedly funny advice book by Judith Martin, "Miss Manners." Previously I had thought of etiquette mainly as conventional insincerities practiced by people too timid or stupid to express themselves in more original ways. Miss Manners had revolutionized my thinking. Etiquette could be subtle, intellectually demanding, as full of emotional tensions and counterpoise as any great novel. For instance, Miss Manners had written that "you look tired" should not be regarded as a generally welcome observation. Therefore the old lady was clearly out of line. On the other hand, Miss Manners had written that younger people, even under provocation, must be *outwardly* seen to be patiently respectful to elders. Then again, Miss Manners had also said politeness didn't require you to give your time and privacy away to strangers. You could gently let them see that they had pulled you away from your own concerns, that your business was your own.

"What?" I said, glancing up and around as if confused, startled from my reverie—surely you don't mean *me*, do you?

"I said 'You look tired'…" But once my face was aligned with hers, the woman faltered. "Aren't you… You work in the office there, don't you?"

"No," I said. The receptionist at the Casa Feliz Apartments was Mexican-American; I was Anglo. I let my limp hair dry however it fell after my bath, while her dark, thick hair was combed into gravity-defying geometric sections. Her creamy, well-tended complexion contrasted with my pimples, blotching, and peeling. Her face was rounder, her features softer than mine. She was shorter than me, and smaller around the hips, more cylindrical than pear-shaped. She favored feminine outfits and accessories, big hoop earrings… Other than both of us being fat we looked nothing alike.

Could the woman be thinking of some completely different person? Her eyesight was probably poor. Grudgingly, I considered forgiving her. Maybe from this distance she could only see a smeary blob anyway. But then where did she get off presuming to announce that a vaguely seen blob looked tired? "I think you have me confused with some other fat woman," I said. I may have missed by a slight margin the genteel Miss-Manners tone I was aiming for.

The old lady's head snapped back as if slapped. "I didn't say *that*," she said. Her voice whined, both defensive and affronted. She struggled for a moment, weighing social anxiety against grievance. "I would never say anything like that—" Mid-sentence, she rallied and found solid footing in indignation— "because *I* have some *manners*."

I pondered a range of responses. It's interesting you mention manners, ma'am, because Miss Manners, my hero, has pointed out that 'you look tired' is not a compliment.... Miss Manners has pointed out that personal remarks should not be addressed to strangers.... You seem to regard the word 'fat' as some sort of obscenity in itself, ma'am, why is that, exactly?

My exercise buzz had ebbed away during this exchange. Dang, now I *was* tired. "Actually, you know, being fat is really not as bad as you might think. There are worse things than being fat."

Such as…? Anorexia and bulimia are worse. Self-hatred is worse. But the old woman withdrew from the window without asking me to elaborate.

the 1980s

I knew that such a thing as a Fat Liberation Movement existed, but not how to find my place in it. The world was making an awful mistake. There was widespread bigotry on roughly the same order as racial or sexual discrimination, there was error and intolerance roughly on the order of Galileo's persecutors, except that in this case the reigning orthodoxy didn't even understand itself to be a religious faith acting to suppress science. Bitterest of ironies, it thought it *was* science.

There was terrible and widespread suffering which was mostly invisible, or was trivialized because the fat were merely ridiculous. *These* persecutors didn't need to burn and torture: the fat punished themselves. It was wrong, it was, yes, why not, it was *evil*, even if mostly unwittingly, and I had a moral duty to combat it.

But what could I do? What was needed was courageous scientists, great orators. During my years of trying to get thin and stay thin, I had flunked classes, changed majors repeatedly, haphazardly. My college career was still in a muddled shambles. I had no professional goals, was nowhere near graduation, and even now couldn't have declared a major with certainty. Reading and thinking and feeling weren't going to change the world all by themselves.

Now I understood that my fat didn't mean I must be lazy or greedy, a failed degraded human being. But what next? I ought to go out and rescue others, but to do it I needed to be a better, different person. Someone accomplished, eloquent. Someone emotionally much larger than myself.

1987–there are worse things than being fat.

Zhenya in 1980

I first met Zhenya in Russian class. Her name was actually Jean, of course, but teachers rechristened us both Zhenya to get into the Russian spirit. Zhenya didn't care for this coincidence and suggested that I go by Zhenochka: "Jeanie." I didn't care for the diminutive so I added a middle name instead: "Kimovna," based in the Russian manner on my father's name, though the result didn't really sound Russian, exactly. Years later I continued to call Zhenya by her Russian name partly out of nostalgia, and partly for the convenience of Paul, who liked being able to distinguish Zhenya from his Jean in conversation.

Zhenya was fat in 1980 too. Not as fat as I would later become, but enough in that pre-"obesity epidemic" time to stand out. She dressed in unstylish clothes, long skirts in subdued colors, dark greens that seemed emotionally deep, alluring in combination with her brown hair, which was restrained in a heavy braid.

1980s seesaw

As my own weight seesawed, I passed Zhenya several times, going up and going down, slightly thinner than she was in the spring of 1980, fatter in 1981, then thin, then gradually fat again…. Meanwhile, her weight had slowly descended, just once, and now it was as though she sat, fashionably dressed, hair cut short, perched daintily at the peak of some hypothetical range of motion, anchored at the other end by me, my butt solidly planted at the bottom, and it looked as if neither of us would ever budge again. I missed the olden days not because I envied her thinness precisely—I refused to envy the thin, and anyway I assumed that Zhenya had gone anorexic—but because any fool could appreciate Zhenya's looks now, it no longer took a special sensibility.

For as long as I'd known her, I felt that Zhenya held me at a studied distance: this intimate, but no closer. And now that our appearance diverged so widely, did it make a best-friendship even more remote? I didn't want to think so. As a good fat activist I shouldn't feel that my body encumbered me in the pursuit of affection.

Zhenya had even, in the intervening years, had an affair with a woman. It should have been me who got close to her, I thought, could have been me, in the olden days when we were both available and both fat.

During the brief time when the seesaw had almost balanced, we once had a conversation about violence. We had just seen the movie *Raging Bull*, and I found it difficult to watch the scenes of boxers' faces and bodies being repeatedly, deliberately pounded. Zhenya couldn't understand why anyone wanted to see prize fights, she said. Me neither, I said, although….

There was something. That made me almost understand. When men, you know, said things. About your body. Strangers, I mean.

"Things": I was too ashamed to mention being fat directly, too ashamed to mention mooing, too ashamed to mention the *shame* that the mooing caused, the feeling that in some sense the humiliation was deserved.

At such times I could understand violent fantasies, I said. I would punish such men if I could. Hurt them.

Zhenya had a fantasy too but hers was different. The men who affronted her would be struck blind on the spot by some righteous supernatural force. Then they would wander the world, enfeebled and weeping ceaselessly from their now-useless eyes. Helpless and fumbling, they would seek after her, because she had been the last person to see them unafflicted. After many groping years, they would find her and fall at her feet, confessing their guilt and begging pardon. And her forgiveness would restore their sight.

It was like a story out of King Arthur. It went so well with Zhenya's green skirt and her braid.

Now

It's a great temptation to lie to you, to fudge the conversations. Just a little. To make myself, in retrospect, into a slightly more effective activist. To articulate the feelings I had at the time in words that only came to me later.

1984

I had a fling with an older man, a family friend who had met me during my peak of teenage fatness. He complimented me on my transformed body: "When I first met you before, I thought—now, there's a woman who has absolutely no interest in sex." Fat women, he explained, fear sex and overeat so as to avoid coming to terms with it.

His theory couldn't be right, I said, at least about me, since he had been wrong about my sex drive. "I came on to you, remember?"

"Yes, but by then you had changed. Obviously you managed to overcome your fear, and once that happened you were able to lose weight."

I told him I'd never feared sex, and he said "Not consciously, maybe."

It would be so nice if I hadn't choked then on my own anger:

So this alleged motive of mine is perceptible to you but not to me? (I might have said.) Here's an alternative account. *You* look at a fat woman and feel repulsed, and you then interpret your own sensations as something the woman has deliberately caused. Kind of like the way a lot of rapists think a woman was asking for it? You know, the basic blame-the-victim? If fat women make fewer encouraging signals to men than others, it's because they fear *rejection*. They have a keener insight into your feelings than you do theirs.

In reality, of course, I only managed to mutter my offended disagreement and he took the emotional vehemence as further proof that he must be right. "Well, then, why do *you* think you gained all that weight?"

I explained, as well as I could, the setpoint theory as I then understood it: "I think a lot of people, when they diet trying to get thin they provoke an overreaction from their bodies and end up fatter."

"That sounds like bullshit," he said.

1987

Sam was an old high-school acquaintance who had known me early on the very first sweep of the seesaw. Abstaining now from alcohol, deeply depressed about his own life, Sam wanted to convince me I must have been molested in childhood: "Think about it. I know when I started to drink. When did you start to eat?" By the time of this conversation I was married to Paul, and nearly back up to 200 pounds.

"Actually, I don't have an eating problem," I said. "I had a not-eating problem, but I got over it."

"Things happen for a reason," Sam said.

"Things": Despite his boldness in embarking on this loving intervention (friends don't *let* friends pork up), Sam wasn't quite bold enough to say the word "fat." Meanwhile, I was having my own problems addressing Sam. My gaze kept getting pinned on his ravaged face as I struggled to treat his wheelchair casually, neither obviously avoiding it nor morbidly interested in it. A couple years before, in a bad part of town, Sam had been shot in the spine by someone he didn't know who wasn't aiming at him. Accidents happen, I wanted to say, but I was afraid of how that would sound. I was afraid of the depths of anguish in Sam's voice, as though another person's unhappiness had the force to suck you in, the way a black hole absorbs even light. Sam had already mentioned suicide. But it seemed that I could also sense despair directly, that I smelled it, perhaps, or felt it pulling at me. He seemed far heavier to me than I seemed to myself.

Was this the kind of thing other people imagined when they looked at my fat body? Gothic ruins, a mangled thing that had once been a person, grotesquely pinned under colossal wreckage, but horribly still twitching; the wish to get away from it…. I made an effort to shake off the gloom. It was childish and unkind. We were two people talking, that's all we were. Stay open, I told myself.

"Not every reason has to be some dark psychological reason," I said. "There's physiology too. Bodies are physical."

"That's too simple," Sam said.

Over the last four years I had developed a rich mental imagery for the anything-but-simple human physiology. Bodies are designed (I might have said)—well, "designed" in a manner of speaking that is, by the cumulative effect of evolutionary pressures through untold ages—designed to be self-preservation machines. They try to hold themselves in homeostatic balance. They try to maintain the same temperature whether it's hot or cold outside; to hang onto their tissue even when food supplies decrease. There are genetic differences in how effectively our bodies do this. Then on top of what's built into our DNA, so many accidental factors that affect the body over a lifetime—temporarily, or, as in Sam's case, permanently. Body chemistry is so intricately woven together that it makes no more sense to say that some gothic psychodrama is the *reason* for being fat than to say there's a reason why a bullet caused the damage it did. You would either have to say there's no particular reason, or that there are thousands of reasons, most either too big or too little for human comprehension: the brain state that led to the electrochemical impulse that passed through the nerve that triggered the twitch of a finger muscle; the rate of expansion of gasses during the milliseconds of the explosion; the friction of the gun barrel and then the air, and then the intervening body tissues. Then the whole mass of the earth creating weight, dragging the gunman's arm down, the total sum of Sam's past that brought him to exactly that point, at exactly that second instead of a second later, instead of a foot to the right or left. Even two inches and his spine would be intact.

I stammered out something feeble, leaving out the bullet analogy though it had sprung into my mind full formed. It didn't seem quite polite to mention.

Sam shook his head in wide swings. "I think you do know what really happened," he said. "You know, even if you don't remember right now. It all had to start somewhere." His voice groaned like the coffin that opens in the depths of the damp crypt, about to disgorge its unspeakable secret. The words banged out dire and slow, like the flapping of shutters against the mildewed walls of a haunted house as the storm begins: "Jean, Jean, *think: when* did you start to *eat*?"

1980-2001

And the doctors! Streams of doctors over the years, haranguing doctors, tactful doctors, doctors who just want to help. Most fat people avoid going to doctors if they possibly can, because it causes so much shame. Not even the most insensitive doctors make barnyard noises, of course, but even the gentlest ones can have the same effect when they see and react to only one trait. When they try to force the fat patient's life onto their preferred storyline.

Before every appointment I used to spend time rehearsing remarks I might make to startle the doctor into seeing me from a different perspective.

"Are you aware of the health risks associated with being obese?"

Gosh, no. The medical profession thinks fat is unhealthy? Maybe you guys should try to publicize that.

"I consider it my responsibility as a doctor to ask you: What are you doing about your weight?"

Okay, now that you've fulfilled your responsibility, can we talk about what I came in for?

"You know, the real problem here might not be your feet your ankle your neck your wrists your Achilles tendon your period…. The real problem here could be your excess weight."

Do any thin people ever come in with this problem?

"Sure, but the issue here is you—"

Does every fat person invariably develop this problem?

"No, but—"

Okay, then I'd like to receive the same kinds of medical information and care you would give a thin patient, please.

I imagined myself controlling the exchange, making my points easily, keeping cool. Of course the reality was never like that. I'd be too shy, too flustered, too irritated. The doctor would have his script too, and he'd have performed it far more times than I had.

"Let's get you an appointment with our nutritionist. She can help you move to a diet that's lower in fat and higher in complex carbohydrates."

You forgot to ask what my eating habits are *now*!

"Let's get you started with an exercise program. Why don't you try going to the gym with a friend? That can really help with your motivation."

You forgot to ask what my exercise habits are *now*!

There was a sports-medicine doctor I went to intermittently ever since I broke my ankle roller-blading in 1998. The ankle continued to interfere with some of my activities. I told the sports-med guy that exercise was central to my life, but he couldn't quite take that in. Peeking into my chart one day when he stepped out of the room, I saw what he had written: "Patient is very overweight. She has recently started doing some aerobic exercise." *Recently*: this was after he'd been seeing me for *three years*.

1989

Zhenya and I were walking along the sidewalk to a movie. Just ahead at the intersection I saw the light turning yellow; meanwhile, a battered white pickup registered at the edge of my vision, though the girls inside hadn't yet done anything to attract my attention. Teenage girls, yes, not men this time. I doubt very many people start out a social evening saying, "Let's cruise the streets looking for fat people to harass," so they must have made an almost instantaneous decision when they saw me, just as I did when I heard them. The whole thing took very little time.

"Lose weight!" the girls called out from the truck—sang, really—chanting the words together, like a squad practicing their cheerleading calls: "Lose weight! …two three… Lose weight!" Their voices were high and delighted and secure, cocooned in their three-musketeers camaraderie. It's tempting to call it innocent, but it can't have been entirely. They must have intended to humiliate, at least, though it's possible they had no clear idea of their target being a fully real person like themselves. I might have been a cartoon character to them. I can't decide if this is better or worse.

The sound of those female voices, possibly coupled with the presence of Zhenya, triggered a reaction in me like the flipping of a switch. All along, unbeknownst to me, there must have been some little measuring device lurking somewhere in my brain and spinal chord, something that automatically sized up the comparative physical power of potential adversaries. The mooing boys and men had provoked feelings as strong as I could feel, but they had never toggled the action switch to ON, presumably because they had measured out in my brain as more dangerous than me. These girls, however, had just made a very foolish error: I was more dangerous than they were.

I didn't think any of these things explicitly; they simply registered directly in my body. Less than a second after I first heard the voices I was bending and searching the sidewalk around me for something to throw, then I was out into the street. Maneuvering my adrenaline-filled body felt like holding a gushing firehose that could easily jitter out of my grasp, levitating itself, whipping around in the air to miss its proper target. Urgent signals seemed to be firing past my everyday mind and directly into my muscles: Careful, now, don't slip! Quick, quick! Nothing mattered but keeping that truck from escaping.

The best rock I could find on the blacktop was disappointing, not much bigger around than my thumbnail. As I threw it I exulted to see the girls' weak skinny arms, their bleached split ends, the three of them sitting in the cab of their shit-kicker truck without even a tight squeeze: I could break these flimsy little skanks like twigs. Even their hair was thin!

The quality of their voices changed immediately when the rock pinged off the back window of the truck's cab. "Fuck you!" "Bitch!" Ragged angry yells, no longer a chorus. Their surprise was comical. They had intended, they must have intended, to have an effect on the cartoonish fat person, but they had not imagined that the cartoon could or ever would make a move to touch them. They must have assumed I'd simply turn away in quiet embarrassment. That was what fat people did, of course.

"You fucking bitch!" said the girl at the passenger-side window. Our eyes met. Her righteous indignation was even funnier than their initial surprise.

"Come on, then, if you have a problem with me," I said. I danced up onto the sidewalk like a boxer, waving my arms. "Come on, babes, I'm right here, let's go!" The wish for them to come and fight me was as intensely physical as sexual desire. I was aware of Zhenya as a silent witness at my side. In the moment I was confident that I could beat up all three girls even together, but probably it also entered into my subterranean calculations somewhere, that Zhenya would alter the balance somehow if I turned out to be wrong.

Was Zhenya admiring my self-respect and courage, or was she furious with me the way sensible girls get when their belligerent dates court violence over nothing?

In any case, there was no fight. The light turned green and the girls drove away.

"Zhenya, I'm sorry about all that."

"That's okay, it's perfectly fine."

That was my best shot, my *Raging Cow* moment. The cleanest most direct blow I can remember striking for fat dignity was the size of my thumbnail. I was never an effective fat activist, and after the 1980s, I mostly stopped trying: you cannot change other people's eyes.

Even now I'd forgive all my old adversaries if I could just make them *see*.

Able Bodies:
a 1990s Mosaic

1990. *The man with no nose*

By our third year of marriage, I understood Paul had given up on sex. From 1987 through 1989, he'd kept saying he was just in a temporary slump, it was just dissertation stress, but by now that was obviously not the whole story. Was it because I got fat again? It's nothing to do with you, Paul said, it's just me. But that wasn't necessarily true. The fact that Paul was fat himself—quite a bit fatter than me at that time, in fact—didn't mean he couldn't find my body repulsive; it only meant that he wouldn't be able to admit it if he did. Maybe Paul's problem was medical. Maybe it was a combination of things. Whatever, he didn't intend to do anything about it.

My own libido was plenty high in those days. I looked at both men and women. I'd been corresponding with a woman who placed an ad in the Women Seeking Women section of the *Tucson Weekly*. Raven, she called herself. I never meant for it to go further than some racy letters. I'd envisioned a steady supply of personalized pornography delivered to my post office box. Somehow I hadn't grasped at the outset that the source of that supply was going to be another person. After a few months of intimate revelations, I fell for her. Just on the basis of words. We had never exchanged pictures but our fantasies were compatible. I was sure what she looked like wouldn't make any difference to me.

I was working in a used bookstore. For a game, each female customer I waited on, I said to myself, This could be Raven. Then I practiced taking my sexual feelings and centering them on that specific body. There was never much trouble except when the woman was far younger than me, but I already knew Raven was older. Therefore, I knew there would be no impediment on my side. Do you have physical preferences? I wrote to Raven. Body types that you prefer or don't prefer? Not really, she wrote…. Well, okay, if I'm honest, there is one thing that puts me off.

She didn't say what was her one thing, and I didn't say I was fat. But I knew all along. What else could it be? She probably suspected, too. We kept writing anyway, stirring each other up.

My Raven correspondence was not a secret from Paul. He even encouraged it, asking about her, offering to fetch the mail from my post office box. It took the pressure off him, I guess. He agreed that I could have a fling with Raven if he could also have a fling with another woman some day. I said all right partly because I didn't think it would ever happen. He had to say that to save his pride. It's a deal, I said, if I actually bag Raven. Deal, he said, and we shook hands. Anyway, I thought, Raven probably won't ever want to.

I kept up my game at the bookstore. When the woman was dark-haired and in her late thirties, my breath would speed up. This really could be Raven, for real. When she was pretty, my lust mixed with despair and a kind of anger. Raven would never want me—she was so shallow! I was capable of desiring her regardless of her body's shape. A woman was black: a black Raven suited me fine. A woman limped, and I thought, yes, let Raven have something physically wrong with her, something serious enough to offset my fat. By now Raven and I were cautiously negotiating—by mail—a first meeting in person. I sent her my phone number and asked her to call me on Friday after midnight. I was aflame. After all we had written I couldn't bear not to actually do any of it. Some of the fantasies had been, shall we say, a trifle unusual. If Raven found my body objectionable, perhaps I might offer to blindfold her. Then there'd be no problem, right? Then I would be whoever, whatever she wanted. I was that desperate.

On Wednesday, late in the afternoon, the man with no nose walked into the bookstore where Mariely and I were working alone. Mariely was pale-skinned, dark-haired, prettier than average without being a raving beauty, a serious student with a thoughtful face. At around 20 years old, she was too young to attract me, but a Raven who was Mariely plus another 15 years would suit me very well indeed.

Mariely took one look at the man with no nose and fled to the back room. I shared her feelings. He was pretty hard to look at. When I say he had no nose, I don't mean that the end of it was missing, or that there was a discreet bandage over a flat place, or even that there was some kind of malformed lump instead of a regular nose. I mean he had a gaping red and black hole in the middle of his face. How are you this afternoon, I said. I made myself look at him and smile. I saw, or imagined I could see, a dangling pair of bones inside the cavern where his nose ought to be. I wasn't usually all that outgoing with customers, but I made a special effort to chat with the man with no nose, because I was ashamed at how he repelled me. I made myself touch his hand as I gave him his change.

The man with no nose stayed by the register, talking cheerfully, for several minutes. My jumpiness subsided slightly. It became easier to keep eye contact and smile. If I knew him for a friend, I thought, I'd get used to him. …What if he were Raven? What if Raven were actually a man, this man? I could do it. I could get over that hurdle. Given time, I could come to love and desire this person, I was sure. Bitterly, I thought again of Raven's likely refusal, and I felt myself morally superior, not that it was any big comfort.

The man with no nose left the store and Mariely came out from the back room. Oh, I'm so ashamed! she said. Don't be, I said. It's only natural; I felt the same way. But I was complacent just the same. I hadn't run; I had conquered my feelings.

On Friday night when the phone rang I found myself short of breath. Raven's voice so disoriented me at first that I thought she had a speech defect. After a few minutes I realized it was simply a Southern accent, all sunshine and slow honey. "You don't sound like I expected," I said. I don't know why, with all the different bodies and faces I'd had her try on, I'd never bothered to imagine Raven as having any specific voice.

"Well, there are bound to be a few surprises," she said.

"Yes," I said. "Listen, you remember we wrote one time about body types?" I felt sick. I wondered if the noseless man ever had blind dates, and what he might say to them on the phone beforehand: *Oh, by the way, there's something I'd better mention before we meet, just so, you know, it's not a shock when you first see me....*

"I'm fat," I said.

"Oh," Raven said, so disappointed that I actually felt sorry for her for a second. "Let's meet anyway, we can be friends at least." She had the grace to be embarrassed about her reaction. "I guess I don't measure up to my own standards sometimes."

"Raven," I said, "don't worry. It's only natural." In the back of my mind, I started planning a longer campaign. If I could get over my initial repulsion enough to imagine making love to the man with no nose, maybe Raven could get over hers too, eventually.

We met the same night in a 24-hour coffee shop. Raven turned out to be a gawky skinny short-haired blonde with a goofy boyish face. She looked like Opie of Mayberry, or Dennis the Menace. Why on *earth* would a *blonde* woman ever choose Raven for a pen name? Inexplicably, my desire, that great burden of desire that had sat on me for months, the desire I breathed and walked around inside, the desire so desperately strong that it was absolutely indifferent to the bodily details of its object—my desire vanished. Temporarily. After a few weeks my scattered fantasies regrouped themselves and realigned around the body of the actual Raven.

For her, it took even longer than that.

1993. Even God has the occasional off day

My fat wasn't a hurdle for Jan like it was for Raven. I had sent her a picture right away, never make that mistake again, right? This was in the late middle era of my marriage, before I had completely given up the idea that it might be possible to have one kind of commitment with my asexual husband, and another kind with somebody else at the same time. I met Jan through a—well, not exactly a dating service strictly speaking. More of a liaison service. In any case, my personal profile attracted her attention ("Prefer emotional, articulate partner: all other traits trivial by comparison") and she contacted me. We wrote and wrote, talked and talked on the phone, and I felt we had both pretty much fallen for each other by the time I flew to Michigan for a visit.

For Jan the big obstacle was that she thought I wouldn't like, or couldn't deal with, her children. She was a single mom. Her boys were three and four, and they were obstreperous. I was awkward with them at first, it's true. But I found the whole package, the kids and her, attractive. We could all get over the hurdle once we got to know each other, I felt.

You're my little drop of sunshine, she would say as she nuzzled the younger boy's body. You're my cool drink of water, she said to the older, graver boy. And to both of them, often, she said, God did a good job when She made you! Some of the women I'd been dating (or "dating") were full-blown goddess-worshipers, with altars and everything. But I didn't see an altar at Jan's house, so I figured the female deity thing was just to instill an open-minded spirit in her kids. Good luck, I thought. Children have their own personalities, I believe; I don't think parents make them from scratch.

Jan had daycare arrangements, but while I was there I babysat several days while she was at work, to get to know the boys, and to advance my case that I was, too, interested in her whole family. I was looking for something long-term, sick of the "dating" scene.

I don't remember how the subject of missing body parts came up, but I do remember it was a natural extension of something else we were talking about, maybe something from the boys' cartoons, the X-Men maybe. Isn't there one character in a wheelchair? I *didn't* bring it up just to be morbid, or as a ploy to win them over by pandering to unwholesome curiosity. Although of course I knew it would be interesting to them. After all, I remembered being a child. I remembered my fascination with a substitute teacher who had only one hand. A stack of papers tucked into the crook of her elbow, the bare stump of the wrist poking out on the other side as she passed them out, one at a time, with her good hand. I was frantic to hear her story and deeply relieved when she gathered us into a circle on the third day and told it.

I knew a woman once who only had one hand, I told the boys. And another time I met a man who didn't have a nose. Of course they were fascinated. How *come*? they said. How *can* people not have parts of their body? In the case of the woman with one hand, it was an accident, I said. I know the story because she was our teacher and she told us. She found a bullet one day when she was a little girl. She thought it was only the spent shell, and she was playing with it, picking at it with a nail, but really it was a live bullet and it exploded and blew off her hand. I don't know what happened to the man with no nose, because he didn't tell me, and you can't ask if people don't tell you. He might have had an accident, too, or maybe some kind of disease that affected his nose. Or maybe he was just born without one. But how *come*? they said. How *can* someone be born without a nose?

I was having an off day. I hadn't been sleeping well. And I was discouraged at my prospects with Jan. She seemed determined to believe we could never work out long-term. I answered the boys with the first thing that popped into my mind: Sometimes God doesn't do such a good job.

Minus the God part, this more or less expressed my actual philosophy. So much of what happens to us, good or bad, comes not by our choice or even any human agency, but the accretion of many random forces both larger and smaller than we are. As a matter of fact, what I said was also compatible with Jan's expressed theology. Indeed, God's doing an extra good job on some occasions logically *entails* His or Her doing a less good job on some other occasions. Nevertheless, I was just a little uneasy about the whole topic afterwards.

When Jan got home from work, the boys rushed to tell her everything about their day. I don't know why I didn't anticipate that that would happen. Is it true that people can be born without body parts? they said. Is it true that God doesn't do a good job sometimes?

No, she said. It's true that some people are born *different*. But that's because God knows those are very special people, extra strong, with extra loving hearts. Over the boys' heads, she gave me a strange look.

I was feeling pretty strange myself.

1999. Access

After Jan, I embarked on a celibate period. Life was calmer that way. In a few years my libido declined considerably, and I was planning to just let that be the end of it. Unless somebody desirable positively flung him- or herself into my lap—which I thought extremely unlikely—I was through looking. I didn't want to go shopping for a fat fetishist, and what else was out there for me? Marketing myself was too humiliating, better to give up. Occasional masturbation and frequent exercise satisfied my sensual requirements well enough.

On a sunny late-spring day during the late part of my marriage—I had separated from Paul but we weren't divorced yet—I went to the pool at the University of Missouri for my regular workout. I was a little early and the lifeguard hadn't arrived yet, so I sat on the bench and waited. Almost everyone who came out of the locker room went straight on past, through the glass doors to the outside pool. But the outside pool had no stairs, only a ladder which, at something like 280 pounds, I didn't feel I could use safely.

Ten minutes past the hour a girl with a lifeguard's whistle approached me, smiling brightly. Uh-oh, I thought. We're short-staffed, she said, so we're only opening up the outside pool for now. Everything is supposed to be open now, I said, according to the schedule. Yes, she said, but we don't have the staff, so we're only able to open one pool, I hope that's all right. Well, no, it's actually not, I said, because I need the inside pool. Her look told me I was being very unreasonable. A lot of people want to swim outside, she said, so somebody would end up unhappy no matter what we decided. Yeah, maybe so, I said, but one decision is right and the other one is wrong. You need to open the indoor pool first, because it's the one with the stairs.

The girl kept her voice professional. You're welcome to wait here, she said, while we call around and try to find more staff. Or you're welcome to change your mind and swim in the outside pool. The outside pool is not *accessible* to me, I said. The girl's face showed her contempt. It was mutual. She was a little twit with no imagination for other people's circumstances. She was able-bodied, so everyone else was too, or should be. I hoped a person minus a limb or two would show up wanting to swim laps. That would shame her.

I could make more of a fuss, I thought. I could demand to speak to her supervisor. Or I could write a letter later. But how much of my time was it worth? Nobody would thank me for making myself a spokesman for disability. And probably this was a one-time event. I'd wait half an hour, I decided, then I'd take my righteous indignation to the ski machine in the aerobics room instead.

Another woman came out of the locker room and asked me what was going on. I told her. I'm not supposed to go in the sunlight, the woman said, because of my medication. Great! I thought. Let her make a fuss, write a letter. A woman allergic to sunlight has more legitimacy than a fat woman. But alas, the medicated woman's will to combat was even weaker than mine. She left after only ten minutes. I thought about just plopping on into the water, an act of civil disobedience, but I refrained. When my half hour was up I decided to take one quick look outside.

I walked slowly around the entire pool, inspecting it, allowing the lifeguard to see me but not deigning to notice her in return. All of the ladders were narrow; I certainly wouldn't fit between the bars straight on. Maybe I could somehow climb sideways? My right leg was strong enough to do its part, but my left was still recovering from the broken ankle. And my wrists were vulnerable, my hands clumsy in the braces I wore to swim. And even apart from the bad ankle my feet weren't in that great a shape to balance on narrow rungs, wet, bare, under a weight like mine. Better not.

But there was the shallow end, four feet deep. I looked where the water came to on other people's bodies. Say I'd be up to my chest. Jumping and pushing at the same time with my arms, could I heave my torso up high enough to roll out over the rim of the pool? It seemed possible. And if I did fail, it would provide a dramatic illustration of her error to the snippy little lifeguard. Anyway, I'd get my workout in first before I tried it.

If I had to be rescued from outside, I didn't want anyone hauling me by the wrists. I looked around for other possibilities and saw a stack of white plastic chairs. That would do. If I couldn't roll out of the pool in a reasonably dignified way, I would ask in a dignified manner for a chair to be tossed to me, or several chairs. I could build a whole staircase of chairs if need be.

It was a pity to go back on what I said to the lifeguard before; unless and until I needed to call for the chairs she would think I was a neurotic faker. I hesitated. But what difference did her opinion make? Nothing I could do would ever make her see me as I wanted to be seen. All that counted here was my own workout, my own good relationship with my body. For a moment I felt bad for the woman on Dracula meds who had missed her swim, and even an abstract sympathy for all the paraplegics who had not shown up to swim, but might have.

I jumped in. The cool water in the warm sunshine was exquisite; I could see why most people preferred it.

Me preparing to entertain in 1999. Note the wholesome food choices.

Chapter 20

Robert Pool Made Me Thin.
But I'm Not Grateful.

Now

There's a mortal feud between Robert Pool and me, but he doesn't know that, since he doesn't know I exist. Robert Pool wrote a book with the same title as mine, but his was published first. Excuse me, reader, but I'd just like to emphasize that I had already decided on my title before becoming aware of the existence of Robert Pool.

Robert Pool is a science journalist, a smart guy, and compassionate besides (well, mostly). I gave his book a good review, which it deserved (mostly), and I used it later as a textbook in a class I was teaching. I have to admire Robert Pool and I can't help hating his guts at times.

Robert Pool made me thin. But I'm not grateful.

I'm in a feud with my mother, too. She knows it. Poor Mom! Poor me!

What about you, reader? Are you on my side? Odds are, not completely. After all, this is the chapter you've been waiting for and I've been dreading. Even though I've explained to my publisher it's not a diet book, I don't believe in losing weight, I think the whole concept of the obesity epidemic is a terrible misunderstanding... still they won't have been able to resist putting before and after pictures of me on the cover. And that's why the overwhelming majority of you picked it up, I'm sure.

"How did you do it?" To me this is the least significant part of the story. The book I originally planned to write ended with me as a healthy fat woman leading a relatively contented life built on excellent habits. I never expected to get thin again and wasn't attempting it; that outcome was a freak accident for which I deserve no credit. The difference between fat and thin, I believe, is primarily a matter of luck. My relationship to food and exercise are no different now than they were at the fattest time of my life. I wouldn't expect you to believe that, but it's true just the same.

All right, then, here's the chapter you're salivating for, go ahead, snarf it down!

This is what happened. This is how Robert Pool (and my mother, and American society in general) made me thin. *Accidentally.*

July 2001, Columbia, Missouri, working on my PhD

My best friend Laura comes to dinner along with Bill and Averill, two other grad students. Bill is my grocery buddy: he doesn't have a car and I take him with me to the grocery store most weeks. Averill's the one who gave me the idea for my dissertation, the manuscript that eventually grew into this book.

I've made Chicken Masala, rice, salad, and no dessert since I never eat them. Also there's bean soup and bread if anyone wants it. I cook big batches of this soup a few times a month, making it from pinto beans and grocery-store salsa, reading the salsa labels carefully to make sure I don't get a brand with any form of sugar in it, or hydrogenated fats, or added anything else I don't want. Laura praises the soup; Averill praises everything. Averill is thin, like Laura. Bill is always on some diet or other and he wants to talk about what foods are "fattening." He and Averill discuss the status of potatoes, of carbohydrates in general, of cooking with olive oil. As usual, I try to tune this talk out.

"And then the doctor said, 'Bill, you're fat!'" Bill laughs in a self-deprecating way. I bet, though, that the doctor's remark hurt much more than he's admitting. I wouldn't have called Bill fat, but these things are relative. What is Bill thinking when he tells this story in front of someone so much fatter than he is? I like the word "fat," like to say it forthrightly as though it were nothing that required any apology, but I know Bill doesn't mean it that way. The conversation moves on, and I drift again.

"You eat quite a bit of meat, don't you, Jean?" Bill turns to me suddenly.

"What?" I try to conceal my exasperation. Bill sees the groceries I buy every week, but the evidence of his own experience counts for nothing alongside the stereotype. "Three or four pounds a month. To me that doesn't seem like a whole lot." I answer in a clipped way without looking at him. Sometimes this works.

Laura stays to clean up when the others have gone. "How's it going," she says, meaning my book. She fills one side of the sink with soapy water.

"I have 40 or 50 pages written," I say. "But the whole project is stirring up my feelings in ways I didn't expect. I thought I got over all that years ago."

Among other things, I'm working on my Robert Pool book review. The title caught my eye because it's the same as mine, though with a different subtitle of course: *FAT—Fighting the Obesity Epidemic*. Pool starts off with a century's worth of scientific evidence that fat people shouldn't be thought of as just "sloths or gluttons," that the body has biological systems for regulating fat. There's a hormone, leptin, that communicates with the brain about how much fat is in the body, and then there's a complicated brain chemistry that sets appetite and metabolism levels. The physiology discussion in Pool's book could be a positive influence on the reading public, except then he undercuts the message with snide jokes. Like this: "No one can honestly say 'My leptin made me eat that cheesecake.'"

I try to explain to Laura how I feel about Pool. "Nine tenths of the book is great," I say, "but his tone pisses me off." What he said about the rats with holes in their stomachs, for instance. In one of the classic experiments on eating and satiety, some rats were surgically implanted with tubes that made anything they ate drain right back out of them. Not too surprisingly, the experimental stomach-tube rats continued eating much longer than the control group of intact rats, trying unsuccessfully to satisfy their hunger.

"Oh, the poor things!" Laura says. Laura is so tender-hearted that when she caught a mouse in a sticky trap in her kitchen, she got up in the middle of the night, drove out into the country, and swabbed it down with cooking oil to release it from the glue.

"Yes," I say, "but listen, the way Pool describes this situation is that the rats were 'stuffing themselves.' But 'stuffing themselves' is just exactly what they *weren't* doing!" With Laura, I don't need to hold back. I let the words come boiling out. "Pool takes this familiar, condescending human attitude, that most of his readers probably are starting with—that there are a lot of piggy people out there over-indulging in food—and he applies it in a totally inappropriate way to those lab animals. When what he should be doing is exactly the opposite: showing how those contemptuous attitudes should be modified in light of the experiment."

"Sorry," Laura says. "I don't exactly know what you mean."

"Bulimia," I say. "People think of bulimic women as stuffing themselves, too, but they aren't, any more than those rats were, because they never get the chance to digest. You have to look at the whole system, not just what goes into the mouth."

"You need to write about this," Laura says.

I've told my mother nothing about my project, but by a strange coincidence she picks July to launch one of her occasional initiatives. "There's an article in the *New Yorker* about an extremely overweight man who had his stomach stapled, did you see it?"

"No," I say heavily. No amount of clipped answering will deter my mother if she's talked herself into the missionary mode. Come hell or high water, she will deliver the message she has charged herself to bring.

"It changed his life," she said. "The description of the way he was living before—it sounds just terrible. He couldn't even climb the stairs in his own house. He slept in the living room."

"Hmm," I say, trying to sound both depressed, which I am, and noncommittal, which I'm not. I'm deeply pessimistic about this article, but I suppose it's a research necessity and I'll have to get it at the library.

My mother assures me that she isn't casting any aspersions on me personally. And she's no big fan of elective surgery, but some people, people who are leading wretched lives—handicapped lives, is what it amounts to—really need to do something. "I'm talking about the kind of people that sit down and eat whole bags of cookies at a time," she says. "It's a sickness."

"You don't know what it's like—" I'm mad but I try to speak gently, choose my words carefully—"to have a very high setpoint. It's something that happens by accident. Nobody does it on purpose. The regulatory mechanisms in their bodies have been damaged by years of deprivation, and now they're driven by physical pressures stronger than anything you've ever felt."

"It's an addiction," my mom says.

"I don't think that's the best way to look at it," I say. "It's instinct."

"The article talks about people who have the surgery but keep on eating anyway, even though it bursts out the stitches and causes terrible complications."

"Well that's just what I'm saying: hunger is an even more powerful force than pain."

"It's like those people who've been operated on for cancer and who keep on smoking through the hole in their throats!"

There are so many different ways I could answer this that nothing comes out. I do think it's possible to get addicted to soda and sugary things, high-fat snacks, and other "foods" like that which don't exist in the natural world. But the drive to eat enough is built into everyone. It's not a deviation from normalcy, it *is* normalcy. I go to my knees, then stretch out on the floor, carefully playing out the phone cord. After all this time, why can't my mother hear me? Probably she's thinking something similar. My chest is heavy and my eyes fill up. Oh, mothers and daughters! It's like a marriage, but with no divorcing.

"Hello?" says my mother. "Hello?"

"Mm, yeah, I'm here," I say, breathing shallowly so that my voice won't break.

Most of the places where I think Pool is wrong aren't hard to refute. But I'm having a serious theoretical crisis over the Pima Indians (Chapter 6). The Pimas were ahead of the fattening curve in the 20th

century. For the rest of the country, rising weights have gone hand in hand with the increasing stigma for being fat and the increasing dominance of the weight-loss industry. So for most Americans, it makes sense that dieting itself, ironically, has been the primary engine driving the "obesity epidemic" from the 1950s onward. But the Pimas got fat in a time before anybody was trying to get thin, so for them the explanation must be something different. Environmental factors, just as Pool says, a response to a changed diet in the 20th century. I can't deny that the Pimas mean something.

It doesn't mean there's no such thing as a setpoint, but it does mean setpoints must be more complex than I'd been used to thinking: the homeostatic systems must include a feedback loop reacting to the *types* of food that are available. And it doesn't mean that fat people could all get thin if they would just live right, as Pool so uncharitably implies. I know in my bones that if it were really possible to get thin, all those women struggling so hard for the last half century would have discovered the right way to do it.

Laura's in Arkansas but she sends me a Lane Bryant coupon by email: $25 off if I spend $75. On the phone she tells me she saw pinstriped suits on sale there when she was at the mall. "I know you like pin stripes," she says. She tells me I should get a suit now to be ready for interviewing when I graduate.

"Maybe," I say. "I'll think about it when the time gets closer."

"But they won't have these suits by then."

"Maybe I'll go take a look at them," I say. "I'll think about it."

I'm going to give Pool a good review. I have no choice. Nobody will ever listen to me if I sound like a fanatic crackpot who can't get along with reasonable people. I make oatmeal for breakfast, measuring out one cup grain and two cups water. A handful of raisins, a teaspoon of canola oil. Except for social occasions, I haven't used butter in the last six years. Oil is cheaper and keeps better, and if the nutrition experts are right it's healthier. I don't absolutely trust the experts to be right, seeing they are so wrong about why I'm fat, but it gives me some satisfaction anyway to know I eat the "right" way. The oatmeal cooks up to about two bowlfuls and I eat it. I work the rest of the morning on my dissertation.

When I start to get hungry, in the early afternoon, I knock off writing and heat a pan of bean soup. I eat two and a half bowls of the soup and put the rest away. All day, while I'm cooking and eating, while I'm writing, in the back of my mind I'm carrying on a conversation with Robert Pool, with my mother, with the world at large which thinks I have to be an indulgent eater because I'm fat. Does this look like hedonism to you? I say. Maybe the average person would only want one bowl of oatmeal, one and a half of soup, but if I don't eat the amount my appetite prompts me to now then I'll be ferociously hungry in a few hours and have to eat a lot more than I want to in order to catch up again. Eating is a chore that it's better to keep on top of. It's only oatmeal, it's only beans—hello! The food I eat is just not that *exciting*!

Secretly I have a science-fiction fantasy about a totalitarian culture where everyone eats the same thing—some kind of nutrient broth or the people equivalent of dry dogfood—something perfected over many generations of clinical trials to be the optimal nutritional balance for human beings. Something that tastes utterly terrible and is provided for free by the government in gigantic public vats for anyone to go and suck as much out as hunger prompts them to. In a place like that it would be obvious that a person who eats more than average must be hungrier than average. That a person with a fat body must be different physiologically, not just in their habits. It's a childish, unrealistic scenario, but still I wish I lived in that society. I really do.

I think about my mother. She of all people should know the intensity of my drive to excel, the level of commitment I can bring to bear. She should *remember* how I drove myself to the point of injury when I was in my twenties. Does she really think that somehow my personality has now changed to the exact opposite? I can sort of forgive strangers who assume I'm weak-willed and lazy, food-loving, addicted to soft easy pleasures. But not my own mother.

I think about Robert Pool. He mentions the statistical argument that only something like 5 or 7 percent of all people who try to lose weight succeed long-term, but he calls it a "convenient excuse." At one point he describes some women who lost weight by eating a diet of mostly complex carbohydrates. Then later, like statistically average dieters, they regained all the weight they had lost. "It is not known whether the women backslid" in their eating habits, Pool writes. Such a sly, nasty insinuation, I think. *I* know what happened to those women. Either their bodies learned to refatten on the carbohydrate diet, or else the women got cumulatively more and more starved, and they finally gave in and ate what would relieve them. There isn't a woman in the world who wouldn't stay thin if she could find a way to do it that was even halfway physically comfortable. I spend most days eating mostly complex carbohydrates too, but at bedtime if I feel hungry I'll drink a glass of milk to catch up on fat and protein. If I don't—I've tried this repeatedly—I'll get into a state of fat deficit and be continuously ravenous even if I eat carbohydrates until my stomach can't hold any more.

To think that Pool is one of the liberals! One of the people who lay out all the evidence about homeostatic control of fat stores and then say, "So what does all this mean for those of us who'd like to shed a few pounds?" One of those who readily agree that diets don't work long-term but still think that "permanent lifestyle changes" surely would. I tell myself these are the people I have to work with; I won't find any better allies. But I don't have to like it. Permanent lifestyle changes! Anger makes me yip out loud.

All afternoon, I make detailed notes from the Pool book, immersing myself in his thoughts, so when I go for my workout I feel like he's still hanging around in my mind, observing me. I go to Bear Creek trail for an hour of my peculiar form of low-impact running—if it's not a misnomer to call a 300-pound woman's fastest form of locomotion "running."

My private word for it, what I record in my exercise diary, is "traveling." I slide my feet out in front of me fast and far, but I don't pick them up high, so they never hit the ground very hard. My hips have to swivel more than a normal person's would, to let my big thighs swing past each other, but when I get going it feels fluid and powerful. I only travel on dirt or turf trails, never hard surfaces like sidewalks. I can travel about three miles an hour, and it's my favorite workout. But I make sure not to do it oftener than once every five days, alternating with swimming and ski machine to protect myself from overuse injuries.

I imagine showing my workout log to Pool. An hour of aerobic exercise, four or more times a week, see? Stretches and strength training too, almost every day, see? In terms of my own body's exertion, I work just as intensely as a thin athlete, though my fastest time per mile is about 18 minutes. At the 1.5 mile marker, I check my watch and my heartrate. My time so far is 28 minutes—a little better than average. My heart rate is around 85 percent of max: I like the drama of intense efforts, and I tend to work out at the higher end of my aerobic range.

I turn around to travel back. My mind churns. Of all the foods I eat regularly, the only one I really consider luxurious is cheese. I eat more than a pound a week, usually, several ounces a day on average—that's not a huge amount, surely? Still, it's the kind of rich, pleasurable food that Pool or my mother could point to if they were trying to show me that my own choices cause my "weight problem." But I know pleasure has nothing to do with it. It's true that I like cheese, but that's not why it's one of my staples. It's a simple way to get myself fed enough quickly, without a lot of cooking. That's all. That's my reason.

The ghostly presences of Pool and my mother exchange skeptical glances. Pool says insinuatingly, "No one can honestly say 'My leptin made me eat that cheese.' "

I know I'm right but I don't know how to prove it. It would be a terrible inconvenience to give up cheese. Then I would have to eat more of some other energy-dense food, like meat, or else a lot more of something less rich, and I don't want to do either. I picture my mother rolling her eyes at my intransigence. More than once she's told me I should drink 1% milk instead of 2%. I've tried 1%, and I have nothing against it, but I always find I need to drink twice as much, so what's the point? My mother wouldn't believe that I didn't care how the milk tasted; she wouldn't believe there was any such thing as a body feeling a fat deficit. "Why don't you buy skim milk, then, and hold a stick of butter between your teeth while you drink it?"

I have half a mile left to travel and I try to hold a brisk pace. My body feels good, well lubricated, and my mind is calmer now, floaty. An idea comes to me from nowhere: tofu.

Back in the 70s, at the height of my family's fling with small-planetish alternative lifestyles, my mother made a few brief experiments cooking with tofu. Tofu is high-fat and high-protein, like cheese. I could eat tofu sandwiches, throw tofu into my rice or my salad. It would do everything for me that cheese does now, and possibly be healthier if the experts are right. Of course, I've always found tofu repulsive, but so much the better, to prove I don't eat for pleasure. It will be just like the government-issue nutrient vats. No more cheese, ever. Simple.

Mr. Pool, I say, I've got your permanent lifestyle changes right here. As I throw my leg forward I slap the inside of my upper thigh. Right here.

I'm back at my starting point and I walk around, cooling off. I have my hands on my hips and I try to project pride and confidence in my body, in case anyone is looking. The tofu plan has me excited, although it is essentially pointless. Because who am I doing it for? I won't be making any announcements to my mother, and I don't even know Pool. Certainly I don't expect any physical results. The only change is going to be if a doctor challenges me, as some do, to describe what I eat. Then instead of saying I eat moderate amounts of cheese, and have the doctor think I'm fooling myself, I can casually mention that I never eat it. The way I now say, Oh, no, I never eat desserts, I never eat junk food. No, that's right, none at all. While I'm at it, I think, I'll cut out the bedtime milk too. If I'm running a fat deficit, I can fix it equally well with some olive oil on bread. Whole wheat bread, of course. I'll eat like a 19th-century Pima Indian, more or less.

August

My first tofu sandwiches made me gag, but I steeled myself and got them down. I've tried different brands of tofu now and different degrees of firmness. I've tried it raw, microwaved, fried, and boiled. If I put it with strong-flavored greens, like escarole or mustard, it's less disagreeable. Gradually, my throat stops rebelling against the gelatinous texture. The flavor isn't really unpleasant, though it's nothing to write home about. It's mild and nondescript. Tofu doesn't taste beany, like you might expect, but it doesn't have no flavor, either, like my mother used to claim in the 1970s. It tastes exactly like tofu.

Sometime in the third week of the tofu exercise, a big white glob falls from the sandwich to my plate and I swipe it up and into my mouth with the bread crust. Only afterwards do I realize that I just treated tofu as if it were herbed goat cheese, or some other expensive delicacy I didn't want to lose any of. I have turned a corner. My brain has rewired itself. I wonder if I could retrain myself to eat other foods I dislike.

I mail my mother a copy of the Pool book review and the next time we talk she enthuses. "It sounds like a wonderful book."

"Yeah," I say. "Well, I had some serious reservations, actually, but there wasn't enough space to go into it, in 500 words." I don't elaborate.

September

I experiment with leaving oil out of my oatmeal and my potatoes. I stop frying anything. I expect these experiments to fail and my body to go into a raging fat deficit, as always in the past, and I warn myself in advance not to let the situation get desperate. At bedtime, or whenever else I need to, I'll eat more tofu, more oil and bread. I expect to go through oil much faster, and I buy a bottle of olive and another of canola (the monounsaturates that experts recommend), but actually after a while it's clear that my oil use has strangely declined.

Something is happening to me. I don't get hungry as quickly as I used to, or as intensely. And my feelings of satiety are more muted too. In the past my hunger patterns were like a series of steep hills and sharp dropoffs. Now the slope in both directions is gentle, almost imperceptible. I thought at first the difference was just my imagination but now I'm sure it isn't.

Food tastes different too, stronger-flavored, like when I was a child. Vegetables in particular seem both stronger and subtler, their component elements weaving together in a complex way. Slices of bread—whole-grain, of course –are rich enough to be pleasant eating absolutely bare, nothing on them. Same for potatoes. A former roommate who was a vegan once told me that she preferred the flavor of food with no oil added to it. I thought at the time she was just striking a pose, but maybe this is what she meant. Maybe your palate makes an adjustment, recalibrates itself for whatever environment it finds itself in. Just like fruit has long been the top of my sweetness scale, now peanut butter, hummus, and tofu are the top of the richness scale. So perhaps vegetables and grains have been yanked upward to the middle.

When I pack lunches, I have a greater sense of freedom. In the past, as I left the house I would have to consider that in four or five hours at the most I would need to eat a substantial amount of food. I'd take with me high-volume foods like fruit or vegetables, and bread or rice, but I'd also have to include something dense and proteiny to make it through the day. If there wouldn't be a fridge or microwave available, the options were limited: peanut butter, cheese, nuts, boiled eggs. Now it's like the leash has gotten longer—I can go six or seven hours with nothing at all—and a couple baked potatoes thrown into my backpack, or a container of oatmeal that I can make in five minutes, is enough to tide me over no matter where I go or how long I stay.

I love not having to spend so much time planning about eating. But there's one other change, too, something alarming. My body is a little bit thinner. Every other time in my life this has ever happened, it's been the prelude to getting fatter.

I can insert two fingers between my body and the side of the bathtub.

Feeling less squeezed than usual in the car, I drive to St. Louis to pick my mother up at the airport. I hope she won't notice that my body is different. I can't bear it if she praises me for this. If she is relieved and happy that I have given up my crackpot ideas.

I feel vaguely guilty, as though I'd been unfaithful to my ideals. But I'm not, I'm not. Really I'm doing nothing different from what I've always done: eat when I'm hungry and not otherwise, and not weigh myself. But what about my metabolism—is it possible to enter into some mild form of starvation, accidentally? I push the thoughts aside. I'll worry about it when I'm alone.

If Mom notices any difference in me, she says nothing. Over the next two days I show her around my new apartment, the campus, the Grindstone wilderness area which is one of my favorite workout spots. We go back and forth across Grindstone, hiking and looking at the late-blooming wildflowers. We get home late and hungry; I head straight for the fridge and lay out food on the table.

"What's that?" my mother says.

"Tofu," I say. It's the extra soft kind; I dip into it with a butter knife and spread it on toast. "Want some? Mm-mm!"

"No, thanks," my mother says. I eat bread, tofu, carrots, tomatoes, spinach. She has bread with peanut butter, the vegetables, walnuts, raisins, and some cheese and 1% milk I've bought especially for her visit. I hope she doesn't notice that I'm not having cheese. I take a small handful of raisins and nuts. They're so rich that I don't want much.

I make excuses not to go to restaurants. I have people over to my place and I serve bean soup, lentils, squash soup, curried potatoes, rice, polenta, tabouli, hummus, vegetables, tortillas, or bread in various combinations. No one says anything about a change in

Thanksgiving 2001. None of my pants fit anymore.

my lifestyle. It's not sufficiently different from what I always did to attract anyone's attention. In the bathtub I can put my entire sideways fist beside my thigh.

November

Laura is the chief hostess at Thanksgiving but her mother, sisters, and in-laws also provide much of the food. Every vegetable dish seems to contain bacon or bacon grease; it's a southern thing. Laura's congenitally thin younger sister goes on about how fat the family dog has gotten, how she wishes her husband would lose weight, but he just won't do it. She asks for someone to pass the bacon rolls again, please. I reflect that the last time I ate bacon was in 1993.

I don't want to be conspicuous, so in the end I have a little dab of almost everything that isn't a dessert or junk food, though I'm aware that my categories are somewhat arbitrary. Bacon rolls are off-limits; green beans with grease-laden onion-ring topping aren't? I take some tossed salad and try to pick around the bacon crumbs. The bacony squash puree hits my mouth as something that has a pleasant flavor but is strangely and undesirably *thick*, like drinking half and half straight. The mashed yams are thick in the same way (with butter, I guess), and too sweet besides. The two types of stuffing are thick and thicker. The slice of turkey seems meltingly tender, as if it were made of velvet scraps. I have a great slab of mostly-whole-grain rye bread that Laura made especially for me and I use it to dilute the rich foods. Laura's mother looks anxious when I refuse the deep-fried hors d'oeuvres, the soda and other sweet drinks, and the pies, but she doesn't press me. Evidently Laura has coached her. I get through the meal decently, finishing about the same time as the others. Calorie for calorie, I think I've eaten less than anyone at the table, but I feel fuller than I have in a long time, and heavily sleepy.

At night when everyone's gone, Laura brings out a wrapped box. "I got you your Christmas present early," she says. "I bet you can guess what it is, can't you?"

I'm bewildered. "No, I have no idea." But when I get the paper off and the lid up, and see pin stripes on dark fabric, it does seem like I ought to have known.

"Size 28, right?" Laura says.

I burst into tears.

"What is it, what's the matter?" Laura says. "Don't worry: I still have the receipt if you don't want it."

"Laura," I say, "something really strange is happening to me."

Chapter 21

Vanity

2003-2004

For a while there I really found it difficult to keep my hands off my ass. It was just so strange! It had been my largest part, the one that required the most managing out in public. I'd case the furniture as soon as I arrived at a party, looking for the chair that could hold that great globe, first of all without breaking underneath, second of all without comically disappearing as though sucked up inside, third of all comfortably. Picking my way through a crowded room, I'd turn my butt sideways and ease it around corners like maneuvering a big couch through an angled hallway. In private, even both hands together felt wispy and insubstantial when laid against one cheek. Now that was all changed. Now a buttock was the sort of thing that a single spread hand could cover, more or less. Whenever I happened to be alone, my hand would wander back and check it again. In the locker room at Student Rec, in the TA office, on the trail at Rockbridge Park: Yes, really. Just one hand would do it.

Like so many other things in my life, I fell into yoga by accident, because I read a book. The author suggested that many of people's chronic pain or repetitive-motion problems were caused by the way modern life constricted their range of motion. Pictures in the book showed people embedded in what looked like a plexiglas box whose height was the distance between their shoulders and their waists. Their arms were effectively imprisoned within this box as they worked at their desks. Their heads and shoulders curved constantly forward as their attention focused inside the box. Exercise as generally practiced wouldn't counteract the long-term warping pressures of the box, because it was still just repetitive, restricted motion, usually chosen to favor whatever major muscle groups already worked the best anyway. It was true that my own favorite workouts put the greatest stress onto my already splendid leg muscles and did nothing to address the caving-in of my chest, the forward creep of my shoulders.

Maybe, I thought, I should simply play more. I envisioned myself learning something brand new, a pleasurable activity that would use many different little muscles in unusual ways. Something like belly dancing, maybe. Right around then Averill told me about some yoga classes that were very cheap because they were at a gym subsidized by university research. I joined.

The clientele at this gym are all either university employees or else the old people who are providing the research data. Barbara teaches the "Gentle" class three times a week to a handful of old people who feel like trying yoga, while Laurie teaches "Vigorous" to five of us from the English Department, plus the yoga groupies who've followed her here from her other job at Wilson's Gym. Laurie is, by general agreement, the most exciting Ashtanga teacher in town. She ripples with upper-body muscle and a guru's charisma. She runs us through rapid sequences of poses which I later learn are called "vinyasas," which include moves a bit like push-ups. She guides us into flowing gymnastic postures that require balance as well as great exertion, like the one that begins in what I think of as "pretzel" pose—a lunge with one arm under a thigh, hands clasped behind the back—and shifts to standing erect on what had been the back leg, with what had been the lunge leg now pointing up to the ceiling, all without letting go of the clasped hands. I'm hooked.

Before or after yoga, I step onto the cardio machines in the main room, since it's never crowded and why not get my money's worth. It feels weird at my age to be the youngest person working out. For a couple decades now I've always been the fattest person in the gyms and student rec centers I've frequented. More recently I've also been one of the oldest. I wish I had a dollar for every time some little twenty-year-old PE-majoring staffer accosted me on the machines in my fat workout days.

"Whoa, take it easy there, don't try to do everything in one day. Getting in shape is a gradual process."

"I'm only doing my regular workout—does something look wrong?"

"Well, you're going at it pretty hard. You don't want to overdo and get burned out. Have you signed up for our fitness assessment and weight-tracking program?"

"I'm not interested in that."

"Well, make sure to drink plenty of water."

Yeah, thanks, you don't know me from Adam and I've been working out since before you were born. Usually I managed not to say this out loud.

And now, and now… Of all the bodies here, mine is actually the one that most closely resembles the gym stereotype of fitness, instead of being furthest from it. It's hard to get my mind around it. I reach my hand back and feel the size of a buttock again. The room's not completely deserted but nobody's looking and anyway the ranking hardbodies at the gym are always entitled to examine their body parts, aren't they? Like the men you see fondling their muscles in the weight room.

The leftmost of the rowing machines faces directly into one of the wall mirrors, so I can see the muscles working in my shoulders as I pull. With the fat gone from my upper body I can actually see the divisions in the deltoid itself, directly under my skin. I find them fascinating.

The gazing into mirrored walls, the intense self-absorption—these are exactly the things social critics decry about gym culture: elevating narcissism to a virtue. Am I doing that or am I doing something else?

M, my mate, is the only person who ever sees me naked. "Your skin has tightened up a lot," she says. On my arms it has. Possibly my face and neck too. But not even the elasticized yoga pants can prevent my two handfuls of buttock from spreading themselves thin as pancake batter over the seat of the rowing machine until two floppy edges protrude on either side and oscillate in the breeze created by my forward and backward thrusting. This is also visually interesting.

Somehow I've picked up a few red bumps on the side of my thigh, from bug bites or maybe poison ivy, I don't know. Instead of getting better they spread and then start to drip. I go to Student Health. The nurse takes me to the scale first thing, of course. How else should you begin a skin treatment?

I've seen this nurse before: prematurely gray, rough skin, a few rogue patches of curling facial hair, a squat pear-shaped body, probably considers herself fat, though actually in this office the average nurse is bigger. Anyway, nobody would call her pretty. I want to feel my solidarity with her and every other less-than-beautiful woman, but right now she's representing the fat-hating medical orthodoxy so she's out of luck.

Some fat activists make a political point of refusing the scale, but I can't bring myself to be quite so conspicuous when all that would happen is I'd get branded as a nut. So my official policy on being weighed is that it's nothing to do with me and I barely notice it happening. Let them engage in their misguided rituals if they want.

As always, the nurse initially underestimates my weight and has to backtrack and shift the larger block. I'm 154 pounds. But I'm roughly the same size I used to be when I weighed 135-140 as a muscular teenager, so does that mean I now have 15 more pounds of skin than I did then? It's possible. Heft a full-length leather coat and you'll see it's heavy.

As the nurse records my number in my chart she also has all my past numbers available. "It's remarkable how much weight you've lost over the last two years," she says. "Congratulations." She's not speaking primarily as nurse to patient, I can tell. In fact this is the very opposite of condescension: the nurse is, so to speak, bowing to me in the ritual offering that feminine friendship requires. Verbal tribute must be paid to any woman who has become thinner, if you don't want to seem like a bad sport, resentful when someone else succeeds. The nurse is acknowledging an achievement that for most women ranks up there with winning a Pulitzer.

But I can't go along with it. Can't, won't, whatever. Not even to avoid getting branded as a nut. It's just not right! This is *not* an achievement and I deserve nothing I didn't deserve as a fat woman, nothing this nurse doesn't deserve now. Okay, Mom, I know, a truly gracious woman would just say "thank you," would accept the nurse's courtesy in the generous spirit she intends. But what about my own values? I have to defend them even though I can't possibly make them understood. I'm stuck between two impossibles and it makes me angry. There should be some way to rise above the impasse, some detour that will take me out in an unexpected direction, through a third dimension.

"Well, I really don't think people ought to put as much importance on that as they do," I say. It comes out more snappish than I meant. Atta girl, to be high-minded, attack the kind-hearted!

The nurse draws back, surprised. "Yes, I think you're right," she says mildly.

Before yoga, just as I'm getting onto an elliptical machine, pulling up the menu, one of the gym employees stops me. "Can I use you for a demonstration?" He's doing check-in for a new person. Without looking closely, I register a soft-looking woman, forty-something or maybe fifty.

"Sure." I get off the machine, readjust the height of its arms, and get back on while he provides a running commentary. He corrects me—safety first!—when I step directly from the floor onto a stirrup, since that's a part that can move. "Oh, yeah, guess you're right," I say.

"And now," he says in a jocular tone, "we will tactfully avert our eyes while she enters her weight."

"I'm sure *she's* not worried about that," the woman says, rather sullenly. She's shaped similar to the rogue-haired nurse but is considerably prettier, with softer well-groomed skin. Unlike the gallant nurse, she begrudges the thin elite their status: why should anyone outrank her? This lady's a kindred spirit and my heart goes out to her.

"You're right," I say mildly, though I know she doesn't mean it quite the way I'm pretending: "That weight business is a big fuss over nothing."

The trainer leaves the woman alone on the machine to my left but in five minutes he's back. "Whoa, take it easy there! Don't overdo it on the first day."

"I'm not going any faster than *she* is," the woman says, pointing at me.

"Well, I'm sure she knows what she's doing, don't you think?"

The woman shuts up and looks sour. I'm indignant too. This kid doesn't know me from fucking Adam! But I keep my mouth shut.

Several months later, the cheap gym eliminates all its yoga classes, "in order to serve the needs of our clients better," and I follow Laurie to Wilson's Gym where the monthly fee is three times as much. Befitting the high fees, Wilson's has a decided corporate sheen. That has its attractions, actually. The equipment is better and there's more of it. There are more classes offered and a bigger yoga room to spread out the mats in, though when Laurie's teaching it gets pretty full anyway.

The lights can be dimmed, and all the teachers do that, but apart from that the yoga room has the same slick look and mirrored walls as the cardio room and the weight room. Two senior professors from the English Department go to these classes regularly and they make me nervous though I like them well enough on campus. The gym atmosphere tends to inspire small talk about staying in shape. This close to graduation, I don't want anyone who outranks me professionally seeing me in my yoga pants or thinking about my physical transformation. I'll need them for job recommendations and I can't risk getting visibly pissed off or acting eccentric.

Since the English Department tends to cluster in the right side of the room, I go to the left. The back left corner seems attractively inconspicuous. Standing here in the seam between the left mirror and the back mirror, I can listen to the teacher's directions and lose my awareness of everyone else in the room, focusing exclusively on my own body. I make sure to arrive early for class to spread my mat in the same corner each time.

The two teachers who aren't Laurie aren't as good, of course, and don't draw big crowds, though each has her die-hard core of fans. Linda was Laurie's student and her classes are basically Laurie lite, with fewer of the poses that require great strength, and more poses like pigeon that you can only do properly if you're as flexible as Linda is, cocking up one elbow behind her head as she clasps the opposite cocked foot.

FAT: The Story of Life With My Body

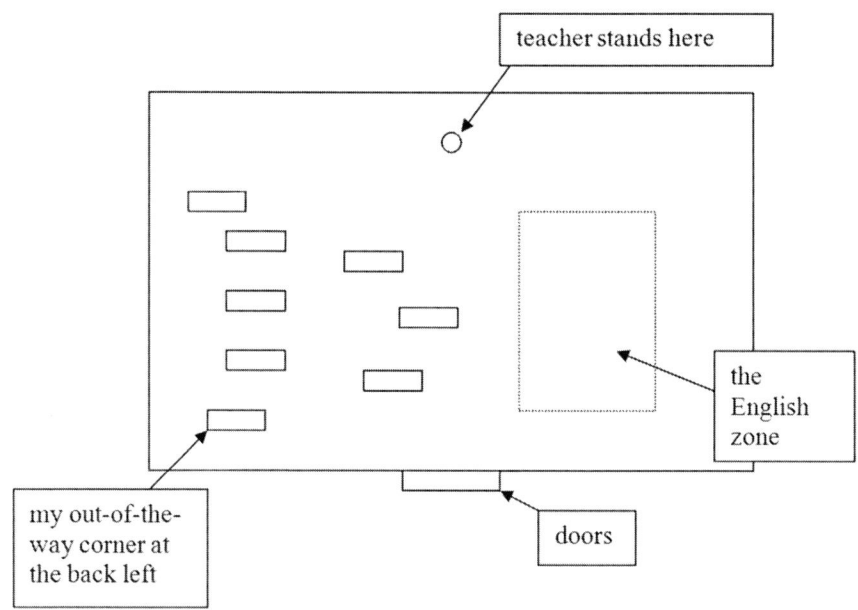

JoAnn is said to be one of the Wilson family that owns the gym; she's been teaching aerobics and weight-lifting for years and only recently added a yoga certificate. Her routines involve a great many push-ups. Before each class she demonstrates the correct "upper plank" position that precedes *chaturanga*. "You might not yet have the upper-body strength to do this," she says and demonstrates two incorrect sagging postures that might be taken by weaker women. "If not, just put your knees right on the ground." JoAnn gives her directions through a microphone, presumably from the reasonable desire to save her voice, not because she's deliberately setting out to sound pompous. "Give up all sense of competition," she intones periodically during class. She strolls among the mats, getting down on the floor to redemonstrate plank position and *chaturanga* to women who are sagging.

M's friend Kim goes to Wilson's too. "After Laurie, my second choice for yoga is Linda," I say, making conversation.

"I like JoAnn's better," she says.

"Ugh, really?"

"You should try her strength-training class. She's more in her element there."

"Yeah?" After yoga, sometimes, I've seen women setting up for something else in that room, with barbells and some kind of blocks. It looks fun. Secretly I have a passionate desire for more upper-body strength. If I could stand on my hands or do forearm balances like Laurie! I've been doing a bit of tree climbing at the park, the exercise-as-play thing, and my arms are a teeny bit stronger, but not a lot.

"It's called 'Body-Sculpting'. Do you want to go with me next time?"

"Um, no. I don't care for the concept of body-sculpting."

"It's not what it sounds like, it's mostly just some weights incorporated into a cardio routine. I think you'd enjoy it."

"Maybe, but I'm still not going to anything called 'body-sculpting.'"

"Why not?"

"Because bodies shouldn't be treated like raw materials for art, and I think gyms have some responsibility to promote health, and that attitude's not health."

Kim has the social skills and self-control not to reveal it by her face if she thinks I'm a nut. "Okay, so it's a stupid name, but it's a good *class*."

"I won't participate in something called 'body-sculpting' no matter what kind of class it is."

"That seems a little…" Kim gropes for a delicate phrase: "disproportionate."

"Would you go to a class that was called 'Harpoon a Fat Chick'? Would you go to one called…." I grope for a phrase powerful enough to catapult my feelings across the gulf that separates me from the whole rest of the female world: " 'Aryan-Elite Supremacy Training'?"

Kim's carefully arranged face shows me that I blew it again: this is one of those occasions on which my eloquence will not be changing the world. Vanity of vanities, I mumble inside my head, trying to rise above embarrassments the Ecclesiastes way. All is vanity.

The Wilson's cardio room has rows and rows of treadmills, ellipticals, stairmasters, and stationary bicycles, as well as a good handful of ski machines and rowing machines. Racks of televisions line the walls just above them. After five o'clock the room fills up with a bobbing sea of hypnotized faces. These people look like cult members. Mostly professional-class white people in their thirties and forties and fifties. More women than men. The few round faces bend lower than the others over their devotions as if in contrition; the pudgy bodies are seeking redemption, while the slender, secure in their salvation, glow in righteousness.

There's a woman I often see in the locker room who looks a bit like me; anyway she's about my age and height, slender, small-breasted, and has dark shortish hair. Her spine as she walks is straight but not rigid, self-possessed and confident. Dressing and undressing, she isn't furtive with her body as many women are in the locker room, but there's nevertheless a reserve in the way she carries herself. Like an aristocrat whose position at the top is so secure that it doesn't even arise as an issue in her mind. Like a prosperous Calvinist's wealth, her body is both the reward and the proof of a life well lived. After a week or two she begins nodding to me as we pass, as if to acknowledge I am also one of the elect.

I don't want it. If I have to be sorted into one group or the other, the high-status or the low-, then I'd prefer to stick with the underdogs I've been with my whole adult life, the fat.

Of course the slender woman's attitudes may be nothing like the ones I've imagined for her. But then what does go through her mind as she steps onto the locker-room scale each day, holding her arms open, as casually reverent as a priest at the altar?

I fly to San Diego for the MLA conference, where I have six job interviews spread over two days. I wear a black-and-white checked suit that's a hand-me-down from M's stepmother and carry a leather briefcase that my mother gave me. Late in the afternoon on the first day I step into the women's bathroom on the first floor of the main hotel. It's crowded with other academic women, mostly dressed in suits like me. The few in their twenties are probably looking for their first jobs, but the others in their thirties, forties, and fifties, will be professors. I blend right in. No one looking at me would know I'm just a lowly graduate student. My burdens fall away from me: I'm finished for the day, I could be the peer of anyone here, and I'm dressed well enough not to be intimidated by the elegant hotel. I get into line for the stalls. This floor is the floor-equivalent of a pin-striped suit: big squares of what appears to be black marble with light-colored veins. The mirrors cover the whole wall opposite the stalls from floor to ceiling. The line gradually shortens ahead of me and lengthens behind me. I can examine the other women in the mirror without seeming to stare. Suddenly I notice: in this lineup of two dozen women my age, give or take a decade, I'm one of the best-looking, if not the best. It's like the floor's dropped out from under me but am I soaring or falling? Mostly what I feel is astonishment. I look again to verify that my first impression was correct: most people would consider me good-looking for a fortyish woman. In my clothes, anyway. Out of sight underneath them is my skin in its convolutions. My awareness of it anchors me.

"How was the MLA?" One of the English profs is early for yoga and chats me up in the hallway. It's the young American Lit guy who's married to the medievalist. Neither one of them has anything directly to do with my work, so I'm at ease.

"It was an eye-opener," I say. "Made me feel like a real grown-up." People from the previous class trickle out past us. "I guess I'll go ahead and put my mat down and stake out my corner."

"I think it's great," he says, "the way you go straight to the front of the room every time."

I say yeah, smile and nod even though I'm flabbergasted—the *front* of the room? Is he crazy? I place my mat in the back left corner as always. As the warm-up starts I'm still trying to make sense out of it. I'm as far away from Laurie as anyone in the room.

"Step to the front of your mats for *surya namaskar*," Laurie says. Well… it's true that the "front" of the mat faces the left wall, the direction we turn for sun salutations and the other vinyasas. So I guess someone *could* perceive the left wall as the "front" one.

"*Chaturanga*," Laurie says. I face the floor. "Up dog," Laurie says. I push my torso upright like I'm rolling along a curved track, and there's my face in the mirror again. "Down dog." My hands are pointed toward the now-unseen mirror. If I think of that direction as *front*, then everyone else is behind me now, it's true. "Left foot forward, warrior one," says Laurie, and there I am in the mirror again.

Oh, my god. If I have an unobstructed view of my body in the mirror, then for every other observer, my body is between their eyes and the mirror. I *am* at the front—how could I have not noticed it before? To everyone else in this room I must look exactly as the slender woman looks to me when she weighs herself: publicly self-satisfied.

It's the longest and least relaxing yoga class I've ever been through.

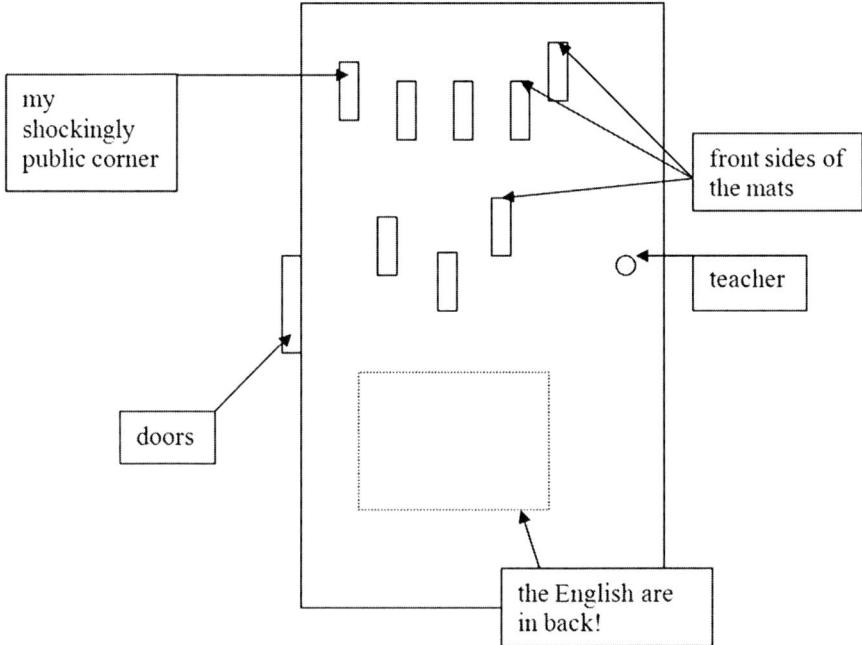

I have to change something but what? It's intolerable if the English Department thinks I've been flaunting my body. Yeah, she lost some weight, next thing you know she's prancing around in form-fitting yoga pants, eager to display her body.... Thin pride, the flip side of fat shame. How can I prove that my real philosophy is the opposite?

All right, instead of wearing yoga pants, I'll put on shorts, and let my thighs show. My thighs, my thighs, the center of my strength. Under the fat, packed in tight, the giant muscles have always been there, powerful but invisible. Now you can see their movements intermittently, like animals inside a big cloth sack. The subcutaneous fat that remains no longer has any firm location, changing position like a compass needle, pointing continuously straight toward gravity no matter what position my thighs are in. That cellulite which most women feel stalking them from behind, from their flanks, can come right around to the front for me: inverted, in plow pose, it dangles over my face. I regard it without distaste. It's been many, many years since I thought of my fat as an enemy and I'm not about to begin now.

There's a great variety of textures to see in the skin of my thighs. From draping like a fabric, it can tighten over the tensed quadriceps if I'm standing, or holding a thigh horizontal in front of me. Then again it can dimple, pleat, or bunch. It can wave or look grainy, making me think of wet soil. The old stretch marks stand out like worm casts, whiter than their background, several dozen nested together. M has expressed pleasure in these loose places of my skin. The softness, the extra-ness of it, she says, are a luxury. "It's sensual, rippling, like the way a rich yogurt feels on your tongue." I know what she means although this is not my own feeling and I doubt anyone else would share it.

I could wear shorts to show all this, bring forward my real pride: that never since my epiphany at age 22 have I repudiated my body. That I am a nonparticipant in the competition to look attractive. That in fact I reject the entire system of self-discipline and self-evaluation that governs so many women's lives and marks their bodies ever since this generation became convinced that thin equals health equals worth and therefore beauty is not, after all, a superficial pursuit.

Not all of this could be read directly from the skin of my thighs, maybe, but at least it would be obvious that my motives for going to the gym had nothing to do with what previous generations used to call vanity....

It's no use. My drive to be an admirable person is hopelessly entwined with my drive never to be less admired than others, and so there can be no absolute escape from comparisons, pride, envy, and resentment. Flashing my thighs would only be an effort to shift the ground of competition from physical to moral superiority.

Certain lines of literature can assert themselves in my mind as familiarly and insistently as my own mother's face, comforting or disapproving, and one comes to me now from Joyce's "Araby": "I saw myself as a creature driven and derided by vanity; and my eyes burned with anguish and anger."

At the next class I wear my yoga pants as usual but turn right instead of left coming in the door. I put my mat down at the back of the English zone.

Chapter 22

Equilibrium

Now

The following things which were true of me at age 14 are not true anymore: (1) I thought I was a genius. (2) I lived with my parents, who were (3) married to each other, and (4) they were vigorous adults in their mid-forties, and although I knew I wasn't really in charge of and responsible for my own life, I felt myself (5) fully competent to understand and control it if only I were free from interference.

Back then I had a few clear ideas, from having read a few books. You'd think the thousands of books I've read since would increase my confidence that I know how to think about things, but it seems to have had the opposite effect: theory upon theory upon contradictory theory. But with my parents in their seventies, divorced, far away, and declining in their powers, I'm it. I'm the ranking adult decision-maker. There's no other alternative, for me or anyone else in that position. The human body doesn't come with an instruction manual. What can we do but try to think for ourselves, sift through the mountains of evidence and then, tossing our own very lives into the balance, make our best guesses?

This is my current theory. It's clear from the recidivism evidence (the patterns of people regaining lost weight) that the human body has some way of encouraging fat stores to return to a constant level. But this designated level is not necessarily set at a single immutable setpoint for a lifetime. At any given time, under specific circumstances, your body has a point of equilibrium, which it will maintain if you eat in accordance with your appetite. If you force yourself below the equilibrium point by fighting appetite, you will be constantly miserable until you return to it. If you somehow wind up above equilibrium point, your body will rapidly return to normal without your needing to diet in the usual sense of that word.

At 14, my body was trying to complete the necessary adjustments of puberty and perhaps it needed another five pounds or so of fat to make me fertile, keep me reliably menstruating. Fat's not an inert ballast, remember, but a live, hormone-generating tissue! The leptin made by fat is in constant communication and interaction with all the body's other hormone systems, including the ones responsible for sexual development, including the ones responsible for appetite. If I'd been willing to leave the new equilibrium alone, I might well have stayed comfortably at 125 pounds until middle age or pregnancy, whichever came first. But I didn't leave it alone. I plunged my body into deprivation conditions, repeatedly, over the course of many years, and my equilibrium point was gradually nudged higher and higher. Perhaps this upward drift is merely some kind of accidental side effect of periodic famines, or perhaps some built-in evolutionary safety device reprograms us depending how harsh the prevailing local conditions appear to be. Women might be more reprogrammable in this respect than men, since they're the ones who will need to carry a pregnancy to term.

Anyway, starting at age 22 I then spent about twenty years leaving my body alone in its now much fatter equilibrium, eating according to appetite, exercising but getting no thinner. The nutritional environment I created for myself was somewhat unusual for an American, since I avoided foods with added sugars and fats, ate little to no refined flours or grains, and relatively little meat. But I did use cheese and milk as nutritional staples.

Something about removing milk products from my nutritional environment had an effect on my established equilibrium, causing some kind of reset. Was it the removal of saturated fat? Or the lactose? The increased total proportion of complex carbohydrates in comparison to other nutrients? Ditto ditto fiber? I have no idea. But since this was the only significant change in my habits, I attribute the cascade of physiological changes to that. After a few weeks or maybe two months of the new regimen, my appetite patterns changed significantly. Not my behavior. I ate smaller amounts and less often that year because I just didn't get as hungry. I was above my equilibrium point. This state persisted for a little more than a year, while my fat stores were decreasing down to my new equilibrium point, and then I stabilized and my appetite returned to something that felt normal to me.

These days I try not to concern myself about my body fat and I never weigh myself and I never try to restrict the amount I eat (though I avoid modern processed foods to a socially abnormal degree). I continue to exercise about as much as I did when fat, and so far I have continued to be fairly thin.

People with a vested interest in the American weight-loss culture will point to my experiences as evidence that people can, too, lose weight. I'll concede this much: It may well be the case that people generally have more than one equilibrium potentially available to them, depending on their activity level and what kinds of food they make available to their bodies.

It seems clear that contrary to what I believed for a long time, it is indeed possible for a high equilibrium point to be readjusted downward, at least under some conditions and for some people, the ones who are like me in the relevant aspects. But which aspects of my case are relevant? Even assuming that I'm genetically typical, my life history has been quite atypical. To dial back an elevated equilibrium point, is it necessary to begin by spending 20 years not dieting? Is it necessary *not* to have weight loss as your goal? For me, those were certainly factors. If I had been trying to lose weight, if I had even believed weight loss to be possible, there's no way I would have created the precise set of circumstances which so surprisingly (accidentally!) made me thinner. My drive to excel is such that I'd undoubtedly have eaten too little, exercised too much, and sooner or later something would have given way or broken. It was only because thinness was not an ideal of mine that I managed to hold onto my harmonious relationships with food and sports when everything else in my world shifted under my feet.

Should I preach now?

If I had the power to change the world, I'd say let's all stop thinking and talking in terms of "weight" when we talk about promoting public health. Instead of an "obesity" epidemic, let's fight the junk-food and sedentariness epidemic. Since the energy-balance equations make such poor predictors for weight gain or loss in controlled laboratory experiments, it means that you can't just weigh someone and say what their past behavior has been. You don't know that the thin person has wholesome eating patterns and is active; you don't know that the fat person doesn't and isn't. The fat person you see on the street may have endured more hunger than you can imagine. There may be large numbers of fat people who should more accurately be regarded as part-time anorexics than as habitual overeaters.

Measuring weight by means of a scale has turned into a convenient shortcut for health providers, because it's so easy to do, whereas habits are very difficult to ascertain. Measuring weight by eye has also become culturally convenient as a way of quickly sorting people into social classes. So then people who want to boost their social status—both fat and thin—are inevitably drawn to focus their energies on what the scale says rather than making their health their foremost concern, as it should be for anyone.

The concept of weight, then, is like a fast food for the mind: quick and soft, easy to chew, superficially appealing, but dangerous in the long term because it tempts us away from the more difficult work of seeking true intellectual nutrition. Weight is an easy scapegoat for all our uncertainties and helplessness in our lives with our bodies, and a steady money-maker for the various weight-loss industries that prey on our insecurities and dreams of self-improvement.

Let's stop telling schoolchildren they can shape their own bodies however they choose by diet and exercise, and start promoting good nutrition and active habits as desirable ends in themselves. Let's stop telling grown men and women that they must be abnormal psychologically if they're fat. Yes, I grant you, plenty of fat people have themselves embraced the idea that they are neurotic and will be able to reap the social rewards of being thin someday when they can fully understand and manage their emotions. But then, there are probably also a fair number of women willing to believe, since experts said so, that they must have unconsciously envied their brothers' penises.

If you are fat and you read this book for advice about weight loss, I have some: Change your priorities.

Fat storage is a very complex biological phenomenon that is not subject to your direct control. It's connected in deep ways to every other aspect of your bodily life, and you can cause terrible harm to yourself by tampering with the mechanisms. The down side of embracing yourself as a biological being is acknowledging that you don't have absolute freedom to remake yourself into something completely different. The up side is that you can stop blaming yourself for moral or psychological defects.

And you're not completely helpless to improve your life. Your body composition is not directly accessible to your adjustment, but your habits are. Without trying in any way to restrict your appetite, you can replace foods you consider to be unwholesome with foods you consider to be wholesome. You can gradually replace some of your sedentary leisure time with pleasurable active hobbies and, if it feels good, gradually increase the intensity and duration. Doing these things may not make you thinner—odds are they won't—but there's a very good chance they will improve your sense of wellbeing, your diagnostic indicators, and your self-esteem. Those things are worthwhile quite independent of what you weigh.

Chapter 23

Body Flow

2008

The hallway outside the activity room is still empty three minutes before 8:30, when the class is supposed to start. I'm here for "Body Flow," and the proportions in my mood fluctuate like my body's a basin under taps running hot and cold. The wrath of the thwarted consumer is diluted by trickling anxiety that I might somehow have gotten something wrong myself. I stick my head around the corner to see if anyone nearby is carrying a yoga mat.

Inside the dark room many bodies are moving, and on top of the lit stage the instructor for "Body Combat" punctuates his kicks and squats with martial yells and gives no sign of winding down. Sweat gleams on his beefy torso. When another woman passes through the hallway, I look only close enough to notice two things. One: her body is roughly proportioned like mine—"pear" is the word you always hear, but I think "bowling pin" is closer. Two: whereas I am an unusually thin bowling pin, rather elegant, really, in the right clothes, she is fat.

I yearn to hold every fat body in tender esteem, but it's easy to lose touch with my creed at the gym. I joined this place even though my new colleagues at the University of Texas have told me it's a meat market, even though most people here are twenty years younger than me, because I want high-intensity workouts. Before signing their contract, I toured another place whose clientele was mostly middle-aged, and the step class I visited was pathetically mild.

At 8:30 the woman returns and peers through the open door. I look at her lycra-clad bottom and thighs. How can I describe them without caricature? She's fat—fatt*ish*—everywhere, thick-waisted and big-armed, but one quadrant of her body—below-and-behind the mid-point—has a much higher concentration of flesh than the rest. In both volume and texture it looks roughly like a standard pillow has been placed in the backside of her black tights. Up top she is wearing a lime green shirt.

Do you understand that comedy is not my goal, nor tragedy either? This is simply her shape (and mine too). Under the fat is muscle, lots of it. "Class will start in a few minutes," she says to me. "There's an overlap with the previous class." She holds her body unselfconsciously, focused on making the next thing happen. From her authority, I know she's either the teacher or a longtime student. On the one hand I hope she's just a student. My former teacher Laurie was columnar with upper-body muscle, challenging the class with arm balances and other gymnastic poses, and that's what I want again. On the other hand I long for this fat woman to astonish me and everyone else with her grace and strength.

I contemplate lime green. In books when you read a gross-out scene involving a fat woman's nether parts, whether the situation is sexual or slapstick or both, she'll be wearing lime-green panties. Like lime green is some kind of uniform. No matter how often I read such scenes I don't get used to them. It's hard for me to hold still, hard to accept that my feelings really are confined to my mind, can't come boiling out upon the writers' own masculine (and presumably relatively taut) bodies. Where were these fictive fat women supposed to be buying the panties? No fat store I ever shopped at offered colors other than white or discreet beige, or less often pale pink. Maybe that's different now, there's a lot more of everything available now, but not twenty years ago when fat people were rarer in public and therefore more freakish.

Around 8:45 more people finally collect in the hallway and the room empties of kickboxers with surprising efficiency. I lay out my yoga mat toward the back and wait, looking at the empty stage. There's a giant sheet of black velvet behind draped strips of gold-colored fake satin and gauzy white stuff. It looks like a low-rent glam-rock concert is about to begin.

Here she comes, yes, she's the teacher and "Body Flow" is now about to start. The fat woman mounts the stage and unrolls a lime green yoga mat.

Cover Artist

Cesar R. Garza is a freelance designer who edits an online literary journal in South Texas. He holds a B.A. in English (Yale), a publishing certificate (Columbia School of Journalism), and a M.S. in Library and Information Science (Pratt Institute, New York)